in the Sunny Caribbee

PO Box 16, Admiralty Bay, Bequia, St. Vincent, Grenadines, West Indies.
Tel: Bequia (809 45) 83425   Fax: (809 45) 83612.

Sandy Island photo Kristina Lagerkvist

"(They) discovered that ...this region possessed a light and heart of its own that ought to be seen and heard."

L. Edward Brathwaite

EXPLORING
THE
WINDWARD ISLANDS

CHRIS DOYLE - text and maps
SALLY ERDLE - cartoons and drawings
ⓒ1988 CHRIS DOYLE PUBLISHING

CHRIS DOYLE PUBLISHING, GRENADA, W.I.

ISBN 976-8063-04-1

U.S. distribution:
Cruising Guide Publications,
P.O.Box 13131, sta 9,
Clearwater, Florida 34621
(813) 796-2469

Caribbean distribution:
Tipi Punnett,
Box 17,
St Vincent, West Indies
(809) 45 84246

Cover design by FIRST BASE DESIGN, St Vincent

TABLE OF CONTENTS

GENERAL INFORMATION

THE ISLANDS

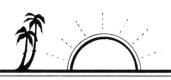

SPECIAL INFORMATION

AUTHOR'S ACKNOWLEDGEMENTS

One of the nice things about writing a guide is that everyone has an idea for you, "Hey you know what you should put in that book of yours...". Well, we listen and a lot of it goes in; unquestionably the book is better for it - thank you, all of you. Special thanks to Peter and Maggie Huff-Rousselle who not only let us run amok in their "not an office" commandeering their computer and laser printer, but who actually seemed to enjoy it! Not only did this help the book it might well have saved what little hair I have left.

The information in this guide was correct to the best of our knowledge at the time of going to press.
No warranty, expressed or implied is made by the publishers for any errors or ommissions in this publication.
All prices given are subject to change without notice.

ANYONE reprinting ANYTHING from this book without the permission of the publishers is in BIG TROUBLE.

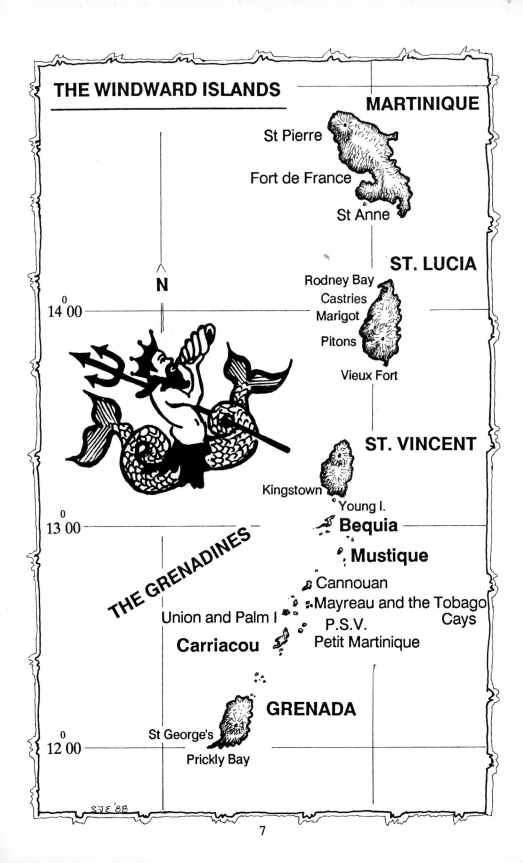

THE WINDWARD ISLANDS

MARTINIQUE

St Pierre

Fort de France

St Anne

ST. LUCIA

Rodney Bay
Castries
Marigot

Pitons

Vieux Fort

N

$14°00$

ST. VINCENT

Kingstown

Young I.

Bequia

$13°00$

Mustique

THE GRENADINES

Cannouan

Mayreau and the Tobago
Cays

Union and Palm I

P.S.V.

Carriacou

Petit Martinique

GRENADA

St George's

$12°00$

Prickly Bay

SJE '88

FOREWORD

We generally travel to the Caribbean for fun, and we feel a guide book should suit that mood. So we keep ours light while still packing in information. We cover as much as we can from the rich and opulant to the cheap and cheerful, you will find expensive super-deluxe gourmet restaurants rubbing shoulders with such basement-bargain delights as "Lambert's Lambi Bar" and "Papa Spoon's Rasta Ranch" (try finding them in another guide!). We tell you how to get around not only by plane and taxi but by bus and boat. Travel is no fun without maps, and we inlcude plenty; one for every inhabited island where you might be able to stay plus blow up detailed maps of the more important areas. We include anecdotes and introduce you to some of the characters you might meet. There are special interest features on Scuba diving, sailboarding, real estate and chartering a yacht. You may also want to know what a restaurant or hotel is going to cost, and you may wish to call in advance or send a telex. We have a 25 page listing of all this and much more....

When most people go to the Caribbean they are looking for sun, good beaches, friendly inhabitants, reasonable prices and enough to do so they don't feel bored. As everyone in the travel business knows this, little distinction is made between the islands - they are all sold on the basis of the Caribbean dream - waving palms, silver sand, smiling inhabitants, bright photogenic colors, and romantic nights under the stars to the strain of a steel band. It is true that most islands share these features, yet each island has a distinctive flavor, and within each island there is often far more than meets the eye - somewhere out there may be that special island, ideal for you. We hope this book will help you find it, or if you already staying on one island, that it will help you find those spots that will make your holiday perfect!

How do we manage all this? Well, your average travel book covers the whole Caribbean - we have just taken the Windward Islands, a small group at the southern end of the Caribbean chain. With a total population of less than a million, they comprise four separate countries and over a dozen inhabited islands, with a wealth of variety in both scenery and culture. Tourism is important, but not the major industry. By limiting ourselves to this area we have managed to work in depth.

HOW TO USE THIS BOOK

Essential nitty gritty; addresses, phone numbers, and details of prices and accept-

us if you find the pricing system helpful, or if you have a better suggestion we'd love to hear it!

When using the listings, keep in mind that prices and management will change from time to time, and as we are only human, there are bound to be a few mistakes. Therefore to be on the safe side use this as a rough guide and confirm anything essential with the business concerned.

"Exploring the Windward Islands" is a companion volume to another book we publish especially for sailors, called "Sailors Guide to the Windward Islands". While we have tried to keep these books as different as possible there is some overlap.

able credit cards, have been put together in a "listings" section at the back of the book. This starts off with international agents and tourist offices and then goes through each island detailing hotels, apartments, restaurants, shops, tour agents, airlines and car rental companies. If you are reading about something in the text and want to know more, just look it up in the listing.

Where possible we have given prices. In the case of restaurants we have tried to give a price range by adding together the least expensive starter, main course and dessert, then the most expensive. Most people like to drink with a meal so on top of our basic sum we added half the bottle price of the cheapest wine. It is of course possible to spend both less and more than the prices shown, and we let you know which restaurants also have less expensive snacks. Tell

In particular we have used the same Food and Scuba diving section in both.

You will also find some advertising. Advertising both helps keep the price of the book reasonable, and at the same time it gives an added flavor to the text. If you enjoy this book and want to help us, just carry it around and let the advertisers know "I read about it in "Exploring the Windwards!"

If you want to let us know how you find this book, or the islands, write:

Chris Doyle,
Box 17, St Vincent,
West Indies.

THE WINDWARDS
WHAT KIND OF WEATHER - WHAT KIND OF PEOPLE - WHAT TO EXPECT

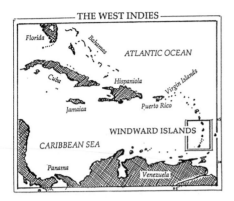

THE WEST INDIES

Florida
Bahamas
ATLANTIC OCEAN
Cuba
Hispaniola
Virgin Islands
Jamaica
Puerto Rico
WINDWARD ISLANDS
CARIBBEAN SEA
Panama
Venezuela

THE WEATHER

Long sunny days, kept from being too hot by trade winds, with warm balmy nights under the moon and stars - in other words perfect weather, right? Well not too far wrong. The Caribbean certainly gets more than its fair share of lovely sunny weather, and the temperature is very constant year round from around 78 to 85 degrees Fahrenheit. However, there are seasons, though these are not as well differentiated as in most other parts of the world. These are called the wet season and the dry season.

The wet season begins sometime in June or July, and finishes around January. For much of the wet season the weather is very pleasant, with plenty of sunshine interspersed with the occasional shower, and indeed Christmas is the area's busiest tourist time. However, a number of small low pressure systems called "upper level troughs", "tropical waves", or "tropical disturbances" do come through. These often generate a day or two of rainy weather. Very rarely one gets longer grey or wet periods. If you come to the Windwards during the rainy season for a week or less there is an outside chance you may have dissapointing weather, but if you come for two weeks or more you would have to have the luck of Job not to get plenty of sunshine!

Between mid-August and early October a combination of the summer and rainy season can make conditions somewhat still and humid, and this is my least favorite time of year, though compared to many places in the world the weather is still quite pleasant. This also happens to be the time when the warm Atlantic ocean produces hurricanes.

Hurricanes are tropical storms with sustained winds in excess of 64 knots (about 70 M.P.H.). Similar storms with less wind are known as tropical storms (winds between 35 and 63 knots) or tropical depressions (less than 35 knots). These storms are associated with heavy rain. The Windwards lie on the very edge of the hurricane zone and so such storms are rather rare. (Grenada has only had one in the last 100 years). The official hurricane season is from June to October. Hurricanes during the months of June, July and October are very rare, most hurricanes occur in August and September. Even during these months years go by without the Windwards being affected so the chances of your being in the wrong place at the wrong time are rather remote! However, if you should be so unlucky, make sure you are in a well constructed building and you will probably end up with nothing worse than a sleepless night and a great story to tell when you get back home!

The dry season starts around February and goes on to June, the driest months being March and April. There are still showers during these months but they are less frequent. The rain forests on the large islands keep lush and green through the dry season, and this is an excellent time to hike in these areas. Some of the coastal areas and the smaller Grenadine Islands can get very dry, and all the green vegetation turns brown. The weather during the dry season is exceptionally pleasant.

The Windwards lie in the trade wind belt,

and winds are normally from the easterly quadrant. This means that the East coast beaches tend to have rough water with breaking waves, while the west coast ones tend to be calm.

Fog and mist are unknown, and often the air has a wonderfully crystaline clarity when one can see far off islands lying on the horizon. Other times, there are mildly hazy conditions, caused by African dust which manages to lift high in the air and blow all the way across the Atlantic! Most visitors would not even notice this unless they were looking out for it. It can make the sunsets lack their usual brilliance and photos of distant views taken on such days lose a little sharpness.

In short, the Windwards have an amazingly pleasant year round climate, and provided you come for more than a whistle stop tour you are bound to get plenty of sunshine.

THE TOURIST SEASON

Apart from the dry and the wet season, there is also a low and a high season. The high season is from mid-December to mid-April which is when most people visit the Windwards because it is cold up north. The low season is for the rest of the year. Many hotels offer less expensive rates in the "low season", and indeed, for those who do not mind when they travel, late April to the end of May combines the best local weather with lower rates! During the slowest time (late August to early October), some of the smaller hotels close down and send the staff off on holiday. During this time the entertainment programs in even the big hotels are often curtailed, so if you come then expect things to be pretty quiet!

11

THE PEOPLE

Despite rumors to the contrary, Columbus did not discover the West Indies; they had in fact been discovered a couple of thousand years before by a people who were still in residence at the time he arrived. These were a short, dark haired, amber skinned people closely related to the North American Indian. The particular tribe in command when he came by were called "Caribs". These had not actually been in residence all that long; further north they were still in the process of evicting the previous tenants, another tribe reputed to be more artistic and less warlike called the "Arawaks". The Spaniards were not that interested in the Windwards, they had larger and more important fish to fry further north and on the mainland where gold was to be found. The Windwards were settled by the French and the English, an action not particularly appreciated by the Caribs. The early settlers had a rather poor opionion of the Caribs, calling them lazy, cunning, and unreliable savages and worse yet - cannibals. On this subject, one early writer waxes poetic saying that they found Frenchmen tender and succulent (tasting pleasantly of garlic, no doubt) whereas Englishmen were too tough and stringy. Then - they made the fatal mistake of eating a friar, whereupon several diners died and the rest got sick, thereafter men of the cloth were struck off the menu. Current thinking suggests that the Caribs probably did taste human flesh after battle as a matter of ritual, but they never really made a meal of it. Just what the Caribs thought of the settlers is lost to history, but I suspect they might have found them smug, self-righteous, self-serving and very hypocritical. Certainly at the end of the day it was the Caribs who were virtually exterminated having been systematically deprived of their land and killed by the settlers. Still in those days it was very much a dog-eat-dog world, and the Caribs had done much the same to the Arawaks. Today the only real settlement in the Windwards containing a few Caribs is at a village called "Fancy" at the very northern tip of St Vincent. Whatever else can be said of the Caribs they had a much more poetic way of naming the islands. For example, St Vincent used be "Hairoon" meaning "home of the blessed". Luckily a couple of their names were kept and in the Grenadines we have "Bequia" (Island of Clouds), "Canouan" (Sea Turtle) and "Carriacou" (Island surrounded by reefs). Another inheritance from these people are thousands of bits of broken pottery widely distributed in various sites much to the delight of many an amateur archeologist. (Pottery may be seen in the Martinique, St Vincent, Carriacou and Grenada Museums, Carib canoes in Bequia by the Clubhouse.)

The early European settlers needed labour to work the rich land and they solved this problem by buying slaves from Africa. The French managed to grab Martinique, and made it their main base in the area. They valued it to the point where Napoleon gave up Canada rather than this pretty island. (Sugar was very profitable at the time and Martinique was also the birthplace of his beloved Josephine). Both St Vincent and Grenada stayed mainly under British control, while poor old St Lucia became a kind of ping pong ball changing hands some 14 times! As a result, Martinique is very French both in lan-

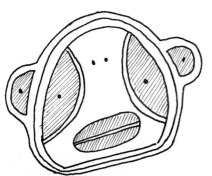

12

guage and culture. It is a part of France, administered by the French government, much in the way Hawaii is part of the U.S. Both St Vincent and Grenada have much more British tradition and the language is English. As St Lucia ended up being British, these are her stronger ties today and the official language is English, but as a heritage from those earlier days most St Lucians also speak "patois" a kind of Afro-anglicized French, which gives them the added advantage of being able to communicate with Martinique inhabitants.

One needs more Indians than Chiefs so the slaves quickly outnumbered their white masters, who philandered enough so that there was soon a significant mulatto population. When slavery was abolished most of the ex-slaves had had more than enough to do with being laborers and refused to work for hire, becoming subsistence farmers or fishermen. In order to fill the gap, indentured East Indian labor was shipped over. Consequently the heritage of today's Windward Islander is very mixed - mainly African but with a lot of European and Indian as well.

MARTINIQUE, with a population of over a quarter of a million, is the largest and most economically advanced of the Windwards, as it is part of France and gets funded by the French government. It is the Riviera of the Windwards, with chic Paris fashions and large multi-story hotels. One can be in the Caribbean yet at the same time have a foot in sophisticated France, and for the gourmand, there are plenty of French restaurants. In the well travelled visitors routes - the big hotels, the tour operators, the large tourist shops - there will be people who speak English. Once

you get off this beaten track it is another matter. You will generally find the people kind and helpful, but some have the Frenchman's quick and sometimes impatient nature where language is concerned. It is a country where a basic knowledge of French pays handsome dividends.

The currency is the French Franc, which has varied very considerably with the U.S. dollar in recent years, between 4 and 9 francs to the dollar. Some taxi drivers and hotels will accept U.S., but you will sometimes get a better rate of exchange at a bank, and if you are changing large amounts it can be worth wandering around and looking at the rates in a few different banks as they can vary quite widely. A few of the big tourist shops offer discounts if you buy with travellers checks.

THE ENGLISH SPEAKING WINDWARDS. At the moment, St Lucia, St Vincent and the Grenadines, and Grenada with both Carriacou and Petit Martinique are all separate nations. (Population somewhat over 100,000 each). All of them are "developing countries" with one foot in the modern industrialised society and the other in a very simple, rural world. To me this is what makes them attractive, because they have a very different but viable lifestyle, which is a refreshing change from the hustle and bustle of the more modern world. In some places cargo is carried and fish are caught under sail. Boats are handcrafted on the beach. Farming is labor intensive, most of it done by hand with the farmer's "third arm", the cutlass. People still have time to stop and chat - sometimes as they pass each other in cars in the middle of the main road - but surely a greeting is worth stopping the

traffic for a minute or two! Services generally hold up, but one gets the occasional power cut or water shortage. There is an island saying "Things don't always work, but everything always works out!" Tourism is an important industry, but second to agriculture. The people are warm and friendly but how you find them will to some extent depend on how far you reach out. Anyone who is genuinely interested in the local people and goes out of their way to smile and talk to them will find them most responsive. But they are not all busboys, and some visitors have come through with a very demanding and petulant attitude, which has put a few locals a little on their guard before they get to know you.

All the English speaking Windwards share the same currency the "E.C." (Eastern Caribbean) dollar. It has for some years been fixed at a set rate of 2.66 E.C. dollars to one U.S. dollar, so you can trade in a few of those green old men and get over twice as many brightly coloured notes covered with flowers and palm trees. Still they are quickly spent - oh well "E.C. come, E.C. go". Nearly everyone will accept U.S., but you will usually get a slightly better rate at the bank. The British pound is easily changed at any bank, but as the rate varies quite a lot, pounds and other foreign currencies are not widely accepted among the tradesmen.

BEFORE YOU COME
NOTES ON VISAS, DRUGS, BAGGAGE AND CLOTHING

VISAS. Right now the French have got on their Gallic high horse about entrance requirements, and to visit Martinique everyone who is not a member of the European Economic Community must (by law) have a visa put in their passport and this includes American citizens. They are not actually enforcing this at the moment with holiday makers, but it would be as well to be on the right side of the law and get one. I suppose there is a sort of justice to it; for years Europeans have had to plough through tedious red tape to get a visa to go to the U.S.

I would most strongly recommend a passport for travelling to the English speaking Windwards, though technically British, Canadian and U.S. citizens can get away with an alternative proof of identity. Other West Europeans just need a passport. Other nationals including those from the Communist block, South Africa and the Middle East may need visas which can usually be obtained from a British embassy. Everyone must have either an onward or return ticket.

DRUGS AND RASTAS. While booze and cigarettes are acceptable, any other mind bending substance that will get you into trouble anywhere else will get you into trouble here, and the jails are probably a lot less comfortable. From time to time visitors have been caught with marijuana and they have usually been heavily fined and deported.

While illegal, grass does in fact grow in the islands, where it is popular with the Rastas. Rastas are a religious "back to nature" group who believe in communion with nature and avoiding anything artificial. They like to eat food straight off the trees and do not believe in soap, but they wash in the rivers and the sea, often cleaning themselves with sand and various plants. They do not cut or comb their hair, but let it dry as is after washing till eventually it forms into thousands of little knots which gives the very unique "dread locks" look. To them ganja is the sacred substance which keeps them in touch with nature, though the serious Rasta will not drink alcohol, smoke tobacco or touch meat. Like any different minority group they are often blamed for anything bad that goes on including theft. This is partly because of Rasta look-alikes. The real Rastas I have worked with have all been honest, gentle folk.

CLOTHING AND BAGGAGE. The Windwards are not "dressy" islands. While there are one or two places where you could really dress up, there are none that you have to. For men slacks and a good sports shirt, and for women a simple dress, are usually adequate. Bathing costumes, shorts, t-shirts, simple skirts and slacks are the basic essentials. You will not go far wrong if you bring half as many clothes and twice as much film as you think you will use! If you use prescription drugs, bring all you need and keep them in your "carry on" luggage.

On the other hand, informality has not reached the point where people wander around towns or villages shirtless or in bathing costumes. If you do so, the locals will stare and make remarks, so once away from the beach you will feel more comfortable to be covered up. For men shorts and a T-shirt are adequate, in the larger towns women might feel more at home in a skirt or pair of slacks.

While on the subject of dress (or the lack of it) topless bathing for ladies is perfectly acceptable on many beaches in Martinique, but people in the other Windwards tend to be more conservative, and in some places even the bra-less look may be frowned upon. Nowdays some people do sunbathe topless near some of the larger hotels. It is best to see what others are up to and use your own judgment.

LOCAL ETIQUETTE
GREETING, BARGAINING AND BEGGING

GREETINGS. Good manners in the Windwards may not always be the same as at home; there are a couple of things you should know. Great store is set on greetings; local people consider it most rude if you approach them for any reason and do not begin with the appropriate greeting "Good morning", "Good night" or if you are in Martinique "Bon jour". People say what they feel much more too, and if you fail to be polite they may well correct you! I rather like the local forth-rightness. When I first came I was surprised when I saw a dwarf walking down the road, and not only did most people stare, but the old ladies would cackle and make rude jokes, and he would answer back and give as good as he got! But on reflection this seemed a much better place to be a dwarf than in a country where you embarrassed people into ignoring you, so that soon you must wonder whether you exist!

Most of us have had "please" and "thank you" drummed into us ever since we opened our mouths and managed to make recognizable sounds. But it is not necessarily this way in the Windwards. If you give someone something, they may say "thank you", but then again they may just take your gift (unopened) and say nothing. This is not necessarily considered bad manners, nor does it mean it was not appreciated.

BARGAINING is not accepted as a way of life here; the price you are offered is the price the vendor is hoping to get. But you can often strike a deal with cab drivers, market ladies and vendors, especially if you are going to be a good customer. Since prices of services are often not fixed (this applies to such people as taxi drivers, guides and laundry ladies) it is essential to discuss and agree on a price before accepting a service, otherwise you may get charged "top dollar" and feel you have been overcharged. In the English speaking islands make sure you are both speaking about the same kind of dollars - sometimes cab drivers work in U.S., and it comes as shock if you thought your bargain was in E.C.!

BEGGING. You could probably count the number of real beggars in the Windwards on the fingers of one hand. They are generally highly eccentric, easily recognizable, and often somewhat lacking "up top". There is one I rather like in Kingstown who wanders up and down Backstreet with a big stick banging all the parked cars! They won't starve if you don't give them anything, but there is no harm in slipping them a little something if you want to. However, with the advent of tourism there are a few perfectly well looked after, well fed kids who go around begging, and who unfortunately look cute enough that they do quite well off the visitors (they wouldn't dare try it with a local). However good it might make you feel to give to such fellows, the effect on them is bad. It really does make them beggars, and a beggar can never really stand tall. If they do well begging it becomes very hard for them to settle down and work later on. Eventually. when they are not so cute and do not do so well, they can become angry, embittered and demanding, feeling the tourist owes them a living.

On the other hand, there is a shortage of employment, so if you can think of something useful for such a youngster to do - carry your bags, or wash your car, you can help foster a spirit of initiative.

NOTES FOR PHOTOGRAPHERS

The Windwards are quite beautiful, and offer enormous scope for exciting pictures. You may want to take more photographs than you can imagine. Keep this in mind when you buy film; film in the Windwards is very expensive and the choice can be very limited, so bring far more than you expect to use, the odds are you will use it anyway! (keep it clear of the airport X-ray machines).

The light is intense, and it is not always easy to catch the full brightness of the colors. Sometimes early morning and late afternoon light is kinder to photos than that in the middle of the day. Often a picture of the sea looks pale and washed out compared to the real thing. The answer to this is to use a polarizing filter. By turning it you will get different effects. If you are taking both sea and sky, be careful not to twist the filter to the point when the blue sky becomes grey.

People are hard to photograph for two reasons, firstly the lighting and secondly the people themselves. Lighting can be a real problem when photographing black people, especially out in the open sun. All too often one gets a picture where the facial features are completely lost. The best solution is to use an extra light source to highlight the face, but most of us don't carry around reflectors, so the other answer is to "overexpose" the picture so that the person turns out sharp and background faded. Often you will have much better luck photographing people in shaded, lower light conditions.

Attitudes towards photographers can be very strange, especially in the English speaking Windwards. For whatever reasons many people feel they are being exploited when they have their picture taken. Of course, it is only polite to ask someone before you take a picture of them, but the problem goes a bit beyond this. There are some very picturesque crowd scenes - sailing ships being loaded with cargo, women washing clothes in the river - but when you go to take a picture someone may well start shouting and waving his fists, and that person may not even be in the picture! This is not universal, and certainly worse in the well travelled tourist areas. Women are sometimes embarrassed to have their picture taken if they are not dressed in their best clothes.

Many people actually like to have their picture taken and certainly if you have a polaroid "now for now" camera and can offer a print you will have no shortage of subjects. Some people may ask to be paid for having their picture taken, and very occasionally they are worth it! Keep in mind it can be a sensitive subject, but do not lose a sense of proportion. Do not take it too seriously if you take a picture of a goat and a little kid runs up to you and says "That's my goat, you must give me a dollar"!

If you want those holiday snaps back right away, you will find quick processing is now available in all the main islands (quality varies).

MARKETS

For a really colorful bustling local scene try visiting the fresh food market on any of the major islands, Saturday mornings are the best (Friday in St Lucia). All the markets sell fresh fruits and vegetables, and if you are interested you can talk with the market ladies - they will tell you what everything is and how to use it (see also our food section). In Martinique you will also find lovely flowers, in Grenada exotic spices, and in St Lucia they have masses of basket work and straw goods. They also have the most wonderfully inexpensive pottery barbecues, made from local clay and baked on an open "ground" fire. Unfortunately they are bulky and fragile, so the odds of getting one back home are slim!

TIPPING

Everyone likes to be tipped, but it is not always expected. In restaurants where no service charge is added, a 10% tip is normal. If service has already been included (this is done automatically by law in Martinique) a little extra is appreciated but not essential. Taxi drivers do not normally expect to be tipped, but if they go out of their way to help you, carrying your bags etc., you can add a few dollars to the fare to show your appreciation. If you get help from kids carrying your suitcases they will expect an E.C. dollar or two.

GREEN FLASH

Nearly every day nature puts on a free color show called sunset. This is the time to find a bar with a comfortable patio facing west, take that evening rum punch, sit back and enjoy! Add to the fun by trying to spot the elusive "green flash". This happens as the very last little bit of the sun disappears over the horizon. For about a second (blink and you've missed it) the very last bit of the sun sometimes turns bright green before it goes. Binoculars certainly make it clearer. If you are in St Vincent and fail to see it, you can go and buy the little photographic souvenir book - "St Vincent and the Grenadines, a portrait of islands in the sun", the pictures (which were taken by our photographer) include a perfect "green flash".

· PAPAYA TREE ·

THINGS THAT BITE IN THE NIGHT....

When one lives in the Caribbean, one gets so immune to those flying, biting things, one almost ceases to think they exist. When I first came here people would ask me home to dinner, and would assure me there were absolutely no mosquitoes at all where they lived. At first in all innocence I would go unprepared and keep slapping at my ankles while everyone else looked at me as if I was suffering some kind of personal paranoid psychosis. Mosquitoes do exist in the Windwards, as does the sandfly, a tiny flying/biting insect which is so small it is called a "no see-um". There are not that many, so most people don't consider them a problem, but some people are so sensitive, that every bite swells into an unsightly lump. Bugs are almost never a problem during the day, but at sunset time and during the night it is best to be prepared. I would recommend any brand of repellent for sitting on the patio at night to watch the sunset or moonrise.

If you are not sleeping in a screened room, you might want to resort to the mosquito coil. This is not a contraceptive device for mosquitoes, but a coil of incense-like material that burns slowly and puts the mosquitoes to sleep. It does not kill them, so if the coil goes out before you awake, they will be up first and you will be breakfast! Mosquito coils are available in almost any supermarket in the Windwards. There is an even better device which is electrical, and warms an impregnated pellet which protects you with an almost odorless vapor. These are harder to come by, but if you are lucky enough to get one, make sure you buy an ample supply of pellets at the same time.

There are poisonous scorpions and centipedes in the Windwards. These are not generally deadly, and luckily very rare, but you might want to look before you sit down out in the open, and take care if you are scrounging in old debris for firewood for a barbecue. Martinique and St Lucia also have a deadly snake, the Fer-de-Lance, which is so rare I've never even met anyone who has seen one in the 18 years I have spent around here!

More common, but not considered harmful, is the cockroach. There are a variety of species, the largest of which can grow to about 2" long! You are unlikely to get them in a hotel, but if you are renting a house you may find them as additional guests. If you only see a couple, give them names and adopt them as house pets, if you get a bad infestation give a good spray with any brand of bug killer. Follow up by spreading bait around in the bottom of cupboards etc. You can make your own by mixing equal parts of boric acid and white sugar. It is best to grind them together in a mortar and pestle.

Contrary to local superstition, lizards are harmless and eat quantities of insects.

GECKOES

THINGS THAT LIVE
IN THE SEA

Any good book on dangerous marine animals will contain enough horrors to send all but the most intrepid adventurer scurrying back to their reclining chair with a stiff drink and a nice safe book. In point of fact for anyone with reasonable common sense, swimming in the Windwards is as safe as taking a walk. Sharks exist, as they do in all the world's oceans, but it seems that although they find old rubber tires and assorted debris acceptable fare along with their fish, they really don't like people, in the Windwards! Maybe the sharks don't attack because the water is generally clear, who knows? All that can be said is that no authenticated shark attacks have ever been recorded here. I have heard just one or two stories of spearfishermen being bothered in other parts of the Caribbean, but the shark has usually been after the catch rather than the hunter. Barracudas are harmless, however some people advocate leaving off shiny jewelry as it might look like a fish lure.

There are more mundane things to think of. Once you get away from the beach, currents can be strong. The prudent swimmer will always keep an eye open for this, and if you are going anywhere rough (like a windward beach) there will be no guards or warning signs, so you will have to use your own judgment. You should always watch where you put your feet, especially near rocks and coral. The main reason for this is the highly visible black spiny sea urchin. This porcupine of the sea is very happy to mind his own business, as long as you don't brush against him or tread on him. If you do his sharp spines will penetrate your skin and break off. This is rather painful, especially for the first few hours. Attempts to remove the very fragile spines are more or less doomed to failure and leave you liable to secondary infection. Better to leave them be, and pour warm lime juice on them to help them dissolve. You are most unlikely to stand on a sting

ray or that rock-mimicking scorpion fish. But just in case step carefully and look where you tread. For most of the time the calm lee beaches are free of jelly fish, though they do exist in the Caribbean. More common are a tiny "sea ant" almost never seen, but felt as a mild tingling which usually goes away soon after you get ashore. A few corals sting - usually not enough to affect your hand if you grab it, but certainly enough to raise a welt if you touch it with a more tender part of your anatomy. All coral cuts should be very well washed with soap and fresh water to help prevent infection. The moray eel is actually a shortsighted and timid creature who would never go out of his way to attack, but still, it would be foolish to stick a hand into some little hole or crevice in the rock where one cannot see. I am hesitant to say that swimming at night is safe, because so few people do it, one really does not know. On the other hand I have often dived at night, and also gone snorkeling without any problem, but I always go with a buddy.

In brief, the sea dangers here are probably less than they are back home, or in most other places in the world, and the water is a lot warmer, prettier and more pleasant!

THREE THINGS TO BE
ON YOUR GUARD AGAINST

The Windwards are both exotic and romantic, therefore one rather expects the dangers to be wild and different. Despite sensationalist articles to the contrary there are really no dangerous pirates, but there are some "deadly" tropical drinks including the famous "rum punch". There is no better way to start your Caribbean holiday than by sipping one of these, but you should also be aware that they slide down deceptively comfortably and smoothly, with a kind of delayed kick, and too many can make the strongest person feel horrible!

Most people come for the sun, and too much sun is probably the worst danger. It

is hard to overestimate the burning rays of tropical sun, and unfortunately by the time you "feel burnt" it is far, far too late. It is best to bring plenty of sunscreen (15+) and use it from the start, building up exposure gradually. The tops of feet are particularly vulnerable, so light cotton socks are essential. Other places people often neglect are the ears and lips. Everyone should have a hat, but we bald headed people should almost never take it off! Long, loose sleeved cotton clothing, and dark sunglasses are a must. Heavy burning can still take place on cloudy days or in the shade. Snorkelers should wear a T-shirt to protect their exposed backs.

There is also a tree you should know about. It is called the Manchineel tree (Hippomane Mancinella). It is a pretty shade tree with small green leaves and yellow-green apples; it grows abundantly along some of the beaches. One can happily shade under the tree, but one should never shelter under it in the rain as the leaves are toxic, and the drips could give you a rash. Avoid contact between your bare skin and the leaves, and do not use wood from the tree for a fire or that song "smoke gets in your eyes" could take on new meaning! The apples are very poisonous. Someone I heard about ate some and as a result had internal blisters from stem to stern. She spent the next few weeks on a milk diet!

"TIEFS"

Everything is so idyllic in the Windwards, that visitors sometimes think they are in paradise and go bananas leaving their things around, then complain bitterly if they get stolen. Most people are honest, but the few bad ones are worth taking precautions for. Nothing special, just keep in mind that it is not wise to put valuables down on the beach then wander far away. If you are staying on the ground floor, it would be foolish to leave something desir-

able close to an open window. If you are staying in a hotel use their safe for your jewelry, passport, surplus cash or travellers checks. Having said that I would like to mention I have also come across some remarkable incidents of honesty in the Windwards, including one night in a dark restaurant where I gave and got change for what I thought was a $20 bill. It turned out it was a hundred and although I never noticed the mistake, ...the next time I went into the restaurant the waiter came up and said: "Mr Chris, you gave me a hundred dollar bill the other night instead of a twenty, here is the change".

While walking at night and hiking in the wilds is fairly safe, it whould be kept in mind, that one can get isolated incidents, just like anywhere else in the world, and it doesn't hurt to "ask around" at your hotel first.

NOTES FOR WOMEN TRAVELLING ON THEIR OWN

In the English speaking islands, young men show their appreciation by going "pssst pssst". One good looking woman I knew was in a restaurant with an even more striking blonde when she heard a "pssst pssst". She turned to the source of this noise who said: "Not you - the other one!" When you hear a "psst" it may not be meant for you because it is also used as a general way of getting attention from someone else. Some women don't mind, others find it a real pain in the neck. Someone I know thought of a great reply, when someone went "pssst" she turned and said "What's the matter with you, has your face sprung a leak?" Another woman tells admirers, "It's much more manly to say 'Good morning' than 'Psst',", and gets a rousing chorus of "Good mornings" up and down the street. On the whole I think the "pssst" is best ignored.

At least you know where you are with local men; they may be interested in more than one thing, but that one thing is certainly high on their list of priorities! If you say "no" most of them are gentlemen, but there are a few who have such a Neanderthal idea of seduction, in most countries it would be called "rape". Occasionally I have heard of women escaping from such situations by expressing their willingness, but using a delaying tactic, such as "lets go back to my room", and using the respite to get themselves in a public place where they can then change their minds!

There have been some great romances and marriages between tourists and locals, but if you are thinking of "fraternising" keep in mind you are in a very different culture and tread carefully. In some places

actions that would be completely innocent at home, such as renting a house and living there by yourself, bathing topless or barhopping on your own at night, can seem like an open invitation to some of the more unruly local men. While many women do wander about on their own at night, my feeling is that two women together are more than twice as safe as one on her own.

In Martinique, expecially in such well travelled areas as Anse Mitan, the attitudes are much more international, and it is probably easier for a woman on her own.

GETTING IN, OUT, AND AROUND
(Notes on transport)

TRAVELLING TO THE WINDWARDS

The Windwards got their name from the old days of sail, when they lay 'to windward' of the other islands, and getting there could involve a long hazardous struggle against wind and sea, with the prospect of pirates thrown in. It is rather easier today! All the Windwards except St Vincent now have big international airports with flights from the U.S.A and Europe. If you get caught at a busy time, and have problems getting bookings you can also come via Barbados. St Vincent's airport is too small for large jets, but it is well linked to the other Windwards and Barbados by smaller airlines so getting in and out should be no problem. If you want to see more than one island, consider arriving at one end of the island chain (Martinique) and leaving from the other (Grenada).

Airlines serving the Windwards include Air France (with an excellent service between Martinique and France), British Airways, British West Indian Airways (B.W.I.A.), Pan Am, and Eastern. In addition some tour companies offer less expensive charter flights from time to time. These include Nouvelles Frontieres (Martinique), Ward Air (Canada) and Pegasus (Europe).

It is worth knowing that St Lucia has two airports, Hewanorra, the big international airport in the South, and Vigie, the smaller inter-island airport close by Castries, the capital. It takes somewhat over an hour to drive from Hewanorra to the north of St Lucia where Castries and many of the hotels are. The cab fare is between $40 and $50 U.S. For around $2 U.S. you can catch a bus from the main road not far from Hewanorra to Castries, but you may not find one in the late afternoon or evening. If you are staying in one of the larger hotels try to find out whether they offer transport to and from Hewanorra. The large Club Med is very close by Hewanorra, and the town of Vieux Fort with a couple of small hotels is only five minutes away.

When it comes time to leave, you will find most all the English speaking islands will have a "departure tax" usually around $20 E.C. a head. It is best to keep some local currency handy for this. If you are making a stop-over, you will normally be exempt from this tax if you spend less than 24 hours in the country. You will have to point this out to the collecting official, who will not know how long you have been there and try to charge you anyway.

FLYING BETWEEN THE ISLANDS

The Windwards are linked together by small airlines. The biggest of these is L.I.A.T. (Leeward Islands Air Transport) with numerous flights between all the different islands. LIAT insists on return flights being re-confirmed at least 72 hours before departure, so why not do this at the airport when you arrive, to save your having to think about it later?

LIAT use a variety of aircraft including smaller 9 to15 seaters. These run daily between Grenada and St Lucia stopping at most of the Grenadine Islands on the way.

22

They are also used for flights between Barbados and Mustique and Barbados and Union Island.

Air Martinique has two flights a day (one morning and one afternoon) from Martinique to Union Island, stopping in St Lucia (Vigie) and St Vincent. In the afternoons they also stop at Mustique.

Grenadine Tours, using Mustique Airways, flies daily between Barbados and St Vincent, Barbados and Union, Barbados and Mustique, and between St Vincent, Mustique and Union. They use a "shared charter" concept. You book as an individual, you are met at Barbados, your bags are looked after, and you are taken to your next flight. Once they have you booked with your connecting flight times, they will take good care of you. However, their flights are not scheduled, so you may find yourself waiting for another flight to arrive so that the charter plane can be filled. Anchor Travel (800 526 4781) are their U.S. agents and can explain further.

Chartering a plane for a group of 5 or more may be no more expensive than going on scheduled flights, and it can be more convenient and a lot more fun too! There are numerous companies that charter planes, or act as agents. These include: LIAT, Air Martinique, Mustique Airways, Tropic Air, St Vincent Airways, Wings, and Anchorage Hotel (Union). Check in our reference section for phone numbers and other details.

TRAVELLING BY SEA
English gentry of leisure can get to and from the English speaking Windwards by banana boat. These large comfortable ships take thirteen passengers, and leave weekly to and from the islands. You can also "island hop" on them. Contact the Geest company. (Box 20, Barry Glamorgan, South Wales, tel:700333. Box 106, St Lucia, tel:22561, St Vincent, tel:61718. Grenada, tel:440 2259).

It is possible to do some island hopping by ferry, as both St Vincent and Grenada have services going to the Grenadines. Details are given under the separate island headings. We also have a complete yacht charter section.

GETTING AROUND
WITHIN THE ISLANDS
TAXIS
There is no easier and more comfortable way to travel than by taxi. Taxis are plentiful and readily available at the airport, in all the major towns etc. Taxi drivers are generally very helpful, friendly and knowledgeable. In St Vincent they really have this down to an art where the good ones will arrange anything for you from organzing a wedding to finding your lost luggage! Fares are supposed to be standard, but often are not. You should always discuss and agree on a fare before you go and if you are dealing in "dollars" make sure you are both talking about the same kind! It can come as a shock to find that great deal you thought you had in E.C., the driver thought he had in U.S.! For long rides and tours, bargaining is sometimes possible.

where the batiks are in full display. Both ventures are involved with Grenada's school for the deaf. Jeanne was born in Mexico and has lived abroad, mostly in Latin America throughout much political turmoil. She used to say "I've come to Grenada, this beautiful and peaceful island, to get away from revolutions and political upheavals..." Then came 1979! Still, even during the revolution Grenada was more peaceful than some other countries she remembers! It all goes back to Mexico when her father was on his way to engineer the building of a road, accompanied by 400 men, horses, mules and supplies. He was ambushed by Pancho Villa, Mexico's well known revolutionary bandit, captured, and was to be shot at dawn. Pancho could hardly let this American die without some "fire in his belly", so he went to see him with a bottle of tequila. The two ended up sitting around the camp fire, spinning yarns and drinking. At dawn when the firing squad arrived, Pancho Villa, overcome with emotion, flung his arms round Jeanne's father and said "Mi amigo you are the best gringo I have ever met - you can go free, and I will only take half your men, animals and supplies!"

Then came Venezuela in a bygone and more lawless age, and the first Tikal shop - in Caracas. Che Guevara was in the hills, and terrorists were looting and holding up banks - locking the staff away in the chilly empty vaults. This became so endemic that employees began to leave extra clothes tucked away there just in case! Carpet tacks were strewn all over the city streets and the only way people could drive was with brooms lashed in front of the car's wheels to swish them out of the way. So Jeanne, tired of the excitement and the sound of a thousand swishing brooms came to Grenada to stay, and had no problems even during the revolutionary days - still Jeanne, like her father, could talk her way out of anything!

The adventurous could try a walk through the Sendall tunnel which was built in 1890 for somewhat smaller carriages of transport. Nowdays huge trucks growl by, almost touching the ceiling and leaving the

pedestrian to try and squash himself flat against the wall in a poor imitation of a fly.

On the other side you have such shops as Gren Craft, a handicraft cooperative (on the Esplanade), Amado's (Granby Street), and a number of stalls at the Shopping Plaza. The once brightly painted Shopping Plaza sign has faded now, but the area can be picked out by by a big new notice sporting the Canadian flag in one corner and the Grenadian in the other proudly announcing "Ocean Outfall Sewer Project!"

Over the years Jim Rudin's name has become synonymous with that of the Yellow Poui Art Gallery and great endevours to find a market place for local artists. His huge collection is spread out between the Yellow Poui Art Gallery (in Halifax Street a few steps down from Barclays Bank) and Yellow Poui Two (in Cross Street). You will see a wonderfully varied collection of Caribbean paintings in all styles, including works by Carriacou's very own primitive master, Canute Calliste. But it doesn't stop at paintings - Yellow Poui sells antique maps, objets d'art, artistic postcards, and more. Plus, there is normally an exhibition of photographs on show at Yellow Poui Two.

Another good reason for visiting this side is to look in Noah's Arkade (Same building as Yellow Poui Two) with their pot pourri of arts, crafts, souvenirs and local books - you are bound to find something in here you really need but didn't know you were looking for!

RESTAURANTS

There are plenty of little places tucked away in odd corners of St George's where you can buy a snack and a beer. There are also larger restaurants where you can expand into a full meal.

Built on a wooden deck out over the harbor, Delicious Landing, informal by day, assumes a becoming elegance at night. Plants, table cloths and a hundred twinkling lights across the harbor that send shimmering reflections almost to your table. Owner Terry Lambert likes to work with fish, shrimp and lambie relying on coconut milk and local spices to bring out the flavor. Begin by ordering a "Spice Island Cinnamon Daiquiri" If that doesn't put a sparkle on your night nothing will! You can take them up on their offer to "call up for a dinner reservation and we will collect you from your hotel and drop you back there at no charge". Things get particularly lively on Wednesdays and Sundays when they have a band. Sunday's lobster special is an even stronger pull. Friday night is happy hour from 4.30 to 6.30 when all drinks are $2 E.C., with an off-the-deck fishing competition open to all (gear supplied).

The Nutmeg is upstairs over Food Fair with a nice view and inexpensive menu.

Restaurant Italia upstairs, at the bottom of the Carenage is owned and run by Italians, so for those of you suffering from terminal pasta deprivation.....you know where to go!

Should hunger take you on the market square side of town there are several places to assuage your needs. Factor (Halifax Street close by the market) does

some first rate rotis, Talk of The Town has an upstairs view, and the more adventurous could seek out Ye Olde Farmhouse Kitchen. This tiny place (3 tables) is set down a little alley at the back of Noah's Arkade. It is surrounded by vines and flowers planted in disused drums. The menu is simple "Big Lunch $12 EC, Small Lunch $6 EC". You take what you get, its good, local, and the "small" was plenty big enough for me!

If town has become altogether too much you can take a water taxi (fare $1 E.C.) over to the far side of the Carenage and walk up to the Sea Scape Inn and view everything from afar.

WHERE TO STAY

Of course most visitors want to stay on the beach, but there are a handful of small hotels and guest houses in town. All are in relatively quiet spots with fantastic views and they tend to be very reasonably priced.

St James Hotel has a view over all those lovely old roofs across the Carenage. An old fashioned building of indeterminate age it started as a private home and became a hotel in 1946 making it one of Grenada's oldest. Plantation Inn sits up the hill behind the Carenage just where town proper begins to peter out and the buildings become smaller, more individual and residential, tiny wooden shacks nestling alongside grand block houses. A quiet kind of area where you would not be surprised to see a goat wandering about. Still, its only a couple of minutes walk to the Carenage or one minute for a bus to the beach, and the view is panoramic taking in everything from the historic old prison right round past Grand Anse to most of town. Meals are available for guests. Mitchell's Guest House, is also in this area, just down on Tyrrel Street.

Sea Scape Inn is a short walk and "water taxi" ride to town. It is set on the far side of the Carenage with great views over the docks and cruise ships all the way round to town. Some rooms have their own bathroom and are air-conditioned.

Let us start at the ruin above GYS. This has a wonderful view all around and is a good place to think about things past and present. Those who cannot make it in person can look at the map. If you look over towards the yacht club you can see the shallow reef with a narrow channel cut through it for the yachts. Back in 1650, when the first French settlers arrrived, this reef was a strip of land, and it was here the first settlement was built, with the sea in front and a great lake behind. This must have helped provide protection against the resident Caribs, who did their best to keep their land. But to no avail - within 4 years they were virtually all exterminated, and by 1690 the town had moved over to its present position. For the next 90 years the island bounced between the French and English according to the spoils of war. It was during this time that Fort George and Fort Frederick were built. Grenada was British from 1783 until independence in 1974.

In the 1950's the black farm labor force lived in very poor conditions with wages of less than $1 E.C. a day. The estates were no longer profitable, but their owners managed to live in good style with servants and horse racing down at Queen's Park, even if some of their buildings were beginning to crumble round the edges. It was into this atmosphere Eric Gairy arrived as a union organizer and champion of the poor, a black David ready to take on the Goliath of the ruling class. He called strikes, organized civil disobedience and managed to raise wages significantly. He later became a politician and ruled Grenada for many years in a flamboyant if somewhat eccentric manner, even raising the topic of flying saucers at the United Nations. He managed to collect a string of titles and letters to adorn his name, and became owner of several businesses (at one time he was reported to be one of the wealthiest black men in the world). As a Grenadian once said: "First Gairy helped the people then he helped himself". However, a new grass roots, left wing political force came into

being under Maurice Bishop and focused a lot of anti- Gairy sentiment, which was made much stronger when Bishop and his close supporters were arrested and beaten up. It was during these troubled times in 1974 that the British forced independence on a largely unwilling island; instead of jubilant celebrations there were general strikes. A lot of people did, and still do, feel allegiance to the Queen and many felt badly let down. In 1979, Bishop, who wanted a Castro-like government, took over the island in a coup while Gairy was in the States. Bishop did his best to effect social improvements, but at a high cost to individual freedom; numerous citizens were locked behind bars, independent newspapers were banned. Bishop's plans were foiled by an even more radical element in his government, led by Deputy P.M. Bernard Coard and his wife Phyllis along with the army who tried to take the island for themselves. They locked Bishop up and put out a rumor he was mentally ill. His followers wouldn't buy that and several thousand set him free and carried him to Fort George. At this point Coard and his cronies sent armored cars from Fort Frederick. When they reached Fort George they opened fire killing some civilians. Many more hurt themselves jumping off the walls of the fort in trying to escape the gunfire. Bishop and half his cabinet were executed on the spot. The Oranization of Eastern Caribbean States, tired of the fiasco, asked the U.S. to help them sort things out and the ensuing "rescue mission" was welcomed with open arms. Grenada once more became a democracy. Coard and his henchmen now sit up there in the jail just below Fort Frederick.

The ruin where we stand, once a proud hotel, (they made the movie "Island in the Sun" here), was taken over by Bishop as Government offices. The damage one can see is not so much the result of the "rescue" forces, but attempts by the communists to destroy records. It looks a mess, but nonetheless 3 tons of documents were saved! It may soon be rebuilt as a new hotel.

WHERE ELSE CAN YOU?

Sunbathe
Be in the shade
Dance to live Steelband
See Historical sights in Review
Swim on fabulous beaches
Fish or snorkel, free.

Be dry and look at underwater life
(Glass bottom window)
Drink lots of free Rum Punch.
Have a fresh shower
Learn about Grenada
Eat a banana or bar-b-que

only on

RHUM RUNNER

The Party Boat!
Book at your hotel desk, travel agency
or call (809) 440-2198/3422
P.O.box 188, St Georges's, Grenada. West Indies.

St George's photo Kristina Lagerkvist

PLACES TO STAY

This is a generally inexpensive area with many guest houses. St Anne's is long established and well frequented. It is popular with young travelers and has a certain style. Occasional youths fail to realise this, which has led to signs on the door: "Natty Dreads (the rough dirty ones) are definitely not allowed on our premises"!

If you are looking for somewhere cheap and basic, you could try Tita's or Traveller's Inn.

Hamilton Inn, Windward Sands, Roydon's and Skyline are all reasonable, middle range guest houses. Mamma has just built her pleasant guest "lodge" overlooking the lagoon. Rooms are simple and inexpensive, each with a bathroom. De Freitas has some cottages which one can rent.

Only in Grenada would someone convert a clinic to an elegant hotel - but that is what you have at Balisier. Perched on top of a 1000 foot hill overlooking town this has a truly fantastic view. It is named after a lovely tropical forest flower and is owned by Stan and Dale Friday. Stan for years has been Grenada's chief surgeon, and had his own clinic here. He has recently become a senator, and spends most of his time in politics, while his wife Dale runs the hotel in a pleasant welcoming manner.

RESTAURANTS

Mamma is huge and black and cooks like an angel. Her restaurant "Mamma's" has become a Grenadian institution, and no trip to Grenada would be complete without a visit here. For a set fee you get a huge feast - plate after plate of exotic local dishes - some ingredients you may recognise (lobster, chicken, fresh tuna, lambi), others will be new to you (manicou, tatoo), and believe it or not Mamma is still discovering new foods. Mamma's has been written up in the "New York Times", "Los Angeles Times", "French Vogue" and formed the basis for a book on tropical cooking. Mamma's is a family business with a very informal atmosphere, you will

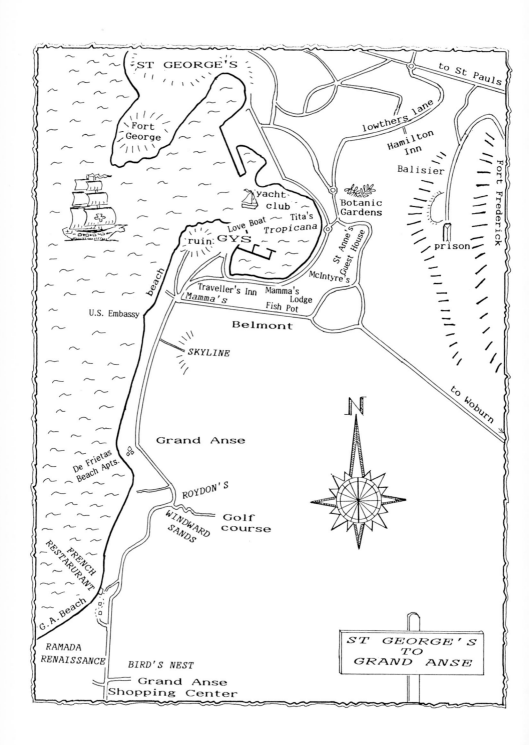

be equally welcomed whether you arrive in rags or riches. If possible go with a group of friends and reserve early in the day, as much work goes into the preparation. Be warned before you pig out - the food is very rich!

Tropicana is probably the best inexpensive place to eat in Grenada. Good, and cheap enough to visit whenever one does not feel like cooking. They specialise in Chinese and local food, the rotis are large and tasty.

The prize for the restaurant with the best view definitely goes to Balisier, here you eat on a patio, and look a thousand feet straight down on the breathtaking panaroma of St George's and the south coast below you. Good food with a local flavor, lobster being a speciality. With its perfect sunset bar, Balisier should be on your list of special places to visit.

Coconut Beach French Restaurant is housed in a lovely little wooden house right on the water's edge on Grand Anse Beach. You eat sitting out right on the beach, the waves almost lapping at your feet. Superb on a moonlight night. Run by Michel and Brigitte, a French couple, the cuisine has its roots in France but uses all local ingedients. This restaurant is often just called "The French Restaurant", but this has caused some confusion because there is another French Restaurant further along the beach (see Grand Anse section).

Other places for local food include The Fish Pot, Royden's, and Windward Sands, and there is always the Patio at GYS, or a snack at the Yacht Club.

WHAT ELSE?

Well, there is a golf course, and if you chase the goats off the green, you can get in a practice round, but its not up to competition standards.

The roads up around Fort Frederick and Balisier afford panoramic views though its a lot easier to drive than walk up there!

While nothing spectacular, the Botanic Gardens are a nice cool place to walk and admire some local trees and plants.

For boat lovers, GYS will be an attraction, but as a notice says "This Dock is in a state of dis-condition!" -so watch your step on the old docks. GYS is to be rebuilt, hopefully work will be well under way by the time you buy this book.

Grand Anse beach is a two mile stretch of white-gold sand, shaded by almonds and palms with a backing of dark green hills. During the day there is a sprinkle of color as bathers in brightly colored costumes lie on the beach or play in the sea. At the town end, beyond the Coconut Beach French Restaurant, the beach is fairly narrow - palms hang sideways over the water, fishing boats and nets decorate the sand, fishermen cook up broth on an open fire, and little dogs chase crabs. Down the beach, by the large hotels it has broadened out to a soft generous sweep, kept immaculate by bands of ladies who walk up and down raking it over. From here one can look over the bay and see the town of St George's nestled into the hills around its harbor. The beach has different moods depending on the weather. Many days it is calm - little wavelets barely brush the shore. It also gets rowdier, with short steep waves growling as they hit the sand - this excites the kids who shout and laugh as they dive through them. The beach is so long, that however many people come, there is always a spot one can find to oneself.

Considered by many to be the Windward's most magnificent beach, Grand Anse is the center of Grenada's tourist industry - here you will find the largest selection of hotels to choose from. None is allowed to be taller than the tallest coconut tree, and the new ones are built a bit back from the beach.

WHERE TO STAY

Let us start right on the beach and work our way along. Ramada Renaissance is beautifully laid out with lovely flower beds and fresh white paint. To me it looks brand new, like the plastic wrapping has just been pulled off. They have a particularly attractive pool area right next to the beach. The Riviera is rather old and looks it. It suffered a bit during the "rescue mission", though reconstruction is going on. Each cottage is self contained, and for the location the prices are very inexpensive. Coyaba, a brand new hotel, means "Heaven" in Arawak. Unlike some other parts of the Caribbean, Grenada has retained a firm hold on its own hotel industry, and foreign ownership is a rarity. Coyaba is owned and run by Andre and Richard Cherman who have been in the tourist business for many years. For a long time Richard was Grenada's director of tourism. The rooms are well designed, they have a private balcony with a view of the beach and if you get tired of looking at that there is satellite T.V! Spice Island Inn is one of Grenada's oldest and best known hotels. Some rooms are right on the beach, while others have a walled garden with a private swimming pool, a luxurious rarity even in these days! Further down there is Jim Needham"s Flamboyant - a collection of self contained cottages. Jim is American, but he's been here so long he almost counts as a local. Behind Flamboyant is Cinnamon Hill,

almost a village of self-contained apartments built in a decorative Spanish style. If we continue out to the next beach, which is smaller but also very lovely, you have the night club Fantasia 2001, backed by the brand new Gem Apartments.

There are actually two roads that run along Grand Anse - one close by the beach and the other a little behind. On the back road, Blue Horizons is owned by Arnold and Royston Hopkin another family of outstandingly successful Grenadian hoteliers. It is a pleasant well run hotel where the rooms are all self-contained and most have a view over the palm trees to the sea and St George's. Next door Hibiscus Hotel is small, personal, but spacious and well run. It is set in a large pleasant garden. Sit by the pool and enjoy the lovely fragrance of the frangipani and ylang ylang trees. Further down the road are the Morne Rouge Beach Apartments, and tucked up a little road to the side are the brand new Sea View Beach Apartments. Having just opened they are offering very attractive rates.

As we walk up the main road going south, still just a few hundred yards from the beach, we find several blocks of self-contained apartments. These are perfectly adequate, pleasant and some have a glimpse of the sea, though in most you would need the neck of a giraffe to get a really good view! They include Palm Court, Wavecrest, Southwinds and Maffekin. The apartments at Palm Court are two stories high and very spacious. Manager Laurel Wardally can be found in her office on the premises.

Down the other way towards the shopping center there is the Capitol Inn. Those on a tight budget can fill Veronica's "barracks style" with about 4 or 5 in a two room apartment and pay very little per head.

Several new hotels have chosen to be built at True Blue. This is convenient both to the airport and Grand Anse, and there are many lovely little hidden beaches to be explored along Point Saline. Godfrey Ventour has worked his way up in the hotel business - he started at the Calabash, then became manager of Secret Harbour, and now has his own No Problem self-contained apartments. "No problem" is a very local expression - you want something, "no problem". Someone dings your car and you angrily face the culprit, "no problem man". You don't have anywhere to stay - try No Problem Apartments! They are built, hotel style, amid an attractive garden and swimming pool, and right next door is Mall 21 with a restaurant, boutique, supermarket and car rental agency. High on a hill overlooking True Blue Bay is Hillcrest, a small 6 bedroom hotel. This is owned by Wellington Friday, the brother of surgeon Stan who has Balisier. Like his brother Wellington is a Doctor - an educator who has been a government minister and ambassador-at-large.

Further down the road the new Foxe Inn is clean, modern and motel style. Some of the rooms are self contained.

WHERE TO EAT OUT

Let us start at the snacky end of things. In the Grand Anse shopping center Sugar And Spice is a fast food pizza and ice cream bar which also serves rotis and chicken 'n chips. It is inexpensive, efficient and the ice cream is some of the best on the island. For rotis, snacks and local plates you have Veronica's and Capitol Inn. A very pleasant place, which offers not only inexpensive snacks and plates, but full meals, is Marielles at Mall 21. Or, further down the road you can try Foxe Inn which offers tasty local food.

The Bird's Nest is a good Chinese restaurant that also specializes in local seafood.

Chez Josephine is a good French-Creole restaurant built right on Grand Anse Beach at the St George's School of Medicine. They specialise in local seafood and lobster. As well as full meals they have a comprehensive snack menu with good salads etc.

If you are looking for something a little grander you can try the hotels. Blue Horizon's La Belle Creole, has for years had the reputation of consistently producing excellent food using all local produce. Go to Coyaba for their 9-12 am Sunday Brunch - a huge Grenadian buffet of wonderful local dishes including salt fish and lambi souse, bakes and sea eggs. You eat to the accompaniment of the Pepsi South Stars, one of the top local steel bands, all at a very reasonable price. Hibiscus has a sweet intimate little restaurant which has earned reputation for doing first rate local food. (Advance booking advisable). Ramada Renaissance has two restaurants and you will also find restaurants at Morne Rouge Beach Apartments, Fantasia 2001 and Cinammon Hill. This latter has a fabulous view towards St George's on one side, and a lovely pool with a rock fountain on the other.

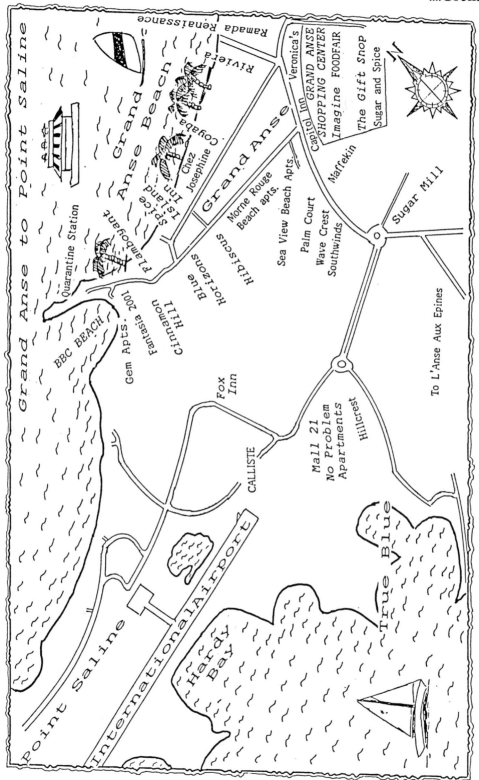

SHOPPING

Your food needs are easily met at Foodfair or Mall 21. Boutiques abound, they have them in all the major hotels and in Mall 21. Go to Grand Anse Shopping Center and visit Imagine - a wonderful handicraft shop crammed with everything from brightly colored batiks to woodcraft, pottery, and hand painted T-shirts. They have a mass of local products including the Spice Island Cosmetics as well as maps, books and their own speciality - a line of lovely local dolls (look at the clown). In the same area you will find The Man's Shop, for men's wear and the Gift Shop for porcelain, bone china, leather and jewelry.

WHAT ELSE?

This is unquestionably the area of beaches. Grand Anse is the most magnificent, but explore also the BBC (Morne Rouge) beach, and all the little beaches along the north shore of Point Saline - there are some real beauties here. At Grand Anse HMC runs a full range of watersports - Scuba, aquacycles, sailboards, Wavecutters, parasailing, Lasers, Sunfish, Jet ski, sports fishing and day sails. Check locations at Coyaba, Ramada, or Spice Island Inn.

In 1957 L'Anse Aux Epines was a derelict acreage of small prickly bushes. The soil had been worn out in the heyday of the great sugar boom, and the only remnant of that era was the old great house over looking Prickly Bay, without even a decent track to reach it. Gordon Brathwaite wanted this land badly and managed to scratch, save and borrow enough to buy it. "What does that stupid Brath Boy think he's doing" spluttered the old timers over their afternoon cocktails "that land is completely worthless, he can't do anything with it".

But Brath knew, all right. He put in a decent road, imported a herd of Jamaica Red cattle and began piecemeal to sell off bits of his farm to all comers. As houses started to build, so the demand grew, and soon the farm was just a couple of meadows in the valley and for the rest there were several hotels and hundreds of houses.

There were few restrictions on building and everyone had his own idea of what a house should look like. Soon Japanese pagoda roofs rubbed shoulders with 1950's modern, and Spanish mansions sprouted like mushrooms. Less ambitious people put up oblong "L'Anse Aux Epines box bungalows", more showy folk produced huge edifices with more arches and pillars than the Taj Mahal and an English pub was thrown in for good measure.

By rights it should be a horrid discordant mess, but in Grenada things that are supposed to work often don't and those that shouldn't often do! L'Anse Aux Epines is a perfectly delightful area. Beautiful gardens abound showing green lawns dotted with red flamboyant trees and bougainvillea in red, white and purple. There is pink oleander and Pride of Barbados, and bush trees grown huge with care. One sees a wonderful mass of green speckled with color, out of which roofs peep like so many cocked hats. At night one is lulled to sleep by tree frogs and crickets, and awakened at dawn by bird song.

L'Anse Aux Epines is a well-to-do residential area, where local and foreign residents get along well. There is a nice feeling of community. People meet and chat on L'Anse Epines beach, down by the boatyard, or in the restaurants. During the season they are joined by visitors looking for rather exclusive, quiet "away from it all" hotels. It attracts all types from young energetic people who spend their days snorkeling and wind-surfing, to the annual British migration of elderly dears who spend a few hours sitting sedately on the beach, and the rest playing bridge and mixing stiff gin and tonics. L'Anse Aux Epines is a hot mile or two (depending on where you are staying) from the main bus route. A bus does sometimes run from the boatyard in the mornings, but renting a car is a great advantage.

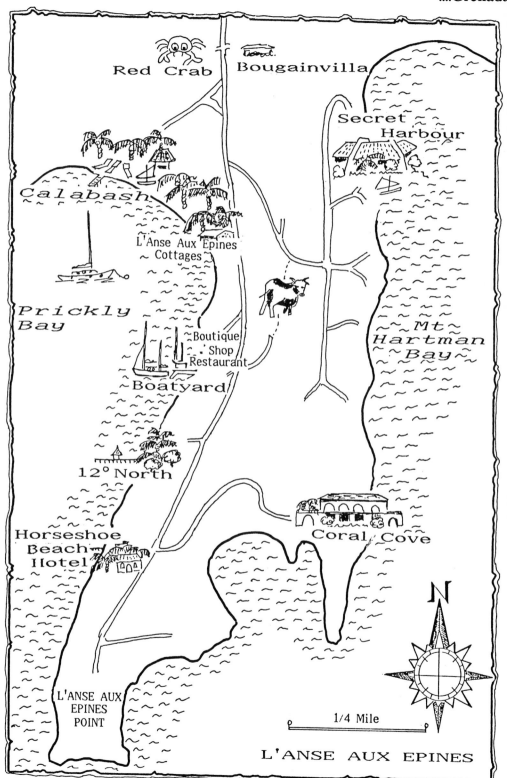

Red Crab

Bougainvilla

Secret Harbour

Calabash

L'Anse Aux Epines
Cottages

Prickly Bay

Boutique
Shop
Restaurant

~Boatyard~

12° North

Mt~ Hartman Bay~

Horseshoe Beach Hotel

Coral Cove

N

1/4 Mile

L'ANSE AUX EPINES POINT

L'ANSE AUX EPINES

47

WHERE TO STAY

All the hotels in L'Anse Aux Epines are small (less than 25 rooms). The emphasis is on space, privacy and seclusion, rather than "lots of action". They are all lovely, and if you are staying here, you can get a taste of them all by migrating from one to the next having a drink in each (this occupation would be much too elegant to described as a "pub crawl").

The Calabash is built on flat land on the main beach. Guests stay in whitewashed cottages built around a pond and lawn shaded by coconut palms. Rooms are simple but pleasing with a living area and patio. The main building is small and quietly elegant, paintings hang on stone walls, the dining room is open at the front with a view across the garden to the anchored yachts in the sea beyond. One eats under a ceiling of flowering vines, and on a Friday night to the accompaniment of a piano. The restaurant has won the prestigious "Golden Fork" award for excellence. A perfect hotel for those that want a tastefully quiet corner of the Caribbean, where they need do nothing more energetic than play tennis or take out a sailboard. On Saturdays in season they have a steel band who play outside on the lawn where their music can mingle with the sigh of surf and call of crickets.

Coral Cove is a new block of 11 self-contained, shore side apartments and cottages which face the breeze and a lovely view of Hog Island and Grenada's indented south coast. There is a tennis court, swimming pool and beach for sunbathing, but the reef makes sea bathing better for intrepid snorkelers. Maids pop in to clean and wash the linen, but after that it is up to you.

Horse Shoe Beach Hotel. This hotel has a lot of character with the atmosphere of a Spanish mansion sprawling down a beautifully gardened hill to the sea. There is a private beach and a dock to take you out into water deep enough to swim in. The older rooms are lovely - all rough whitewash and stained wood, each with a lovely authentic antique four poster bed in local mahogany. There are also more modern

suites for those who prefer them. The restaurant has a pleasing view over the bay. There is a nightly happy hour between 6 and 7 p.m. with two drinks for the price of one, and snacks. On Fridays, happy hour is accompanied by a live band. During the season they plan to host a champagne brunch on Sundays.

Lance Aux Epines Cottages. 7 largish units perfectly located for those who want to be right on the beach. In just a dozen steps you can be swimming before breakfast. These cottages come with a full maid service which includes cooking and clothes washing.

Secret Harbour is unquestionably Grenada's most majestic hotel. Italian tiles, brick pillars, heavy wooden beams, sunken baths and much more. The main building is up the hill where one can sit and take a drink in a perfect little alcove looking out over gardens of bougainvilla, frangipani and waving palms to the bay beyond. Guests stay in private suites which almost lean out over the water. It is enough to impress even your most blase friends.

There is a swimming pool, tennis, volley ball, and table tennis, with sailboards and dinghies for the adventurous. If you are staying elsewhere in Grenada come and enjoy Secret Harbour for a drink or meal.

Jo Gaylord's Twelve Degrees North is an exceptionally private and exclusive group of rental apartments. There are only 8 of them. You are not shown in and left to sort things out on your own. You have Jo and Pat as hosts backed by a special assistant assigned only to you. She will cook, clean, wash your clothes and tell you all about the island. She knows how to move silently and when to vanish. She can leave your dinner before she goes, but like all the staff she has left by 3 p.m. It would be hard not to love the totally private secluded garden with its own miniature beach. It is too shallow to swim here but a long wooden dock takes you out to deep water. You can stop on the way and sit under the little gazebo. Here, way out over the water you can feel the breeze on your skin and listen to the laughing gulls. Stare at the wavelets passing under the dock and they'll wash away your

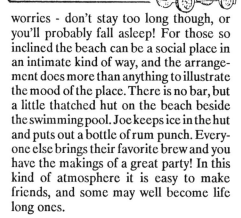
worries - don't stay too long though, or you'll probably fall asleep! For those so inclined the beach can be a social place in an intimate kind of way, and the arrangement does more than anything to illustrate the mood of the place. There is no bar, but a little thatched hut on the beach beside the swimming pool. Joe keeps ice in the hut and puts out a bottle of rum punch. Everyone else brings their favorite brew and you have the makings of a great party! In this kind of atmosphere it is easy to make friends, and some may well become life long ones.

EATING OUT AND ENTERTAINMENT

The Boatyard Restaurant looks out past a lawn studded with palm and almond trees to the yachts beyond. The best time to introduce yourself to the restaurant (and some of your neighbors) is at happy hour, daily 5.30 to 7 p.m. Stay for dinner, you can have anything from a snack to a full meal including delicious local lambi or best steak.

Further down the road is the Red Crab, an English style pub serving draught beer and such items as fish 'n chips or steak 'n chips. You can relax here with your friends and have a game of darts, or sit out under the spreading flamboyant trees.

If you want to tour the local nightspots, then head on down the road to Panache, rounding off your tour at the Sugar Mill. Both feature disco music into the wee hours.

L'Anse Aux Epines has its own grocery store, the Essentials mini market down at the boatyard. Alongside all the essentials you will find a great selection of local handicraft in their imaginative boutique.

WHAT ELSE?

Horse Shoe Beach hotel is the place for waterports in this area - Hans Dijkman can arrange Scuba, parasailing, deep sea fishing and waterskiing. He also operates a watersports section at the Calabash hotel.

Laughing Gull

TOURS

Tours in Grenada are not yet at the stage of "On Thursday we have a round the island trip..." Often the tour operators have groups going and it is possible to join them. Other times if you call up a tour operator he will try to "fix you up" - this means he will scout around and try to find a few other people to make up a group large enough to be viable on a per head basis. Some tour operators run small groups using taxis rather than buses. The answer to this is to try to organize your activities as early as possible. There are exceptions to this. The aquatic tours are well organized, run to fixed schedules, and anyone can join.

The Rhum Runner is a huge steel "catamaraft" with a blue and white fringe on top - a sort of ultra-wide aquatic double-decker bus with an upper viewing platform and downstairs dance floor.

When I arrived on board the whole cast was assembled - steel band, barman, crew, captain, snorkeling guide and palm hat weavers. They were all gathered at the stern of the boat peering into the cavernous depths of the starboard hold giving advice to a mechanic who was having an argument with a recalcitrant second engine. "Look man - it sparking - you must make she tighter" "Try hitting it harder" "Go fetch a big grip - we go get it fix". The mechanic worked away ignoring the advice, till at last, with a final twist of the wrench he declared himself done and the motor burst into a throaty roar. By the time we reached the cruise ship, everyone was back into place and the steel band started on a slightly wobbly version of "Yellow Bird". This was probably due to the weather, which chose to be unseasonably steel grey, and the usually flat calm sea was as lumpy as a horse hair mattress. However, as I was soon to find out, the Rhum Runner is all-weather fun.

About a hundred passengers climbed on board, all cameras, Panama hats, scarves and bright shirts displaying more birds and flowers than could be found in your average jungle. The bar man started handing round rum punch and we headed to the inner harbor for a sightseeing tour. Part owner Andrew Bierzynsky took to the microphone and while everyone looked he re-created Grenada's history from the days of the old sailing ships, and battles between French and English to the exciting recent events of revolution, treachery, and rescue. It was all there before us - the town with its forts, prison, the ill-fated Butler House, and even a wrecked Russian truck. No sooner was the talk finished than we were passing over the reef and the glass viewing platform was lowered. Everyone went to catch a glimpse of bright tropical fish darting about below.

Next stop was a lovely hidden beach, so secluded its only occupants were two beach guards and a cow. While the Rhum Runner nosed into the sand, the two uniformed law officers chased away the unwilling cow who was dozing on our spot. By now the sun had dispelled the clouds and the rum punch had worked its way into everyone's joints to the point they were jumping up and down in the surf singing.

But the real party started on the way back. Rum punch flowed freely, and the band had found their stride. Never before had four chromed steel drums and a shac shac made so much good sound. Everyone was dancing, jumping up and down to the rhythm. The wooden dance floor bounced with them, as if trying to imitate a trampoline. There was an amateur limbo contest going on for a bottle of rum punch, and as if that was not enough excitement, someone fishing over the side caught a barracuda. Every cruise comes to this climax, and on a previous, never to be forgotten cruise, this was the time that a young Spanish lady rushed up to Andrew - "help help - my seester have gone over the side". The picture froze. With a last tinkle the band stopped, the person doing limbo crashed to the floor - everyone looked. "Where?" - "back there - one minute she seet beside me and the next moment she

51

did gone". Andrew ordered full reverse, returning to the spot she marked - nothing. It seemed the impossible had happened, someone had scaled the four foot high safety rails and gone over. Regardless of his wallet, car keys and watch, Andrew leapt over the side and swam down 20 feet, the salt stinging his eyes as he looked around - nothing. By the time he came up a crew member joined him with mask and fins. They searched again but it was futile. In a deathly hush Andrew returned on board and picked up the emergency radio "Grenada Coast guard, Grenada coast guard, this is a Mayday we need immediate help in a search....."

It was at this moment the missing "seester", freshly made up, with every hair perfectly in place appeared from the toilet to where she had slipped away unnoticed, wondering why the music had stopped!

The picture unfroze; the coast guard was cancelled, Andrew breathed a sigh of relief and tended to the soggy mess that had once been his wallet, the band struck up, the dancing continued and the limbo contest was won by BoBo from Buenos Aires - another fantastic trip!

Rhum Runner does half day tours with steel band for $20 U.S. per person. They also do a moonlight tour on a Friday close to full moon, and some much more local day tours for swimming, snorkeling, and exploring Grenada's coasts. At $20 E.C. these provide exceptional good value, and an opportunity to meet some Grenadians in a relaxed atmosphere.

The Loafer. There is no question that the Rhum Runner was built purely as a "party boat". The Loafer, by contrast, although equally huge, is a sailing vessel designed to win transatlantic races. This is the boat for those who wish to sail; to feel the breeze on their faces, the gentle rhythm of the seas, and the peace of movement without the internal combustion engine. She also does half day, full day and special snorkeling trips, and, if you come in a group large enough, is also available for two day trips to Carriacou.

Back on dry land we will now look at some other things Grenada has to offer. All these can be done as a tour, if you arrange it early enough with a tour agent. For the real "bush" trips involving hikes, then Henry of Henry Tours is your man. You can also do most of these things by bus, rent-a-car and taxi. Let us start by looking at our map of Grenada and pointing out places of interest. The map is for orientation - for navigation buy the survey map available in most boutiques.

THE WEST AND NORTH COASTS

As you go up the west coast from St George's you pass a deep little bay called "Halifax Harbour" - sometimes yachts are anchored here. Not too much further on you come to the tiny village of Concord at the bottom of a hill. A narrow road leads off to the right, and winds upwards through beautiful land laden with nutmeg and fruit trees. At the top is the picturesque CON-CORD WATER FALLS. All Grenada"s water falls come with natural "built in" swimming pools below them, and taking a dip is something special - the water is clean and cool and leaves your skin and hair wonderfully soft. Those that would like a little hike can go on up the river (take the left branch) to the Upper Falls - about a half hour walk with a little scramble at the end. You will be rewarded by a perfectly secluded, private and delightful tropical waterfall.

Continuing up the coast from Concord you come to the fishing town of GOUYAVE - those who want to visit a working estate should check out DOU-GALDSTON. The heart of the town is on the beach where the fishing boats are pulled up and the nets laid out. From here you can continue northwards, or ask someone to direct you to the "Belvidere" road towards Grenville. The BELVIDERE ROAD is a narrow minor road, rough in places, but probably the prettiest in the island. It cuts right through Grenada's rich agricultural land, winding over hills and dropping down valleys - its like a hike through the mountains without having to get out of the car! Hikers could take an early bus from St George's to Gouyave, walk to Birch Grove and catch a bus back to town.

Going on northwards from Gouyave you pass through another fishing town called VICTORIA, then on to SAUTEURS. In the early days when the French first settled on Grenada, they "bought" the island for some axe handles, brandy and beads. The Caribs were probably not fully aware of the ramifications of this real estate deal, and after the French had been there a while, they decided to push them out. After some skirmishes, they mounted an all out attack on the French fort in St George's. The French had meantime received reinforcements who hid behind the fort walls, muskets and cannons loaded, until the Caribs were almost upon them. They opened fire with devastating effect, destroying the main Carib forces. They chased the rest north, killing men, women and children alike, till they came to Sauteurs. Here, it is said, the few remaining Caribs leapt over the cliffs into the sea to their deaths rather than being taken as slaves. Thus came the town's name from the French "sauter", to leap. From Sauteurs you can look northwards to Grenada's Grenadines: Round Island, Carriacou and Petit Martinique. If you arrange it in advance, you can have lunch near here, at a traditional old estate called Morne Fendue. To eat here is a real experience - it is a home rather than a restaurant, and it gives you a feel for what it must have been like to live in the old days of great plantations. The food comes straight from the estate and is both good and local.

Just at the exit to Sauteurs is the tiny road to LEVERA BEACH. This is rather deteriorated now, but certainly passable with a four wheel drive, and not too far to walk. Taken together, the approach, the beach and the views here are some of Grenada's best. Use caution about swimming - waves and currents can be very strong.

NORTH AND EAST COAST

On the way from Sauteurs to Grenville you can turn off to BATHWAY - a lovely wild area close by Levera development. Here one finds huge natural pools formed by rocks which provide safe swimming and are a popular picnic spot on weekends. Those with a spirit of adventure can take the little road from Tivoli to LAKE ANTOINE. (four wheel drive preferable). Lake Antoine is a picturesque old estate that produces rum. It still runs today much as it did 200 years ago. The cane is all crushed by a huge water wheel, the husks fuel a fire for the heat - the juices make the rum.

Hot bubbling sulpher spring baths are supposed to be excellent for the health, and Grenada has a completely natural one of its own - CLABONY SPRING. It is just a little rock pool tucked away in the hills under Mount St Catherine. The water is pleasantly warm. Follow the river up from the turning place just before the road ends; it is about quarter of a mile. If you want to be sure to find it call Clifton Joseph (440 7225, 7048) and ask him to guide you.

GRENVILLE is Grenada's second largest town. It is on the windward coast, with a huge harbor protected by reefs. The market on Saturdays is excellent. There are a few small restaurants where one can get a bite to eat, best to ask around when you get there. At the back of Grenville you can visit the NUTMEG STATION. Nutmeg is Grenada's main export. It is a tough crop; it takes five years before you even know whether the tree is going to bear (there are males and females), and even longer for good production. But in the end it is all worth it. You wait till the nutmegs fall to the ground and you can use every part. The outside fruit-like husk makes jelly, then the nut is wrapped in a pretty red spice called mace. There is a hard shell, which contains an oil making it perfect to put on your garden where you don't want weeds to grow, and the real prize is the nutmeg inside. At the station you will be shown how the nutmegs are washed, dried, shelled and graded, and you will love the spicy smell.

Just outside Grenville on the Grand Etang road is the Carlton St Andrews COCOA STATION. When you eat a piece

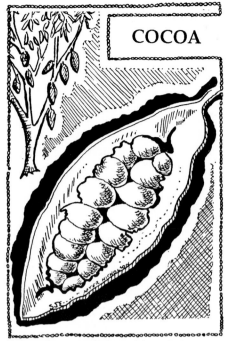

COCOA

of chocolate, you have no idea of what goes before! Inside the cocoa pod, the cocoa bean is surrounded by a sweet tasting fibrous goo. This has to be fermented for 8 days, then dried in the sun. During the drying ladies walk through it, turning with their feet for even drying, then it is further machine dried, and the outer husks taken off, before grading and packing! There are many other nutmeg and cocoa plants you can visit in Grenada, but these are two convenient ones.

THE GRAND ETANG ROAD

The most exciting main road in Grenada is the Grand Etang Road which winds up through the mountains from St George's over to Grenville. Along the way you come to the turn off for ANNENDALE FALLS. You twist down a small road which at one point narrows to accommodate a huge and ancient "Silk Cotton" (Kapok) tree with a wonderfully convoluted trunk. The falls themselves are in a pretty hollow beside some tall mahogany trees. The surrounding rocks are covered in giant "elephant ear" vines whose falling roots make "Tarzan ropes". A lovely garden has been made behind the falls and you can walk up the paths for a perfect picture from above. Herbs and spices are for sale at the visitors center. Before you leave, look upwards - there is a huge samaan tree absolutely covered in every kind of "air plant".

Back on the main road, you wind up and up and up the mountain - then, when you reach the top, pull into the little parking spot and look back - you can see the whole south west coast laid out before you. Just a few yards down the road is another parking spot with a sign "Enjoy camping, hiking, fishing, photography, picnicking, boating, swimming, birdwatching". A trail here leads you to little wooden seats in the peace and quiet. Ahead the wind-swept trees cling to a mountain in a strange pattern reminiscent of a giant sea fan.

GRAND ETANG,
MT QUA QUA AND THE
CONCORD VALLEY TRAILS

Grand Etang lies right in the middle of Grenada - a lake formed in the crater of an old volcano. It is an eerie place, surrounded by a band of wind-pruned trees that often take on a bluish hue. Even up to recent times people have held it in awe - it was not too many years ago I once came here to find a group of white robed religious people, banging on drums, and sending out food on a leaf to feed the "Lady of the Lake". Wonderful stories abound about the lake's fathomless depths, too deep to measure. I was even told of a diver who tried to find the bottom, only to disap-

pear, his drowned body being washed up on a beach in St Lucia. A few years ago I heard with no little amusement an announcement on Radio Grenada "The G.B.S.S. (a local school); sent an expedition to to Grand Etang lake and found it to be 12 feet deep, not bottomless as previously thought". Well, those were the past days of unimaginitive scientific socialism; for me the lake still has a feeling of mystery and romance, and until it becomes full of pedalos, canoes and Sunday trippers, I still think of it as "bottomless".

THE FOREST CENTER

The whole area is the preserve of Grenada's National Parks. Their Forest Center is housed in a pictureque building overlooking the lake. The gardens surrounding the center are immaculate and you can find all sorts of flowers and herbs here. They have marked quite a number of forest trails to enable you to explore on your own. If you visit the center you can read all about Grenada's wildlife, see pictures and videos, get maps of the trails, and ask any questions that may arise.

CONCORD TRAIL

The lake is in the very heart of Grenada's rain forest - a vast expanse of tall trees. Because one views it from the road, the forest seems smaller, and the road bigger, - in reality the main road is just a tiny swathe cut through the jungle. If you want to explore further you can - there is a

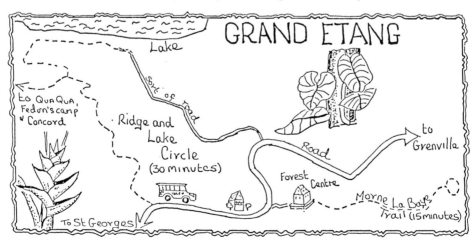

marked trail through to Concord on the island's west coast, here you will find the next nearest road - a good four hour hike away. Luckily the forest is generally cool, but it should not be taken lightly - it is no "safe" trail with steps, handrails and litter bins - it is a rough trail often slippery, steep and treacherous. You will probably find yourself at times hanging onto trees for support and sliding on your bottom. Great for the adventurous but no place to go on your own or to drag along aging aunt Hetty with her gammy knee. Never go in times of really heavy rain, and all through the wet season the path will be a quagmire, and you are likely to arrive the other end looking like "the thing that came out of the swamp". It makes sense to start off early in the morning, giving yourself as much daylight as possible. You will soon find yourself far away from civilization, walking under massive trees which drip with strange vines and mosses. Now and again you will come across some brilliant red or yellow balisier flowers with their banana-like leaves. As you get nearer Concord you start crossing the river - if you explore a little you will find several water falls with pools big enough for a dip. One of the small ones we found was covered in an emerald-green moss, and a flock of little "Doctor" hummingbirds darted in and out of it for a drink. When you finally join up with the "proper" footpath the other side of the Concord river, turn left, not right. - Even though you feel almost dead, it is only five minutes to the wonderful "Upper Concord" falls, where you can swim, relax and laugh at your achievement and aching limbs. Now it is all downhill.

MT QUA QUA

This is part way along the Concord track and gives you a good feel for the rain forest without going all the way across. The trail is better laid out here, and the journey time of one and a half hours each way from Grand Etang is at a reasonably easy pace. You get well away from the road till the only sounds are the birds and tree frogs. From time to time you will have wonderful glimpses across the island. When you reach Mt Qua Qua (2373 feet) you will, clouds permitting, have a wonderful view over Grenada's mountains to the east coast. Here you can sit and look and feel the breeze. Close your eyes - listen - it could be now, or a year ago, or hundreds of years ago; time means nothing to a mountain.

FEDON'S CAMP

This is one for those who eat their spinach and take lots of vitamin pills - it's an extra up hill slog detour half way to Concord - but worth it for those that make it. Fedon was a free mullato planter who, in 1795, inspired by the French revolution, rose against the ruling British who had been giving the French Catholic settlers a rough time. He persuaded some slaves to join him. They captured the governor and 42 other hostages, and controlled most of the country but failed to take St George's. Eventually reinforcements arrived and the rebellion was quelled, but during the assault Fedon carried out his threat to massacre the hostages. In the aftermath, the British proved themselves equally bloodthirsty, hanging nearly 40 rebels. The most unlucky rebel to be hung was Pierre Alexander who faced his departure in an extremely sullen mood, which was not improved when the rope broke leaving him sitting on the ground till they could find a stronger piece! Fedon never suffered this fate: he disappeared never to be found.

OTHER TRAILS

If all the above sounds much too energetic, do not despair, there are also some much easier paths. MORNE LA BAYE TRAIL starts right at the forest center and only take 15 minutes. There is also a half hour RIDGE and CIRCLE trail which takes you a short way on the Concord route, then brings you back by the Grand Etang Lake.

TRANSPORT NOTES

Thrifty independent-minded people can take the Grenville bus from St George's and get out at Grand Etang. If you hike from there over to Concord you can walk back down to the main road and catch a bus back to St George's. Others can make arrangements with a taxi. Otherwise, and for many this makes a lot of sense, you call up Henry of Henry's Tours. He is the only tour operator I have found willing to do real "jungle trips" including several days in the bush if you so wish. Contact him as soon during your stay as possible, as he may have to find some like-minded people to make up the tour and keep the price reasonable. Also, unless you are lucky enough to find a Grenadian friend, he is probably the only man who will take you to Grenada's most beautiful SEVEN FALLS.

BALISIER
(Heliconia)

SEVEN FALLS

These ultimate tropical water falls, with lovely pools for swimming, lie about one hour's muddy downhill hike through dense rain forest. They are very hard to find and lie on private property, making it difficult

as a "do it yourself" project. I suggest you try Henry of Henry's Tours who has permission to take people there. This is only for the fit and adventurous - others could buy the little color picture book "Grenada, Carriacou and Petit Martinique", and admire the photograph of Seven Falls on the back cover.

ST PAULS

Returning to more civilized areas, there are a couple of interesting places at St Pauls.

The Tower. The first time I saw the Tower I was driving from St David's to St Pauls. After miles of twisting round bends, avoiding chickens and admiring the little wooden houses, the Tower came as a kind of shock. An almost ghostly apparition - a massive turreted house dominating the landscape. Partially hidden by trees, it looked out of place, mysterious and more than a little Gothic, summoning up images of wicked butlers and damsels in distress. On turning a bend it disappeared, I thought I might have dreamed it - but round the next corner there it was again. On closer inspection, it is still grand, but perhaps in the more friendly manner of a French Chateau than Dracula's lair.

Undoubtably one of Grenada's most fascinating buildings, the Tower is of quite recent origin - built by C.F.P. Renwick in 1916. Renwick was an immensely rich lawyer who was so astute in business and such dynamite in the courtroom he became known as "Diable Negre" - Black Devil. Among other properties he owned L'Ance Aux Epines. He often went on trips abroad and ended up marrying an English girl. It was for her he built the "Tower" - a massive demonstration of his riches, power and affection with its single layered tower. She tried living there a while, but couldn't take the life, left him and returned to England where she had his baby. Once she left, he closed it up and never lived in it again. But he did use it for private gambling parties played for high stakes. History is a bit cloudy, but he lost a lot of his wealth before he died. Those that are interested can still see his old brass lawyer's sign in Church Street not far past Barclays Bank.

The Slingers, who now own the tower, accept visitors by appointment, and this is an excellent way to sample a little of Grenada's history. You get a tour of the main level, with its magnificent mahogany panelled ceiling and dining table that seats 16. There are paintings, historic documents and maps along with poisoned arrows and other artifacts from the Amerindians of Guyana. You also tour the estate, through fruit orchards and spice trees, past cashew nuts trees to one of the only two Macadamia nut trees in Grenada. There are of course endless flowers. The best part of the trip is, that having taken the tour, you get to relax on the terrace, and drink tea or coffee, and rum punch made of limes from the estate. This will help you, as no museum can, feel a bit of Grenada, both past and present.(call 440 3243/3343, to arrange a visit - there is a $6 U.S. fee which includes refreshment). If you do not want to come by taxi, or cannot find a suitable tour, you can get here by taking the St Pauls bus from the market square. Ask them to put you off at "The Tower".

BAY GARDENS. To find Bay Gardens you turn right at St Paul's Police station and right again at the sign. You will find several acres of lovely gardens, with all manner of trees, plants and flowers. The gardens are privately owned and there might be a nominal charge to enter.

GRENADA'S SOUTH COAST BEYOND PRICKLY BAY

Grenada's south coast is relatively dry - an area of palms, sugar cane and prickly acacia bushes. In the sheltered waters of its deep bays and little islands one finds mangroves and tiny beaches, the favorite haunt of the big blue heron and the smaller blue crane. Here and there cattle are kept, and they are nearly always accompanied by elegant white cattle egrets who search in their footsteps for little insects. If you want to explore the south coast by sea you can go down to Woburn and make a deal with one of the local fishermen who will take you round by boat. Calivigny Island makes a good point to be dropped off; there are secluded beaches and you can walk to the southern tip where the waves crash into the shiny black rocks and the air is full of spray.

The south coast also boasts some lovely developments, which make a pleasurable drive. The oldest established is Westerhall, always immaculately gardened and tended. Take "Old Harbor Drive" down to the tranquil little bay and beach. Fort Jeudy is still fast growing, and right out on the point you get some memorable views.

A special place go for an inexpensive lunch and day by the shore is La Sagesse Nature Reserve. It has been created out of an old estate house and adapted as a small hostelerie. There is a little bar and restaurant, and for those who want to really get away from it all there are three self-contained apartments. Around you have miles of walks through nature, and beaches for swimming. An ideal retreat for those that need to do some walking and thinking. Call and ask about their special guided nature walks which includes eating fresh fruit off the trees as you walk!

THE HASH HOUSE HARRIERS

As a final thought, anyone who likes cross country running is welcome to join the Grenada Hash House Harriers, a sort of "not very serious, lots of fun, cross country trot", specially designed to keep the fast with the slow. Takes place once a fortnight, call Paul Slinger 440 3343 3243.

PUBLIC LIBRARY - ST. GEORGE'S

CARRIACOU

Many travelers talk about wanting to find an "unspoilt" island, but few of them actually enjoy a completely unspoilt island - one virtually untouched by tourism or influences from their own world. The average traveler wants other travelers to talk to, he wants activities that have been created for visitors, he wants to get there after the island has been "discovered" but before the mob arrives. However, for the very few that are independent-minded enough to appreciate a really unspoilt island there is Carriacou.

Carriacou is a naturally beautiful island. Everywhere you walk there are lovely views into the hills and out to sea and surrounding islands. Even their pests are pretty - there is a creeping vine (called Coralita) that covers everything and spreads everywhere, and would you know, it has abundant clusters of charming pink-mauve flowers!

Carriacou people have their roots in Africa, some even know which tribes they came from and keep a lot of African traditions including the "Big Drum" dance which is a way of communicating with the ancestors. The island is out of sight of St George's and "out of sight is out of mind". An active history of smuggling has kept them in the past from being keen on too much influence from the mainland. They are very active culturally, but they are not "westernised" and the traveler will have to make some effort to get to know them. However, for those that do, it would be hard to imagine a nicer, kinder and more friendly people.

They live by farming, fishing and seafaring, which includes the building of boats, and the Carriacou sloops are the best in the islands. Neither is this a static art, their designs have been so improved and refined over the last years that their boats can outsail many a yacht. They race them every year in the Carriacou regatta, a long weekend festival of local fun which takes place in the first weekend in August. One year some Bequians came down to show them a thing or two. They came in what was in fact sleek yacht hull that had been rebuilt from the deck up as a local sloop. However, they were no match for the home grown Carriacou boats who showed them their clean sweet sterns!

What you will find in Carriacou are the most wonderful hikes, very secluded beaches, and a host of lovely outer-islands with some of the best snorkeling in the Windwards. You are unlikely to find more than a handful of other visitors. There will be almost no activities designed for tourists and night life tends to be limited to the odd dance at the "City Hall", and games of checkers and dominoes played on the road outside the rum shops. By all means take on a local at a game of checkers - but be warned, they play be very strange rules. I am used to the slow British rules and couldn't believe it when my opponent got a king and he whipped it all over the board eating up my men like a crazed pac man!

The only town, Hillsborough, is built on the beach with one main street. It is very sleepy, with flowers that pop out between the houses. There is a tiny museum and botanical garden which are worth a visit.

However, Carriacou will change. Tourism is already beginning to come and if it stays low key it will be good for everyone. However, if you want to see it before the others arrive, come now!

WHERE TO STAY

Up to now, Carriacou has suffered from a sort of hit-and-run hotel industry, where the hotels kept opening and closing, and managers changed as often as the weather. However, it looks at last as if we may have started with some good and consistent management. The largest hotel is the Silver Beach Resort with 18 rooms, situated just out of town on the pretty beach that sweeps around Hillsborough Bay. It has just been expanded, and completely renovated. Some rooms are self contained, and some air conditioned. The hotel is large enough to support a nice boutique, a tennis

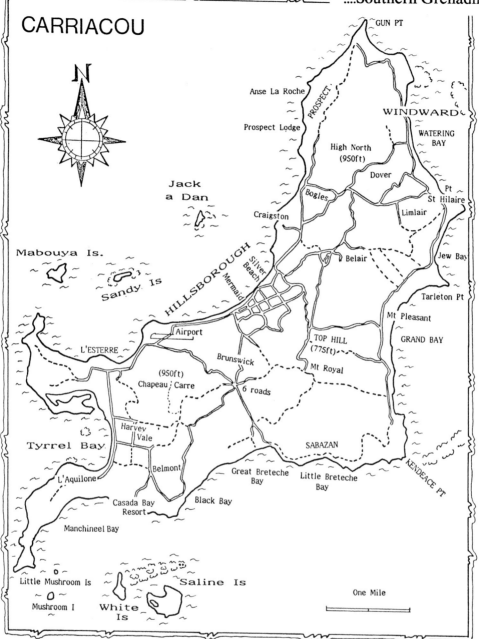

CARRIACOU

N

GUN PT

Anse La Roche

Prospect Lodge

WINDWARD

WATERING BAY

PROSPECT

High North (950ft)

Dover

Pt St Hilaire

Bogles

Limlair

Jack a Dan

Craigston

Belair

Jew Bay

Mabouya Is.

Sandy Is

Silver Beach

Mermaid

HILLSBOROUGH

Tarleton Pt

Mt Pleasant

Airport

TOP HILL (775ft)

GRAND BAY

L'ESTERRE

Brunswick

Mt Royal

(950ft) Chapeau Carre

6 roads

Harvey Vale

SABAZAN

Tyrrel Bay

Belmont

Great Breteche Bay

Little Breteche Bay

KENDEACE PT

L'Aquilone

Casada Bay Resort

Black Bay

Manchineel Bay

Little Mushroom Is

Saline Is

One Mile

Mushroom I

White Is

court and a couple of rental cars. They have boats for hire for exploring the coasts and islands, and scuba is arranged for certain days.

Cassada Bay Hotel is built on a hill with a gorgeous view southwards over little islands down to Grenada. Rooms are cabin style, built out of wood, and they all have a patio overlooking the view. Free ferry service is provided to White Island,

which has both a fantastic beach and excellent snorkeling.

Mermaid Beach Hotel is also on the beach, right in Hillsborough, and the building has a certain charm with a flower filled patio. Some rooms have their own bathrooms, other share.

Cosy Nook just outside Hillsborough is cheap but very basic.

One feels Prospect Lodge is just the way

a guest house should be. It sits way out in a beautiful deserted spot in the north west part of the Island. The Lodge is high up a hill, with land that falls all the way down to the sea. The communal room is light and airy with huge white windows framing a perfect view across the bay. It is owned by an American couple, Lee and Ann Katzenbach. Lee is an artist who creates powerful pictures in bright water colors. Ann likes to take photographs, but spends most of her time keeping the Lodge running. To visit here is like going to stay with good friends in their gorgeous island home - it works both ways too; without the occasional guest, Lee and Ann might well go crazy staring at each other! This is the perfect hide-away for the fit and healthy who want to hike and swim. A boat is available for exploring the islands, and a Sunfish for sailing round the bay. The accomodations are spread between several buildings and two of the rooms are self-contained. Since Prospect Lodge is quite a way from anywhere, you want to take the half board option. They do all their own baking and serve only good fresh foods, chicken and fish being the staples. They grow their own lettuce for the salads, and for desert make their own ice cream, or serve home made cakes.

TRANSPORT

There are buses, but you wait a bit longer here than on the mainland, and as is natural on a small island prices are a bit higher. There are plenty of taxis and you may be able to rent a car from Silver Beach Resort

or Leo Cromwell. Local boats go to Union on Mondays and Thursdays.

EATING OUT

In Carriacou you could just eat out every night of one week and not go to the same restaurant twice! Not only that but every place is rather special in its own way. Cassada Bay is a must if for the view alone! They serve nice local food, including lobster in season. Silver Beach Resort also goes in for good Caribbean seafoods and you can sit practically on the beach. One night you must go out to L'Aquilone, a tiny but very sweet Italian restaurant built out of a cute little wooden house sitting right on top of a hill looking out both over Tyrrel Bay and to the south. They make their own fetuccini with a hand crank pasta machine! Another time you should visit Barba's Oyster Shell restaurant, the lively spot in Tyrrel Bay - you can get fresh fish, lobster and both chicken and lamb from Barba's farm. There is also Bubbles Alexis' new Turtle Dove Beach Bar just down the road from The Oyster Shell. Back in Hillsborough you can go and arrange for customs officer Paddy (ask down at the customs house, everyone knows him) to fix you up a good meal at his bar The Coloured Lantern. You could also go and take a look at the Tip Top Scraper restaurant in town. The Mermaid is Carriacou's original hotel, and makes a pleasant place to take meal - best book in advance. Prospect Lodge does not really run as a restaurant, but call them up and see if they can fit you in with their other guests one night; you

will love the place, get a first rate view and meet some interesting people. In town at lunch time? Try a conch roti at the Golden Eagle - just a little rum shop, but great rotis. If they don't have any you can get chicken or beef rotis just across the road in the Rooftop Restaurant.

SHOPPING

Those in a self-contained apartment will find some grocery stores in town, and may even get a little fresh produce in the market. But if you have a car, go out and visit Barba's supermarket in Tyrell Bay. Apart from a good food selection he has the very best prices for all kinds of liquor, not only in Carriacou, but in the Windwards!

If you are interested in art, arrange to see Canute Caliste. He lives in a tiny wooden house in L'Esterre, and his naive paintings are the best known in the lower Caribbean. You will probably end up paying more for a frame than you will for the painting! There is also an active handicraft industry centered around Tyrrel Bay catering to the yachts. They mainly make turtleshell, coral and coconut shell jewelry. Go down and ask around - ask for John Bedeau, or Randolph Alexis. You may find a handicraft shop in town.

WHAT TO DO

Carriacou is ideal for hiking, or if you are too lazy, driving. There are certain places you must visit. Windward has a lot of Scottish ancestry, and is traditionally the home of Carriacou boatbuilding though many boats are now built in Tyrrel Bay, and it is a sight to watch them being hand-crafted right on the beach. If you are lucky enough to be around when one is going to be launched, make sure you come for the launching. Sabazan is a lovely area to walk to, and up at the end of the beach is a cliff full of pieces of pre-Columbian pottery. As the waves wash the cliff away so more is exposed, and you can find pieces on the sand and under the water. Drivers will want to go up to the hospital for the fabulous views, while the more energetic can hike up High North and Chapeau Carre, where the views are unsurpassed.

But don't spend all your time ashore, get a local fisherman to take you out to Sandy Island, an enchanting desert island of lovely beach surrounded by good snorkeling. If snorkeling is your bag, then go out to the long reef which sweeps out from White Island past Saline Island. The current here is very strong, so have your boat man drop you at the western end of the reef and follow you as you drift down to White Island (sometimes the current goes the other way).

One day should be devoted to a day sail aboard Sweetheart, an aptly named locally built sloop. You sail with her shipwright Zepharine McLaren. She is fully authentic, built right on the beach at Windward, no engine, but swift and powerful under sail (winner of her class in the Carriacou Regatta). You can go visit one of the other Grenadine Islands - a day on this boat will give you, as no other experience can, a feel

for the "local way". (call Zeph 443 7340).

You could also take a boat for a trip over Petit Martinique. This island looks so small from afar, but actually when you start to walk around it it is quite big. You will find scenic walks, pretty houses, boat building, pleasant people and rum shops, of course!

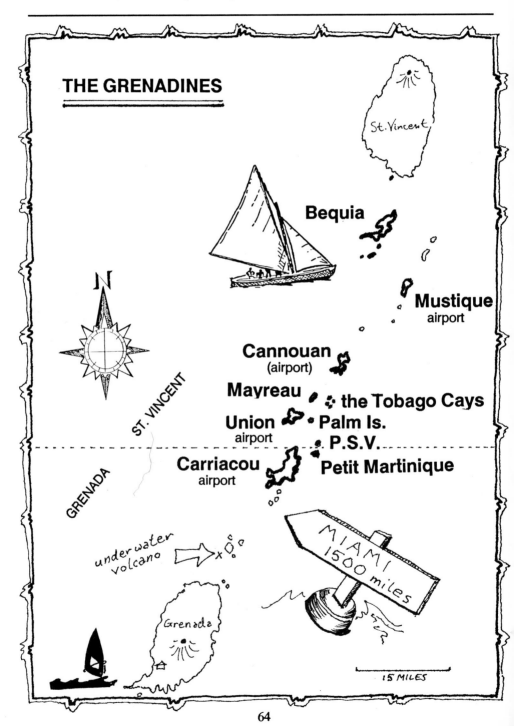

THE GRENADINES

St. Vincent

Bequia

Mustique
airport

Cannouan
(airport)

Mayreau
the Tobago Cays

Union
airport
Palm Is.

P.S.V.

ST. VINCENT

GRENADA

Carriacou
airport
Petit Martinique

underwater volcano

MIAMI
1500 miles

Grenada

15 MILES

ST VINCENT AND THE GRENADINES

To the adventurous traveler, St Vincent and the Grenadines beckons irresistibly - here you have a whole string of islands, well off the beaten track, each with a completely different personality. All the inhabited ones are special enough to attract bands of dedicated adherents, who return year after year to their special island, feeling they have found their personal Shangri La.

St Vincent itself is volcanic island whose dramatic scenery and steep convoluted mountains are covered in dense tropical vegetation. Much of the interior is so wild and inpenetratable that there is no road running all the way round the island, neither one across the center. It is a perfect contrast to the smaller, gentler Grenadine isles which offer the kind of palm fringed beaches and bright blue-green water that forms the core of many a vacationers dream. Some of them are large enough to have rolling hills or small mountains, others are flat sandy uninhabited cays.

The Grenadines include Mustique - the legendary secluded playground of royalty, rock stars and high society; Bequia - an island of industrious mainly artisan inhabitants, which attracts artists, writers, poets and yachtsmen; P.S.V. - the quiet hideaway for successful people who need to "get away from it all", the spectacularly beautiful Tobago Cays, mountainous Union, and other hideaways such as Palm, Canouan and Mayreau.

It is typical in this country of contrasts, that although St Vincent and the Grenadines has perhaps one of the least developed tourist industries in the Windwards, it contains two of the Caribbean's most successful resorts - Young Island and P.S.V. It is also a mecca for yachtsmen, and the main cruising ground for the area's charter yachts.

TRANSPORT WITHIN ST VINCENT AND THE GRENADINES

AIR TRANSPORT

There are airports in St Vincent, Mustique, Canouan, and Union. You can fly to all except Canouan directly from Barbados, or hop down from St Vincent, or up from Grenada. LIAT has daily flights from Barbados to St Vincent, Mustique and Union. Air Martinique flies twice daily from Martinique via St Vincent to Union and back, stopping in Mustique on their second flight. Grenadine Tours using Mustique Airways on a "shared charter" concept are perhaps the most flexible, running as many flights as are necessary to service the demand at a cost comparable to the other airlines.

SEA TRANSPORT

BETWEEN ST VINCENT AND THE REST OF THE GRENADINES
All times are approximate (re-check schedule with the tourist office before packing your bags).

On Mondays and Thursdays the motor vessel "Snapper" leaves St Vincent at 1000, she calls at Bequia (1100), Canouan (1330), and Mayreau (1445), arriving in Union at about 1500 and overnighting there. On Tuesdays and Fridays she sets out from Union at 0700, calling at Mayreau (0730), Canouan (0845) and Bequia (1100) reaching St Vincent around noon. You might be able to arrange rough accommodation on the boat in Union overnight. Also check at the Grenadines Wharf in Kingstown for other vessels which include the Vicki, also the Robert Jr and Geronimo which go to Mustique. The one way fare to Canouan is $10 E.C., Mayreau $12 E.C. and Union $15 E.C.

BETWEEN UNION AND CARRIACOU.

Two boats usually leave Union on Monday and Thursday at 0745 bound for Carriacou, returning later in the morning. (fare $10 E.C.).

Petit St Vincent (otherwise known as P.S.V) is unquestionably to some the ultimate dream island. It stands all on its own, 113 acres of woodland and meadow bounded by white sand beach and set in waters of turquoise and blue. It is partially surrounded by a reef that provides some really beautiful snorkeling.

It was bought by a small group headed by former charter yacht owner Haze Richardson who imagined their idea of a perfect hotel and made the dream come true. The hotel was to be the ideal hideaway - a retreat for those who wish a holiday of quiet relaxation in elegant style well away from bright lights, cruise ships, and the maddening crowd. The geography of the island helps - the beauty is of a serene sort with gentle rolling hills and quiet corners, and it is accessible only by boat.

The accommodation stresses comfort and privacy. Guests stay in spacious, comfortable cottages which are dotted around the island. Each contains a pleasant living room, a large bedroom (twin queen-size doubles) and a bathroom with separate dressing area large enough to suit the most demanding Hollywood star. The best feature of all is a completely private patio and garden area with easy chairs, or maybe a hammock, and a perfect view of the sea. The only telephone is in the office, and for room service each cottage is equipped with a flag pole. If you want to be left alone hoist the red flag, and if you want room service hoist the yellow one - soon a waiter will arrive down the path in a tiny open jeep. If you have never seen a car quite like it do not be surprised, they are built right at the hotel!

P.S.V. does not really feel like a hotel at all, it has more the feel of a huge luxurious private estate with the main hotel building

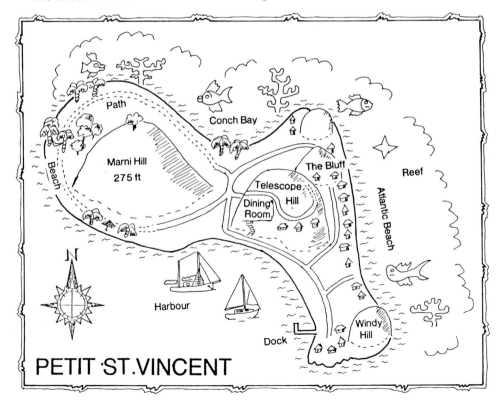

PETIT ST.VINCENT

(bar, restaurant, boutique and offices) as the baronial hall and dining room. This illusion is further engendered by the family of golden labradors that loll aristocratically on the stone steps or chase crabs in the shallows. If you are not a dog lover you will rate no more attention than a lazily rolled eye as you walk by, but it you talk with them you quickly acquire a pet!

Guests spend much of their time swimming and relaxing on the beach, but tennis, table tennis. full watersports and a trimaran for day charters, or speed boat for trips further afield are all available.

UNION ISLAND

Union Island is in the center of the lower Grenadines. It has a little airport, a small hospital, 2 banks, numerous tiny supermarkets and a colorful, bustling harbor packed with yachts.

The island has a dramatic mountainous outline highlighted by the "Pinnacle", a thousand foot peak so steep that from some angles it looks like a cathedral spire. There are many beaches and the surrounding waters are brightly colored from pale green through turquoise to aquamarine.

Union has a well developed day charter industry and is for many the gateway to the Grenadines. Every day a fleet of small planes descends on the island unloading a flock of brightly dressed tourists who are shepherded onto waiting yachts and taken for a cruise around some of the islands. By mid afternoon they return and get whisked back to their hotels in Barbados, St Lucia or Martinique in time for dinner.

Apart from these fleeting migrations, Union is not a tourist island, though there are three hotels all in Clifton, the main community. Staying here and joining the day charter boats could be a cheaper way to see the lower Grenadines than chartering your own yacht. With a little exploring you could certainly find a beach to yourself, and hikes back into the mountains would afford many fabulous views.

The best hotel is the attractive Anchorage Yacht Club which is set in about 20 acres of waterfront property, a perfect location right in the harbor but just out of town. Manager Charlotte Honnart is French, and you can expect good French and Creole cooking. On Mondays and Fridays there is a grand buffet and jump up to a steel band. The French have a "thing" for shark pools. So anything you don't eat for dinner you can toss to the sharks - but do not worry they are only "nurse sharks" and people are more likely to worry them than the other way round. In fact at one time there was a notice saying "Please do not touch the sharks!" The whole bar area is very pleasant and well situated to watch the movement of yachts, most of whom use the Anchorage dock for tying up their dinghies. The accommodation is in beach cottages and rooms, each with its own patio and a view of the harbor. Anchorage also manages the island's airport and if you are thinking of coming in your own plane, the runway is a little over 2000 feet long, takes planes up to five tons and has full customs and immigration facilities. Passengers landing here are charged a small landing fee to cover airport maintenance. Anchorage arranges charter and sightseeing flights. There is an excellent boutique, and up-to-date U.S. newspapers are often on sale! Anchorage also act as yacht charter agents for anyone wishing to spend a few days sailing in the Grenadines.

For other activities and entertainment one has diving, sailboard rentals, deep sea fishing, scuba and a glass bottom boat.

The other hotels are right in town. They are locally owned and somewhat basic, but what they lack in "spit and polish" they make up for in local atmosphere and lower prices.

The Clifton Beach Hotel owned by Conrad Adams is an old style hotel with

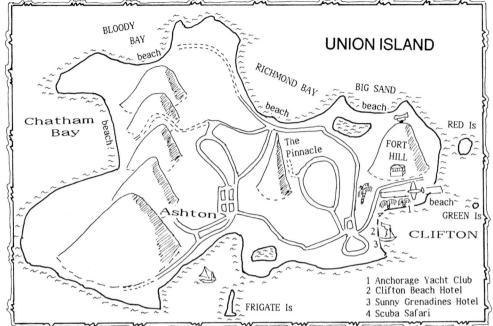

Map of Union Island showing: Bloody Bay, beach, Richmond Bay, beach, Big Sand beach, Chatham Bay, beach, The Pinnacle, Fort Hill, Red Is, Ashton, Clifton, Green Is, beach, Frigate Is

1 Anchorage Yacht Club
2 Clifton Beach Hotel
3 Sunny Grenadines Hotel
4 Scuba Safari

most of the rooms upstairs in a large building. Down below they have a bar and snack bar, and a restaurant looking out over the harbor. Avid shoppers can check the "Chic Unique" boutique opposite, and the local handicraft store down the road.

Mr Mitchell's Sunny Grenadines is further down fronting the harbor. He has rooms and cottages some of which have cooking facilities. Just a short walk up the hill is the brand new 6 room SeaA View Hotel. They have no phone, but their low rates offer a great bargain for those on a budget.

The Sunny Grenadines Restaurant is run by a cheerful French couple Brigitte and Philippe who even butcher their own meat and smoke their own fish! French cuisine with a band and buffet on Thursdays and a lobster party on Fridays.

There are one or two other small local restaurants where you can get a meal - the most entertaining of these is Lambert's Lambi Bar - built of lambi shells, open to the breeze, filling local food at reasonable prices.

Away from Clifton, Union is a very quiet island where you will see more goats and sheep on the roads than cars. There is one other residential village, Ashton and you can find many lovely hikes. The view from the summit of the pinnacle is one of the most breath-taking in the Windwards (you will definitely need a cutlass and you may need a guide). Determined hikers should also make their way over the western mountains to the desolate but lovely Chatham Bay.

UNION'S DAY CHARTER BOATS

Every day the planes arrive and tourists from St Lucia, Martinique and Barbados come to get a glimpse of the Grenadines. They do this by joining a fleet of vessels that head out each day to different islands. Most of the chartering is done by a group of yacht owners who work together. (Unofficial spokesman is Capt'n Yannis). One boat will visit the Tobago Cays, Mayreau and Palm, another P.S.V., Mopion, Palm, etc. Guests eat lunch on board (usually featuring fresh fish and lobster in season), and there is plenty of time to explore, swim and sunbathe. The yachts themselves include the 72ft ketch "Hurricane", the 60 ft trimaran "Sea Rose" and the locally built 78 footer "Scaramouche". All of them are large and stable enough to make even Granny feel at home, and they carry about 25 people a trip. Some offer overnight and weekend tours.

68

Petit St. Vincent Resort

The Grenadines, St. Vincent, West Indies.

On Petit St Vincent our guests live in luxurious secluded cottages on the slopes and by the sea. Outdoor patios with glorious views offer a perfect setting for a leisurely breakfast delivered by our "Mini Moke" room service.

Pleasures are simple, food and drink sophisticated. Our open air pavilion has a large lounge and dining room, and an excellent bar.

Yachtsmen are very welcome. Cube ice, block ice, bread, banana bread, eggs, fuel and water are available. We have a bountiful boutique filled with exotic gifts and clothes. Overseas telephone calls can be placed at our office during normal business hours.

We offer a special overnight rate for yachtsmen who would like a comfortable, quiet and private night ashore. Call us on the radio for availability and rates or inquire at our office on arrival. Dinner reservations can be made by calling :PSV" by 5 p.m.

PSV (US Office) Box 12506, Cincinnati, Ohio 45212. Phone 809-654-9326

Cannouan   photo Kristina Lagerkvist

Anchorage Yacht Club

The Anchorage Yacht Club is the true center of the Grenadines

The AYC resort with its private airport and water sports base, is the gateway to the national park of the Tobago Cays and other marvelous Grenadine islands such as PSV, Palm, Mayreau, Carriacou, etc. An unspoilt world of white coral beaches and crystal clear turquoise water.

Our Dive Anchorage scuba shop features daily dives to the most beautiful coral reefs and wrecks, as well as resort courses for beginners.

The AYC offers you a wide variety of programs - Sailboarding, Sailing excursions, Water skiing, deep sea fishing, or just simply relaxing on our own beautiful private beach.

Excellent French/Creole restaurant with fresh fish year round and lobsters in our pool in season. Two steel jump up nights, and our bar which is the meeting point of yachtsmen coming to the Grenadines, will provide you with lively entertainment.

All beach front air conditioned rooms, direct dialing telephone connections.

Visit us for a day, a few days or longer... write or call: Charlotte Honnart, manager, AYC, Union Island, St Vincent Grenadines, W.I. tel:(809 45) 88221. telex:7595 AYC VQ. We will organize everything from there on.

At **PALM** we're proud of our barefoot informality, friendliness, glassnost and eagerness to please. Our food is good, as is our service - and, always with a smile. Our accommodation in superior, all rooms on the beach.

John and Mary Caldwell are world cruising yachties, who welcome all sailors, and offer them a special overnight rate (with breakfast) in our lovely rooms (makes terra firma a joy to embrace) especially that hot shower!

PALM is not a dull little paradise - no way. We have watersports (sailboarding, Sunfish, Hobie cat, small boats) including scuba diving and instruction, guided snorkeling safaris, fishing trips, fitness club (John's HIGHWAY 90 jogging trail and aerobics sessions) dining out on Union Island, Saturday night steel band "jump up" and barbecue (Wednesdays too in season.) Day sailing, yacht charters.

We have grocery store, dining room, classical bar, ice, tennis, snorkel gear, phones up to 9 p.m. Yachties can call us on VHF channel 68, 7am to 5pm.

Our specialty is peace and quiet, with oceans of sea, sand sun and sailing - open all year.

Ask about our summer special "Fun at Sea" sail away/loaf ashore vacations.

Send a deposit, inclusive dates and flight info. come via Barbados and take LIAT to Union Island, where we will meet you.

See your travel agent, or write John, Palm Island, St Vincent, W.I. or telex 7500 CW agency VQ, or phone (809 45)8 4804.

PALM ISLAND

Imagine acres of palm-fringed silver sand dotted with flowers and and small trees leading into a sparkling sea of transparent greens and blues, so enticing that it is hard to see it without wanting to run across the sand and dive in. That describes Casuarina Beach, for my money the most beautiful beach in the Grenadines and also the home of the Palm Island Beach Club Resort. This little island has received such accolades as "probably the most beautiful place in the world" (L.A. Times).

It wasn't always like this; many years ago there were no palms or flowers, no-one much went there and the island was known as "Prune Island". It took the imagination and pioneering spirit of John and Mary Caldwell to make it what it is today. After the second world war John, an American, found himself stranded in the U.S.A. unable to get back to Australian Mary down under. He hit on the unusual idea of buying a small boat and sailing there. The idea was particularly novel as John had never sailed before and knew nothing of boats! Not surprisingly everything went wrong. John got caught in water spouts,

storms, calms and a hurricane. He was dismasted, he had his boat half wrecked by a shark he caught and imprudently hauled on board. He starved to the point of eating slime scraped from his hull and was finally totally wrecked on a Pacific island. (These stories are told in his book appropriately called "Desperate Voyage".) He eventually got a ride to Australia and met Mary, then in a spirit of true marine madness he bought himself another boat and sailed to the Caribbean. Here he was known for his passion for palm trees, and bunches of baby palms were frequently seen strapped to the back of his boat. Whenever he went ashore he planted a few, thus greatly enhancing many of the beaches. Prune came under his green thumb and several thousand palm trees later, it became Palm Island, and John and Mary built their resort.

From the air Palm Island has a striking resemblance to a whale in shape, it also has funny contours - flat in the middle with steep rounded hills in the corners. A few tracks cross the island, but there are no roads, and there is nothing here but the resort and a few private houses owned by

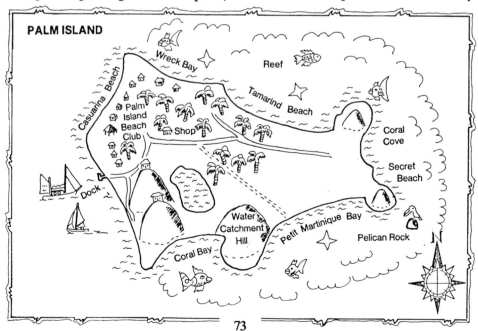

PALM ISLAND

people who came to the hotel and fell in love with it. Although Casuarina Beach is the most spectacular, it is by no means the only beach, there are at least six more within walking distance of the hotel and all are beautiful. Some offer excellent snorkeling and for those wanting to get away from it all, there is no problem finding one to yourself.

Access to Palm is from the airport at Union which is only a mile away by small boat. The style of Palm is very informal, and the rooms are all on the beach. Tennis, paddle tennis, full water sports and a day charter yacht are available. There is a boutique, and a small shop selling basics. On Saturday night a steel band arrives from Union for the lively weekly jump up. A couple of times a week in season cruise ships visit.

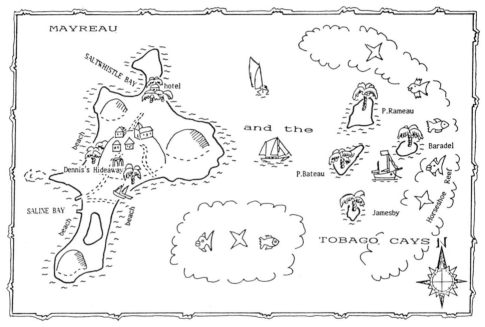

MAYREAU

This is a tiny island in the middle of the Grenadines with one road, no cars, no phones and only about 150 inhabitants who live on the highest hill with panoramic views of the other Grenadines all around. The village has a sweet church, some picturesque houses and a couple of very small basic stores. One time I was there an elderly man shouted "come and see my boutique". We went over and sure enough he had converted his bedroom by laying out a selection of local handicrafts on the floor. We sat on the bed while we made our choice - prices were good too!

Mayreau is surrounded by pristine white

beaches and several of them offer good snorkeling. Paths lead from the village to most of them.

There is only one hotel tucked up in the northern end called "Salt Whistle Bay". It is set on a perfect half moon beach which is one of the safest and calmest in the Grenadines making it ideal for families with children and a favorite with yachtsmen. The hotel with 25 rooms is very low-key and well hidden - so much so that some yachtsmen sailing in there find it hard to believe it exists! But this is its charm - a perfect blend into the scenery, all the buildings being hidden away in a prettily gardened shady 22

SAIL IN THE
GRENADINES...

CAPTAIN YANNIS

acres. It is very quiet - the kind of place where you start the day with nothing to do and only get it half done. The restless will have to satisfy themselves with sailboarding, volley-ball and day trips to other islands.

There is one other restaurant in Mayreau, "Dennis Hideaway" on the main path overlooking Saline Bay. Here you can drink beer at sunset and eat fish, conch, and turtle from the surrounding reefs.

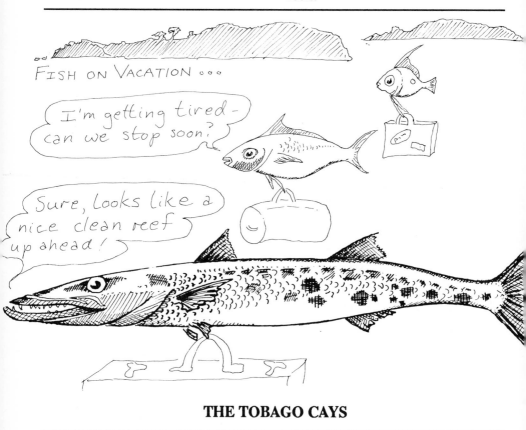

THE TOBAGO CAYS

Here the sounds are those of the wind, surf and bird calls. Four tiny islets are set in a huge horseshoe reef giving miles of clear shallow water of endless color. This nature reserve is one of the world's great beauty spots and a snorkeler's paradise. Chart your course here on a privately rented yacht, or join one of the big yachts that visit it daily from Union Island.

CANOUAN

Set in the middle of the Grenadines, Canouan is a tranquil island of dumpy hills surrounded by deep blue sea. There are just a few hundred inhabitants most of whom live by farming and fishing. All around the island magnificent beaches are tucked away in every corner. A few roads exist but the one or two cars on the island are often "out of service". The small airport has just been resurfaced. Walking in the hills it is hard not to feel a sense of deep peace and and timelessness. In fact when one winds along a tiny path among dry scrubby plants, to the tune of bird calls and goat bleats, and sees a young boy tending his flock, there is a feeling of something positively biblical about this island.

Having re-charged one's batteries of spiritual peace, one can step back into the present world by walking into the Canouan Beach Hotel (CBH). This light and pleasant resort is situated on a long narrow strip of land joining Glass Hill to the rest of the island. It is built on a spectacular beach whose golden sand merges into acres of luminous pale turquoise sea, broken only be powdery white surf along the shore. To cap it all there is an exquisite view southwards over the Grenadines. The hotel is French, as is the restaurant, but the clients are international. Guests stay in pleasant airy little cottages, which are air conditioned and tastefully decorated in bright colors.

Activities include sailing dinghies, scuba, snorkeling, volleyball, tennis, table tennis and day sails to other islands. If you really want to "get away from it all" to a place of great tranquility and perfect beaches, CBH fits the bill.

For those preferring something more local there are two other possibilities. The Crystal Sands Hotel, set right on the beach in the main bay has 10 rooms and a small bar/restaurant. Otherwise there is a charming and inexpensive little guest house perched on top of a hill with a panoramic outlook all around. Called Villa La Bijou, it is the retirement dream

of Michelle De Roche and her husband. Michelle is a French lady who moved to the States where she met and married Mr De Roche (whose family came from Canouan, half the population seems to bear this name!). Building the guest house has been a long slow job - they started in 1974. But Rome wasn't built in a day and the wait was worthwhile. Villa La Bijou, now completed is indeed a little gem, nicely designed with textured walls of stone and pebbles and 6 clean, simple rooms. However, if none of the local cars can be found, be prepared to walk uphill!

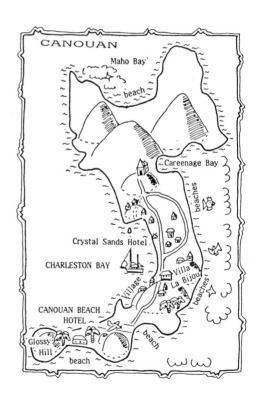

MUSTIQUE

What do Princess Margaret, Raquel Welch, Mick Jagger and David Bowie have in common? The answer: property in Mustique, a name almost synonymous with rich and famous people - a sort of Caribbean Beverly Hills where rock stars and royalty can relax together in their own way far from from the media and the mass market.

It is a small but beautiful island of rolling hills set in sparkling clear water with more than its fair share of lovely beaches; large areas are wild and deserted. Access is provided by a small air strip with connecting flights to Barbados, Grenada, St Vincent and Martinque. The island is privately owned by the Mustique Company which maintains and develops it. The company is in the process of being taken over by the house owners who wish to keep the island much as it is now. There is no town, and only a couple of restaurants and shops. Only the wealthy can afford to build, so the island is dotted with about 70 really gorgeous homes, many of which more closely resemble small castles than the holiday homes they actually are. The main social life of the island takes place privately in these homes.

WHERE TO STAY
The only hotel is the Cotton House, lavishly created regardless of cost by the late Oliver Messel. It includes some lovely Georgian style bedrooms, an elegant lounge and a spectacular pool built amid "ruins" on a hill that offers commanding views all around. It is currently French owned and managed by Christophe Lajus, a hotelier trained in the hotel management school at Lausanne, Switzerland.

There are two guest houses. Billy Mitchell's Firefly was the very first house built on Mustique. Billy was an avid seawoman who traversed the globe under sail. Firefly is located overlooking Britannia Bay so that she could "talk to her yacht". The communal room is quietly elegant with a view of the harbor. The bedrooms, each with its own bathroom and refrigerator, are spacious, private and well above the standard of many hotels, .

There is also Charlie's Guest House, a small and fairly basic place built on a hill

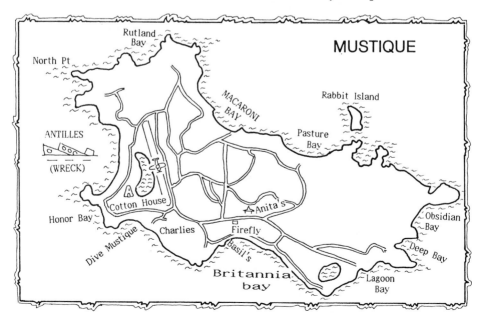

78

with a broad view over the north of the island. It has plenty of personality starting with a managerie of rabbits, dogs, parakeets and cats.

People have discovered that they can holiday well in Mustique without spending a fortune by getting together and renting one of the lovely private homes from Mustique Villas. They all come complete with full staff and a car, and some of the more expensive ones have such amenities as tennis court and swimming pools.

EATING OUT

Yachts congregate down at Britannia Bay. Here you will find BASIL'S BAR, built on stilts out over the water. It is a good sea-food restaurant, with fish, lobster and shrimp being the most popular dishes. (Newsweek voted them one of the best bars in the world). The atmosphere is informal and everyone collects here on Wednesday nights when Basil has his weekly barbecue followed by a jump-up. Monday is another party night to live music when a large passenger ship puts in.

The island's other restaurant is the Cotton House. This is much more elegant and formal and one want to dress up accordingly. They have large buffet lunches up by the pool, and dining on the veranda in the evenings. Saturday night is barbecue time with a band on the beach. More entertainment is planned in the near future.

SHOPPING

The only food store is Basil's General Store, down at Britannia Bay, which does a good job of selling all the essentials, which in Mustique include French champagne and tenderloin. (open weekdays 8 a.m. to 1 p.m. and 3 p.m to 6 p.m.)

Mustique has three good boutiques (opening hours weekdays about 9 - 10 a.m, close around noon, re-opening at 2 or 3 p.m. untill 5 or 6 p.m.). There is Basil's Boutique at Basil's Bar, with special lines from Bali. Treasure at the Cotton House, and don't miss Anita's boutique in the Japanese House. Not only does she have

BASIL'S BAR

Mustique, St. Vincent, W.I. Telephone 84621 84421

When Newsweek instructed their scouts to venture to the far reaches of the globe in search of the perfect martini, the most amiable companions and the ideal background for a wine-fired encounter - the only place they found in the Caribbean? BASIL'S of course! Scout Richard Lee reported:

"Sooner or later every Mariner navigating these islands sails into Mustique's main harbor and heads for Basil's. Alternatively laid-back or lively this breezy little pier bar-restaurant hosts both islanders (some celebrated) and mariners, many of whom message ahead to order dinner of West Indian Lobster and homemade ice cream.

Most however, come for basic libations like rum punch and to gossip about vacationers, to leave messages or just use the phone, one of the busiest in the island (when it's working) In season there is dancing under the stars to the music of live combos. The dress code is whatever's comfortable and cool, including sandals, sneakers and bare feet. Owner Basil Charles, a tall, handsome islander is usually on hand to keep drinks, food and service moving. But then this is an island and no one is in a hurry." (Newsweek November 1987).

Don't miss BASIL'S BOUTIQUE - world famous Basil's bar t shirts and a wide selection of designer batik cotton clothes from Bali.

an elegant collection of clothes and jewelry, there is also a lovely view down the hills to the sea.

WHAT TO DO IN MUSTIQUE

Mustique is essentially a very quiet island. There are many small roads (many better described as dirt tracks) where you can wander and look at the large homes and views. One enjoyable way to see Mustique is by a small motorbike which can be rented by the day from Tech Serve. Another is by horseback, and they have a stables with horse riding at about 7 in the morning and 4 in the afternoon. The prices are reasonable, and you can select a mount as lively or docile as you need. Be sure to visit the lovely Macaroni Beach.

Down at the Cotton House you will find Dive Mustique, a complete dive shop run during the season by New Zealander Lesley Dunning. Diving in Mustique is pleasant and very suitable for learners. You can get fully certified as you dive in just a few days. Both Cotton House and Basil's offer water-skiing, sail boarding, small sailing boats etc.

Bequia is about 8 miles long - a small island of rolling hills and pretty beaches. It is endowed with a large protected harbor called Admiralty Bay. Port Elizabeth, the only town, is a picturesque collection of houses built overlooking the beach at the head of the bay. The beach is where everyone gathers, for here tall palms and broad almond trees reduce the sun's glare to a dappled shade. One can sit on the wall of a flower bed and watch life go by, sandwiched as it were between the two main thoroughfares. Inland lies the road, a casual place dominated by shoppers who stroll along unconcerned about the scanty traffic. On the other side lies the sea, busier by far than the road. Schooners, freighters and yachts come and go, dinghies and water taxis pull into the dock, little "two bow" sailing dinghies dart around like colorful butterflies.

Bequians are of mixed decent, from Scottish farming stock, French freebooters, North American whaling crews and from Africa. They are industrious, adaptable and many are skilled artisans. The majority are seafarers - many travel the oceans as crew on coasters and large ships, and a few end up owning their own. Others fish, putting to sea in in all weathers in small open boats, and several have taken advantage of the burgeoning yachting industry to skipper or crew on charter yachts. Bequia is one of the main centers of the traditional boat building industry in the Grenadines. Boats are designed by eye and built on the beach often with only hand tools. These have varied from tiny "two bow" fishing boats to trading schooners up to 130 feet long. Bequia used to be a thriving whaling station, and although the trade has all but died out now there are still a couple of open whale boats that occasionally put out under sail between the months of February and April, equipped with hand thrown harpoons.

All this adds up to a confident people, who love their island and are cosmopolitan enough to enjoy sharing it the right kind of foreign traveler. The magic of Bequia is in the way locals and visitors blend, each learning from the other so both come away enriched.

A big daily event is the arrival of the local ferries early in the afternoon - a colorful crowd gathers on the dock to meet people and unload their goods. The pace of life is slow and leisurely, yet just enough goes on to make it interesting; bars and restaurants abound, and the atmosphere is pleasantly social. It would be almost impossible to stay here for a few days without making a lot of new friends! It is an easy open atmosphere that attracts artists, writers, musicians and "yachties". Bequia is many a traveler's ideal of the "unspoiled island" - familiar enough to be comfortable, discovered enough to be fun, but protected from being over-run by a 9 mile sea passage that must be traversed by boat. An airport is planned, and one hopes this will not over-stimulate things too much.

82

SEA TRANSPORT
BETWEEN BEQUIA AND ST VINCENT

At the moment the only way to get to Bequia is by sea. The journey takes about one and a quarter hours, and a regular service is provided by two boats that leave Bequia weekdays for St Vincent at 0630, arriving about 0745. One is the famous Bequia-built schooner the "Friendship Rose" who motor sails over. The other is a steel motor ferry the "Admiral". The Admiral has an air conditioned bar where you can watch a video movie, The ship always docks before the movie ends, though no one minds if you stay to watch the end! The Rose stays in St Vincent till 1230, when she returns to Bequia. Between Monday and Friday the Admiral makes two trips daily. She leaves St Vincent for Bequia at 1030 and 1630 (4.30pm) and leaves Bequia for St Vincent at 0630 and 1400 (2pm). On Saturday the Admiral returns at 1230. The one way fare on either vessel is $5 E.C.

On Sundays the Admiral and the motor vessel "Snapper" sometimes do a Bequia excursion leaving St Vincent for Bequia at 0830 returning from Bequia at 1700 (5 pm).

If you miss the ferry or want to go at a different time, there are a number of very small power boats that act as taxis. The fare is considerably higher than by

Friendship Rose SJE

ferry. You can try Bequia Marina (83272), William Gooding (83257), Orton King (83245), or Caribbee Cove (VHF ch 16, 68), or for a local sloop "Trait"83202 (ask Elaine to get in touch with Nando). In St Vincent you can try Danny Sorren at 74582 or at the Dolphin 84238. Or call any of the larger Bequia Hotels and ask them to arrange it for you.

There is another way of getting to Bequia which is well worth your consideration. If ferry times are not suitable, then for a small water taxi the journey between Mustique and Bequia is actually easier than between Admiralty Bay and Kingstown. You can charter a small plane to Mustique and arrange for a water taxi to take you over to Friendship Bay (call up Friendship Bay Resort and ask for their water taxi details).

WHERE TO STAY

ADMIRALTY BAY

For many, this is the place to be - for here one finds the pleasant waterside bars and restaurants strung together by a tiny path that threads its way along the water's edge. In some places one must cross the beach, and on rough days it takes a nimble person to stay dry by running the gauntlet between swells. The path follows the coast as far as the lovely Tony Gibbon's (Princess Margaret) beach, and the energetic can even hike over the next hill to Lower Bay.

Two of the best hotels here are the Frangipani and the Sunny Caribbee Plantation House. The Frangipani is based on a charming old building whose upstairs used to be the old family home and whose downstairs was the storeroom for the 131ft "Gloria Colita", the largest schooner ever built in Bequia. (In 1940 she disappeared and was later found abandoned drifting in the Bermuda Triangle.) The hotel belongs to "Son" Mitchell, Bequia's most popular politician, and currently Prime Minister of St Vincent and the Grenadines. Son first came to power by winning a parliamentary seat as an independent in a closely contested election. The other two parties got six seats each giving Son the balance of power. Neither side could form a government without him. From this perfect bargaining position he become Prime Minister! The position was too precarious to last long, and the other party was soon back with a massive victory, but their popularity did not last long, and in the last elections it was Son who fielded the landslide.

The Frangipani bar area opens onto the waterfront and everyone gathers here to talk and watch the goings on in harbor; it must be one of the easiest places in the world to make friends! Some rooms are in the main building and others cottage style in the pleasant garden. Every Thursday night people gather for a barbecue and jump up to a steel band. A few steps away one finds their "Clubhouse", a center for watersports, with a bar/restaurant upstairs. Nancy Boake runs the sports section with complete sailboarding (including a

frangipani

Bar, Restaurant, Hotel, Yacht Service.
Bequia, St Vincent, West Indies.
telex:7587 FRANGI GIVQ phone:809-45-8325

Perfect location Admiralty Bay just a few minutes walk from town, the natural gathering place for sailors and castaways.

THE FRANGIPANI BAR is just a few steps from our dinghy dock It specializes in fresh fruit drinks, pina coladas and lime rum punch. Ice available.

THE FRANGIPANI RESTAURANT is open all day for breakfast, lunch and dinner. You'll enjoy the local tuna sandwiches on homemade bread, real coffee, or for the hungry, a New York steak or baked red snapper. After 7.30 p.m. dinner is served by candlelight - reservations are advisable. The famous Frangipani Barbecue is Thursday night with charcoal steaks, a fabulous buffet table and live music.

THE FRANGIPANI HOTEL has twin-bedded rooms in a lush garden setting with hot and cold water and a large porch overlooking the bay.

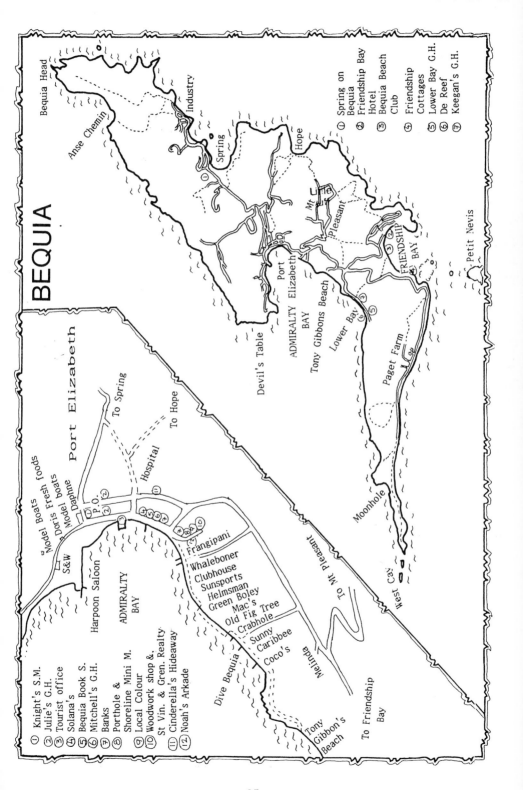

BEQUIA

Bequia Head

Anse Chemin

Industry

Spring

Hope

Mt Pleasant

Urle

Port Elizabeth

Devil's Table

Port Elizabeth

ADMIRALTY Elizabeth BAY

Tony Gibbons Beach

Lower Bay

FRIENDSHIP BAY

Paget Farm

Petit Nevis

Moonhole

West Cay

To Mt Pleasant

To Friendship Bay

Tony Gibbon's Beach

Melinda

To Spring

To Hope

Hospital

Daphne

P.O.

"Model Boats

Doris boats

Model boats

S&W

Harpoon Saloon

ADMIRALTY BAY

Frangipani

Whaleboner
Clubhouse
Sunsports
Helmsman
Green Boley
Mac's
Old Fig Tree
Crabhole
Sunny
Caribbee
Coco's

Dive Bequia

① Spring on
   Bequia
② Friendship Bay
   Hotel
③ Bequia Beach
   Club
④ Friendship
   Cottages
⑤ Lower Bay G.H.
⑥ De Reef
⑦ Keegan's G.H.

① Knight's S.M.
② Julie's G.H.
③ Tourist office
④ Solana's
⑤ Bequia Book S.
⑥ Mitchell's G.H.
⑦ Banks
⑧ Porthole &
   Shoreline Mini M.
⑨ Local Colour
⑩ Woodwork shop &
   St Vin. & Gren. Realty
⑪ Cinderella's Hideaway
⑫ Noah's Arkade

beach simulator for learning) and full Scuba facility.

The Sunny Caribbee Plantation House is ideally positioned midway between town and the fabulous Tony Gibbons (Princess Margaret) beach, both being just a short walk away. It is a very pleasant place to stay, set in a spacious garden of lawn shaded by palm trees, and has its own tiny beach. The main building is an attractive colonial style house which has a few rooms, but most of the accommodation is in decorative wooden cottages, each with its own porch. The hotel's main building suffered a serious fire in the middle of 1988, but should be back in shape by the end of the year.

The Plantation House is the home of Bob Sach's Dive Bequia. Bob, usually assisted by a team of attractive young ladies, is the area's most enthusiastic scuba diving exponent and the beach bar has a big salt water fish tank which has helped persuade many guests to have a go at Scuba. The bar draws a good crowd from about 5.30, and on Wednesdays and Fridays in season they have a barbecue and jump up to a steel band.

Several guest houses are also available. Julie's the largest, is right in town. The rooms are simple, clean and comfortable, each with its own bathroom. If you take the half board package you can expect good local food. The Wallace's Old Fig Tree is smaller with just 6 rooms, but it positioned right on the water looking out over the bay. Because it is small, Adlene Wallace makes you feel just like one of the family. "Papa" Mitchell's guest house in town is basic but the cheapest place to stay.

LOWER BAY

Lower Bay is a two mile walk from town. There is a small fishing community and a long and beautiful beach. Most mornings you can watch the fishermen cast their seine nets, pulling their catch to the shore. On Sundays and holidays people come from all over the island to hang out on the beach and at De Reef bar and restaurant which is built right on the sand. There is a convenient "kiddie pool" created by a reef

close to the beach. Apart from youngsters, this protected swimming spot is a favorite with those trying to cure a terminal hangover. Many people staying in Admiralty Bay come down here for a day on the beach. It is one of the most inexpensive places to stay in Bequia. Both Keegan's and Lower Bay guest houses offer excellent value. Keegan's, owned by Grace and Mac Ville is simple, clean, and cool, and just over the road from the beach. Lower Bay Guest House is pleasant with nice rooms, and lies just a stone's throw from the beach.

SPRING

Spring is about a mile from town, but has the feeling of being completely "away from it all". There is nothing here but rolling hills, coconut trees, cows, and a palm-lined windward beach. Spring on Bequia (open November till June) is an ideal hideaway hotel for those who want quiet privacy. The main building is picturesque forming part of the estate which provides much of the food they serve. The rooms are built of

stone and lie on a hill. The top rooms are really special with picture windows opening onto the sweeping view. Hiking is excellent and the hotel has a swimming pool for those who don't want to move.

INDUSTRY

Industry lies a mile further along the coast from Spring. Hiking trails have been cut right up to Bequia Head, and over to Anse Chemin. The beach offers privacy. There is a restaurant, and for those who want to stay, three double rooms.

FRIENDSHIP BAY

Friendship Bay is on the south side of Bequia. It is a huge bay with a gorgeous palm-fringed beach facing southwards over Isle de Quatre and Petit Nevis (the whaling station) to the other Grenadines. This bay offers some of Bequia's best snorkeling. There are two hotels to choose from. The Friendship Bay Resort is Bequia's largest hotel with 27 rooms dotted about a lovely rambling 12 acre garden that climbs back up the hill from the beach. One gets a pretty little cottage with a patio

there is a smart sport and beachwear shop-Helmsman. Further along you come to the Green Boley; clothes, applique wall hangings, jewelry, and souvenirs. You might by now need to stop at Mac's for coffee and while there get one of their famous T-shirts before pressing on to the Crab Hole where they specialize in fabrics and clothes made from their own silk screen factory out at the back.

While in Bequia there are a few forms of art, which are not cheap, but well worth looking at. One is the Bequia model boat industry. There are two shops, Mauvin's not far from Daphne's and Sargent's a short walk from the Harpoon Saloon. Both shops make beautiful model boats of all types. My favorite are the Bequia whale-boat series. These lovely little miniatures are complete in every detail with mast, sails, oars and harpoons, and are artistically painted in traditional Bequia Boat colors. They can be packed for shipping.

Then there are several artists with completely different styles who painstakingly handpaint beautiful T-shirts. Melinda

paints by hand, birds, fish, whales and flowers, and you can find her T-shirts at Solanas, Noah's Arkade, the Crab Hole or better still get a discount by walking up to her house any afternoon (walk up to the main road from the Plantation House turn right and look for the red and white oil drum saying "Melinda" which marks the house) Although Melinda's T-shirts are her best known line, she is a very capable artist who also does lovely stained glass work. Bob Demmans paints with an air brush, all different kinds of scenes, but especially beautiful underwater ones, on T-shirts, pareos and wall-hangings. They can be found at the Crab Hole, and you can go out back and watch him at work in the Crab Hole factory.

WHAT TO DO IN BEQUIA

One of the nice things about Bequia is that one need do very little, yet stay entertained by watching the goings on around the harbor. Bequia is an ideal size for taking walks (non-hikers can go by bus or taxi). Watch a sunset from Mount Pleasant, walk to Friendship Bay, Spring or Industry for lunch and dinner and enjoy the great variety of views along the way. Actually not a bad idea is to get a taxi out to Industry and hike down one of their trails to Bequia Head or Anse Chemin. Bequia has many lovely beaches, one of the more remote is Hope, where the rather shallow water sets up long lines of breakers often suitable for body surfing (watch the undertow). Although Hope may seem deserted, it is a working plantation, so please do not pick the fruits or coconuts.

Bequia is excellent for sailboarding and you can rent boards or learn at either Frangipani or Friendship Bay. Scuba diving is also superb in this area, both for novices and the experienced - you can learn to dive here and return home certified. You will find dive shops at the Frangipani, Sunny Caribbee, Friendship Bay Resort and Bequia Beach Club. Tennis courts are available at Spring, Friendship Bay Resort, the Plantation House and the Frangipani.

There are many yachts available for either day or longer charters. You can usually meet some of the skippers having a pre-dinner drink at the Frangipani or Sunny Caribbee, or enquire at the Frangipani Yacht Services or your hotel. The cheapest deals are often from passing cruising boats picking up beer money; it is probably wiser to go with the slightly more expensive "old hands" who really know the waters and anchorages well. If you come at Easter you can get involved in the Bequia Regatta - a four day extravaganza of local boat races, yacht races and lots of partying.

Nightlife usually takes the form of a jump-up to a local band and the action moves according to the day of the week. The main ones include the Frangipani on Thursdays, Plantation House on Wednesdays and Fridays in season, the Friendship Bay Resort on Saturdays, The Bequia Beach Club on Wednesdays and the Harpoon Saloon is planning Country and Western night on Tuesdays with another band on Fridays.

THE ISLAND OF ST VINCENT

St Vincent is an island of amazingly steep mountains and lush tropical vegetation. Everywhere you drive you will be treated to majestic views. Much of the interior is unexplored, though there are feeder roads and paths that lead up to the central mountain range.

While St Vincent has many beautiful beaches, most of them are made up of black sand which does not look quite so inviting on the tourist brochures, and is toasty on the toes. This is possibly why in recent years the main thrust of tourism has been towards the Grenadines with their spectacular white sand beaches. St Vincent does have good hotels, and there is plenty to see, though there is little in the way of organized activities. This will be a plus to those who like to get out and explore on their own, and nowhere in the Windwards is the terrain more dramatically rugged for those who like to drive and hike. It is fitting that they have adopted the slogan for the tourist industry that St Vincent is the "natural place to be". People who would like to do some adventuring and some lolling around on the beach can make up an ideal vacation by spending part of their time in St Vincent and the rest in the Grenadines.

IXORA

EARLY DAYS

Because of her steep mountains, St Vincent was hard to subdue and one of the last of the Lesser Antilles to be colonised. She had rather a unique early history owing to the creation of the "Black Caribs".

Like the other islands, her early inhabitants were Caribs, an amber skinned race related to the North American Indian. In about 1675 a slave ship was wrecked on the coast of Bequia. The Caribs decided "finders keepers", and took the slaves for themselves. They proved to be a mixed blessing, a troublesome bunch who were restive and hard to control. The Caribs, realizing the situation was getting out of control, tried to contain matters by killing off all the male children, just keeping the girls. This incited the adult slaves who rebelled, managed to kill a bunch of Caribs and fled to the hills. Here they settled successfully and their numbers swelled as they were joined by slaves who managed to escape from the other islands.

They called themselves Black Caribs, and kept their Carib names and many of the Carib customs, including a penchant for going on the warpath, killing all the men and stealing the women. This aggression was directed at their former masters the Red Caribs, who soon found themselves a diminishing race! Hoping to stabilise the situation they asked for assistance from Martinique, and by 1710 the French had a de facto footing on the island. The French did not really help the Red Carib's cause much, but did a certain amount of double talking, supplying both sides with arms and letting them shoot it out. Meantime they kept grabbing a little more land for themselves, mainly at the cost of the Red Caribs, so that by the time the country was ceded to Britain in 1763 it had 3000 Black Caribs, 4000 French and only 100 Red Caribs!

The British had quite a time dealing with the Black Caribs; matters came to head when they were trying to build a road up the east coast right into Black Carib territory. The Black Caribs managed to sur-

TRANSPORT WITHIN ST VINCENT

TAXIS

There are plenty of taxis in St Vincent with stands near South River Road and the market in Kingstown, at the airport and at Young Island Dock. Most St Vincent taxi drivers are very knowledgeable and make first rate guides. People living in the Grenadines often depend on them to run errands, and ship them goods from St Vincent; this has led to the wide spread use of VHF radios by the taxis. My own favorite is Robert taxi who runs a quiet efficient service and does much of the work for Mustique.

BUSES (prices in E.C.)

These are the mainstay of the local transport system. The buses gather near the market. Generally the long distance buses to Georgetown or Chateaubelair park opposite the market towards the sea. Those going to the Mesopotamia Valley "Mespo" park beside the market, and the buses going to Calliaqua (the main tourist run), park up in front of the Mespo buses. The fare to the Mesopotamia Valley is around $2 and the last bus comes back at about 8 p.m. The fare to Chateaubelair is around $3.50, but the last bus comes back at about 1 p.m. You can get to Georgetown for about $3, last bus returns about 4 p.m. Buses run down the main drag from CSY (Calliaqua) to town till quite late (often 10 p.m. or later). The furthest stop on the bus route is Fancy, but unfortunately buses usually only come into town from Fancy in the morning and return in the afternoon. It should be noted buses are a private enterprise system without fixed time tables, so you should discuss your return with the driver.

SELF DRIVE RENTAL CARS

There are plenty of rental cars available, and Vincentians, knowing their own island, are good about offering 4 wheel drive for exploring. You will need a local license which can be arranged by your hire company. In case of an accident you will normally be liable for the first few hundred dollars worth of damage. Don't forget to drive on the left and lock your car when you leave it.

round the workers and drive them away, but the respite was temporary and four years later under massive military protection the road was completed.

However, they got another chance at the British when in 1778 France declared war on England and, in a winning streak, captured St Vincent with the support of the Caribs. France's luck did not last for long and in 1780 it was returned to England. The Black Caribs were unable to do much for the next 15 years, but after the French Revolution their chance came again and under their leader Chatoyer they launched an attack on the British and almost succeeded in recapturing the island. They drove the English back to Kingstown, a poor position since the Black Caribs commanded the surrounding hills.

For the British the day was saved by a dawn attack on the Carib position and Chatoyer was reputedly killed in hand to hand combat with Major Leith who was commanding the attack. After the Black Caribs were finally subdued they were all taken prisoner, detained on Baliceau and shipped to Honduras. There is a plaque in the Anglican church in town commemorating Leith, and more recently in post colonial times, Chatoyer was made a national hero so a monument was erected to him as well. I think it is rather nice that St Vincent with her mixed heritage can end up honoring both heros!

IN AND NEAR TOWN

The Botanical Gardens and Pre-Columbian Museum (an hour or two)

St Vincent's Botanic Gardens, established in 1765, are the oldest in the western hemisphere. It was towards these gardens that Captain Bligh was bringing the breadfruit trees on the Bounty, when he was thwarted by the the infamous mutiny. However, Bligh was a determined man and he not only sailed over three thousand miles in the open boat into which he was cast adrift, he also later succeeded in getting the breadfruit all the way from the Pacific to the St Vincent Botanic gardens in 1793. A sucker from the original tree is still on display.

When you reach the gardens you will soon be selected by a local unofficial guide who will show you around and tell you about the different plants for a small gratuity (negotiate fees in advance).

Housed in the Botanic Gardens you will also find the Pre-Columbian archeological museum. It is only open on Wednesdays (from 9.45 a.m. to 11.45 a.m.) and on Saturdays (4.00 p.m. to 6.00 p.m.). The museum was largely put together by Dr Kirby, who is often in attendance and well worth talking to. Large maps show the early migration of the different inhabitants starting with the Ciboney who probably arrived about 4000 B.C. There are many examples of Arawak and Carib pottery including a spectacular and ferocious b₁ head. There is also jewelry made of shel and stone, and just how they managed to drill the tiny holes is still a mystery. (There are plans to move the museum to Fort Charlotte)

Fort Charlotte (half an hour)

Built in 1806 to keep Napoleon at bay, Fort Charlotte is built on a 600 foot hill with a commanding and photogenic view of Kingstown. There are well preserved cannons and battlements, and a series of paintings depicting the story of the Black Caribs. The paintings are locked in a museum and you get the key from the keeper in the radio tower. Many years ago we wanted to to look in and the keeper couldn't find the key, and decided his mate must have it. We all went looking for his mate, shouting; he wasn't to be found. We went once again to look in frustration at the iron grill door, and a hand came out through the grill with the key and unlocked the padlock from the inside - shortly afterwards an embarrassed keeper's mate and a girl emerged from within!

Cathedrals

Visitors with an eye for architecture may enjoy visiting St George's Cathedral (late Georgian) and St Mary's Roman Catholic Cathedral, school and presbytery (mainly Romanesque). Both were originally built in the 1820's.

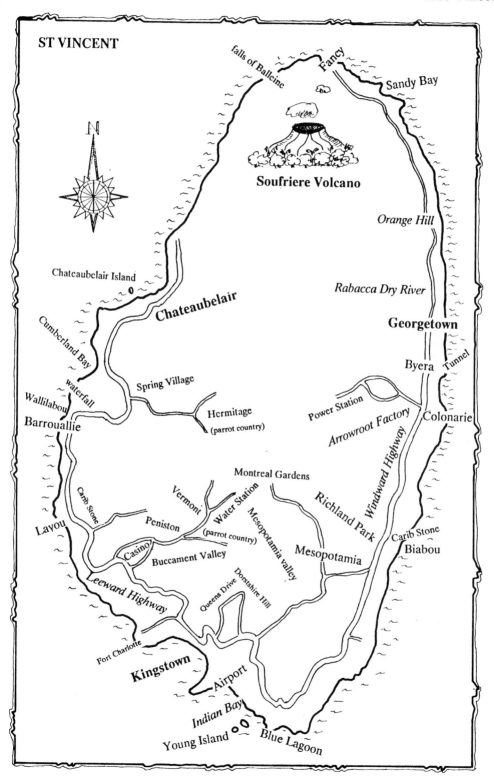

ST VINCENT

falls of Balleine

Fancy

Sandy Bay

Soufriere Volcano

Orange Hill

Chateaubelair Island

Chateaubelair

Rabacca Dry River

Georgetown

Cumberland Bay

Spring Village

Byera

Tunnel

waterfall

Wallilabou

Hermitage
(parrot country)

Power Station

Arrowroot Factory

Colonarie

Barrouallie

Montreal Gardens

Carib Stone

Vermont

Water Station

Windward Highway

Richland Park

Layou

Peniston

(parrot country)

Mesopotamia valley

Carib Stone

Casino

Buccament Valley

Mesopotamia

Biabou

Leeward Highway

Queens Drive

Dorsshire Hill

Fort Charlotte

Kingstown

Airport

Indian Bay

Young Island

Blue Lagoon

TOURS, ACTIVITIES, ETC.

SCUBA

Diving around St Vincent is excellent and anyone with the slightest interest should give it a go. There are two good dive shops both located in Young Island Cut - Bill Tewe's Dive St Vincent is the biggest dive shop. Bill does literally hundreds of resort and full certification courses anually, and runs a flourishing efficient business. It is located right by Young Island Dock. Sue Halbich's Mariner's Scuba Shop is smaller and more low key with an easy relaxed atmosphere. In addition to diving, Scuba Shop rents sailboards, takes people water-skiing, and organizes charters down the Grenadines. Both dive shops offer first-rate trips to the falls of Baleine.

YACHT CHARTERING

St Vincent is ideally located for a cruise through the Grenadines - In Blue Lagoon there is CSY and Bimini Yachts, and in Young Island Cut you have Scuba Shop's charters.

SPORTS FISHING, TRIPS

Danny Soren has a "Longshot" 30 ft twin engine Kustom suitable for sports fishing or day trips to the Grenadines. You can usually find him at the Dolphin restaurant in Young Island cut or call:74582/74238.

Gunn's (Middle Street) offers their 32 foot cabin speedboat "Bacchanal" for day trips to the falls of Baleine etc. They also charter a 22 foot power boat "Halli-Pa-Dalli" for fishing trips. (tel:71706/61250).

TOURS

The idea of conducted tours is still in its infancy in St Vincent, and the traffic is not large enough to carry daily scheduled tours. However, agents will try to fit you in with others wanting to go on tours, so contact them as early as possible during your stay (see our listing). Tours include day tours to Mustique, Bequia and other Grenadines. Also climbing the volcano, island tours, the Botanic Gardens, Falls of Baleine and Mespotamia Valley. Agents include Barefoot Holidays, Grenadine Tours and Sailors Tours.

THE CSY YACHT CLUB

A complete hotel and yacht resort situated in Blue Lagoon on the southern tip of St.Vincent. Our eighteen rooms are the finest on the island and feature air conditioning, telephones, swimming pool, beach bar, boutique and restaurant. The CSY Yacht Club is also the base for our world famous charter fleet, we offer all kinds of charters, including local day charters when yachts are available. For reservations and information call:

In St Vincent: (809) 458-4308
U.S.A. and Canada: (800) 631-1593 (toll free)

FRIENDSHIP BAY

RESORT

Romantic isolated beauty in the
Island of Bequia, Grenadines, W.I.

*Saturday night beach barbecues
*Live music by Exotica
*Watersports, Diving, Sailboarding school
*Day and night tennis
*Excursions aboard Hotel's Classic Yacht
*Mini Market, Boutique, Bread, Ice and Water for Yachts
*Unique swing seat beach bar
*Panoramic restaurant

Friendship Bay Resort, Bequia, St Vincent, West Indies.
tel:809 458 3222. telex:7483 FRIENBAY VQ. radio:VHF ch68.
or Ralph Locke P.O. Box 800, Wacca Buc, N.Y. 10957 U.S.A.
tel:(800) 223 1108. telex:423282

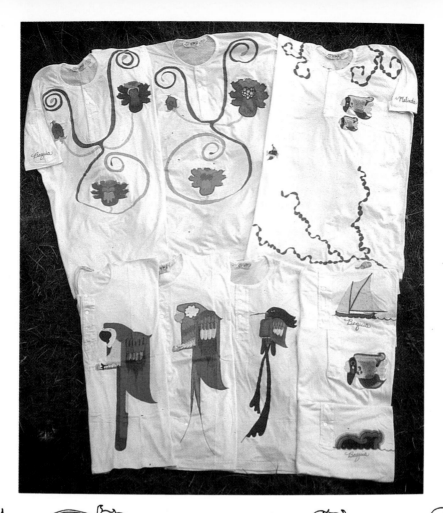

MELINDA'S

HAND PAINTED T-SHIRTS

I ROW OUT IN BEQUIA HARBOR MORNINGS
OR SEE MY ENTIRE COLLECTION AT HOME AFTERNOONS
(phone 83409)

VISA

ALSO CONSIGNED TO

BEQUIA
CRAB HOLE (SEE SALE RACK)
NOAH'S ARKADE (FRANGIPANI HOTEL)
LOCAL COLOR
SOLANA'S
FRIENDSHIP BAY HOTEL

MUSTIQUE
TREASURE BOUTIQUE (COTTON HOUSE HOTEL)
ANITA'S AFFAIR (SHOGUN HOUSE)

GRENADA
IMAGINE BOUTIQUE

LOOK FOR "MELINDA" ON THE SLEEVE.

A private Caribbean Island resort, limited to only 60 guests, 200 yards off the southern coast of St.Vincent. Accomodations are in private cottages with ocean view terraces and over head ceiling fans. As you step ashore we greet you with our Island Special, an exotic blend of local rums and fruit juices topped with a hibiscus. Fruits in your cottages daily, sailboarding, Sunfish, snorkeling, lighted tennis court, two 44 ft yachts for day sailing and extended cruising in the Grenadines.

young Island
the grenadines
St. Vincent, W.I.

U.S. RESERVATIONS:
Ralph Locke Islands
P.O. Box #800 ● Waccabuc, N.Y. 10597
800/223-1108   914/763-5526
TX: 423282   FAX: 914-763-5362

U.K. RESERVATIONS:
Unique Hotels Worldwide
Horsepools House, Edge, Gloucestershire
GL6 6NH England (0452) 813551
TX: 43205   FAX: (0452) 813470

YOUNG ISLAND
Vidal Browne-Mngr.
St. Vincent, W.I. (809) 458-4826
TX: 3217547
FAX: 809/457-4567

ST VINCENT'S HOTELS, SHOPS AND RESTAURANTS

In St Vincent, hotels are primarily family affairs; some have been in the same family for years. They are therefore relatively small, highly individual and usually very personal.

YOUNG ISLAND

Young Island Resort. This resort is so successful and well known, that there are probably people who have hear of Young Island before they hear of St Vincent! Young Island is just a few hundred yards from St Vincent - just far enough to make it self-contained and special; so much more romantic to arrive in a tiny ferry and be greeted as you step out by a welcoming person holding in his hand your first huge tropical drink, topped with a real flower!

Young Island is a magic fairy tale island whose hillside is covered with luxuriant tropical plants - a carnival of color with bright flowers, towering trees and dense vines all tumbling down to the clear blue sea. It is the ultimate "Robinson Crusoe" hideaway. Cottages of natural stone and wood are tucked away among the trees. You can relax in a hammock slung between two palms on the beach, or take a dip in the tropical pool - it looks as if mountain water had collected in a natural hollow among the flowers, but is in fact a swimming pool.

Accomodation is in cottages, which all have large bedrooms and private patios, but some are even bigger with a living room too. Each has a perfect garden setting; some on the hill where they look through a frame of trees to the sea beyond and the only sounds are the wind and the distant cry of parrots. Others are by the water's edge where you can hear the surf and in a few steps be swimming off the beach or snorkeling over the brightly colored reef.

There is a well-balanced entertainment program for guests and sports facilities that include a tennis court, sailboards, full scuba and the island's own fleet of yachts for visiting other islands.

Lunch is served in the open amid the flowers, in the shade of little thatched roofs. Dinner is set in a romantically lit inside "rock garden". One should certainly visit Young Island, and those not staying here should pop over for drinks and maybe dinner one night. On Friday nights there is a barbecue and Saturday night a steel band. There is background music on Tuesdays, Wednesdays and Thursdays.

If you are in St Vincent on a Friday, under no circumstances miss the Young Island Resort Fort Duvernette cocktail party. It's hard to imagine a more romantic spot, all lit up with burning torches - There is plenty to drink and ample snacks which are barbecued on an open fire. (call up for details).

YOUNG ISLAND CUT (Villa)

Sunset Shores lies right on the beach with a view of Young Island, Fort Duvernette and the sea beyond. It is perfect for people who want somewhere quiet, dignified, and run in a very proper and orderly manner. The rooms are set around a garden whose focal point is a swimming pool. The beach is at the bottom of the garden and for those who want to snorkel or sail, Sunfish and snorkeling gear are kept for the complimentary use of guests. There is a restaurant and sometimes in season there is a Saturday night poolside barbecue and jump-up.

The Mermaid Inn is a small very new hotel built right on the beach. Some rooms are self-contained. They have a restaurant specializing in local food, including such delicacies as curried goat.

The Mariners Inn is down at the other end of Young Island Cut. The main structure is a pretty colonial style building, and there is garden featuring a bar built like a boat. There is a sailboarding shop on the premises and a dive shop a few steps away. The restaurant is inexpensive. From time to time they have a Friday night barbecue and jump up.

Located right on the waterfront next to the French Restaurant (they are both run by Simon and Miguele Despointes), the Umbrella Beach Apartments is a small, pleasant and relatively inexpensive place to stay, offering good value. (see also French Restaurant below).

Not far away one finds the Belleville apartments.

The French Restaurant is not only good by St Vincent's standards, it is in fact one of the Windward Islands' really good restaurants, and the food is generally excellent. This is the place to go and eat lobster in season, which you can choose yourself out of the pool. It is moderately expensive, but well worth it, and the house wines are often reasonable. It tends to be very popular, so it would be wise to book in advance.

Just down the harbor wall the Dolphin offers a pub-style atmosphere where you can play darts, chat and get a bite to eat.

The Aquatic Club is the best known nightlife spot in the area. Sometimes they offer an air-conditioned disco and ocassionally they have live music. They also have a little restaurant offering local dishes.

the FRENCH RESTAURANT

VILLA, ST. VINCENT.
TEL: 84972
VHF CHANNEL: 68

SHOPPING

There are a few nice boutiques in Young Island Cut, all within an easy walk. These include The Dock Shop (behind Young Island Dock), The French Restaurant boutique, and Scuba Shop Boutique. Why not take a stroll and visit them all?

BLUE LAGOON

About a mile to the east of Young Island Cut we come to the Blue Lagoon. Hills overlook a reef protected bay. This is the center of St Vincent's charter yacht industry and another popular spot for visitors.

C.S.Y. (Caribbean Sailing Yachts) is St Vincent's largest charter company and their C.S.Y. Hotel has been built with the holiday sailors in mind. Modern, practical and comfortable, each room has its balcony overlooking the yachts and Blue Lagoon beyond. It is a great favorite with yachtsman who want some time ashore before or after their sailing holiday. They have a good restaurant and bar which happens to be an ideal viewing platform from which to spot the "Green Flash" at sunset. A few steps away, their Beach Bar offers snacks and occasional evening entertainment.

Just above Blue Lagoon set on a hill with a perfect view one finds the Ridge View Terrace Apartments and the Ratho Mill apartments.

On the other side of the lagoon at Bimini Yachts one finds a cosy bar and restaurant with a view of the lagoon.

Both CSY and Bimini yachts have boutiques.

About half a mile from Blue Lagoon, down the hill to Calliaqua one can see a tiny, brightly painted shack on the edge of the playing field. This is Papa Spoon's Rasta Ranch, a good, inexpensive and unusual place to get a meal. Papa Spoon serves all Ital food (no meat, only natural ingredients) - you can get roast corn and various kinds of vegetable dishes all served in calabash bowls. Although he's often open in the evenings, this is a more popular lunch spot - seating is appropriately primitive!

St Lucia, nicknamed "Helen of the west", is a beautiful island, with tall mountains, dense rain forests, and superb beaches, but St Lucia really stands out from the other Windwards by the effort her people have put into making tourism a success. St Lucia manages to strike a perfect balance between being unspoiled yet at the same time offering the visitor plenty to do with good service. One can find a wonderful array of restaurants from gourmet food in a perfectly restored old great house, to a snack in a cheap and cheerful lean-to precariously propped on the water's edge, and everything in between even includes an art deco copy of a 1920's Miami style Speakeasy where the waiters wear shoulder holsters. It is fun to go out at night, and there is always something to do.

Of all the Windwards St Lucia stands right on the leading edge for new ideas and innovation in tourism - It is interesting to watch the trends and see what the rest of the Caribbean will be doing next year! One is the resurgence of the "ultimate luxury holiday" where you get totally pampered. Hotel La Toc's new suites are the leaders in this field, but the St Lucian is now planning a new luxury wing, and both Eastwinds and the new Windjammer Landings should be right up there. In terms of restaurants the same style may be found at San Antoine.

Another innovative idea is the all-inclusive holiday - you pay a set fee which covers nearly everything from meals and accomodations to all kinds of activities. This concept has its roots in the Billy Butlin camps in England and the sports minded "Club Meds" world-wide. The originator in the St Lucia was Couples, who made their holiday truly all-inclusive by even throwing in drinks and cigarettes! The all-inclusive package holiday is coming of age - apart from Couples and a new Club Med, there are Club St Lucia, offering first rate holidays as bargain prices, Le Sport, with the emphasis on health, including Thalassotherapay, and Eastwinds, a luxury hotel where you can sit around drinking French Champagne and eating caviar all day!

Innovations don't stop here - ideas in the pipeline include an art deco restaurant based on a turn of the century railway station!

St Lucians welcome visitors, often warmly inviting them to share in their fun; this is obvious to anyone who visits "Friday Night at Gros Islet", a very local way for a small town to entertain itself of an evening, where visitors have had such fun it has become a major attraction, to both tourists and St Lucians.

Visitors adventurous enough to come to the Windwards, yet who want to avoid the time and hassle involved in exploring and discovering things all by themselves, will find that St Lucia has very well organized tour operators. There is almost nothing to be done in St Lucia that cannot be done as part of an organized tour - shopping, hikes through the rain forest, sport fishing, sailing, trips to other islands and visits to plantations, are just a few of the things available through hotel activities desks, or from the tour agents in town.

St Lucia is the center of the charter boat industry in the Windwards, with large yachting centers in Rodney Bay Marina at the north of the island, and Marigot Bay to the south of Castries. From here yachts catch the trade winds north for weekend trips to Martinique, or south for longer trips to the Grenadines.

Yet although St Lucia is well geared to tourism, it is by no means a "Tourist Island". The people support themselves mainly through agriculture and fishing. Food is grown not only in the accessible valleys, but also on steep hillsides. Planting and reaping are done by hand and the produce is often bundled up and carried to the nearest road balanced on the farmer's head or strapped to the back of a donkey. Fishing is mainly from open boats. As in pre-Columbian days, these are hollowed out of a giant tree, though paddle and sail have given way to the outboard motor. The countryside around Soufriere including the Pitons and the rain forest is as magnificently beautiful and wild as can be found anywhere in the Windwards, and the St Lucian government is showing a very enlightened attitude towards protecting its beauty spots and wild terrain. St Lucia is the kind of place where there is plenty of organized activity, yet the adventurous can get "well away" from it all.

GETTING AROUND ST LUCIA

You will find taxis at the airport, all the major hotels, and in Castries along Bridge Street and just beyond the market on the Chausee Road side.

There are several quite large car rental companies (see our listings section). You need a St Lucian driving permit, which you get by paying $30 E.C. and showing your own. The best time to do this is at the airport when you arrive - ask the immigration officer.

St Lucia has two airports, Vigie a smaller inter-island one in the north, and Hewanorra, a large international one in the south. It takes about one and a quarter hours to drive from Hewanorra to the north end of the island where many of the hotels are. (It costs around $40 U.S for a taxi.) If you are traveling on your own find out if your hotel offers airport transfers. Alternatively, call up some of the tour companies we have in our listings some days before you arrive and see if they can arrange a transfer for you. There are also buses which run between Vieux Fort and Castries passing by the main road a short walk from the airport. However, you may not find one in the evening or on a Sunday. Vigie is close to Castries and taxi rides to the major hotels less expensive. If you want to use a bus, you will have to walk a hot mile to the bottom end of the airport down to the main road to find one. Alternatively, you can take the path across the airport and turn left which quickly brings you to another part of the main road (still quite a walk to where the buses stop).

Buses are the local way to go, and St Lucia has plenty! We give the locations of the bus stops in Castries on our map. The stretch between Castries and Gros Islet is particularly well serviced, and you can often get buses from early in the morning to almost midnight. Vieux Fort to Castries buses are also quite frequent and you can usually get buses going either way up to about 6 or 7 p.m. Soufriere is more difficult, buses often come into Castries in the mornings and return in the afternoons. Friday and Saturday are the best days when you may be able to get a bus back from Soufriere as late as 3 p.m.

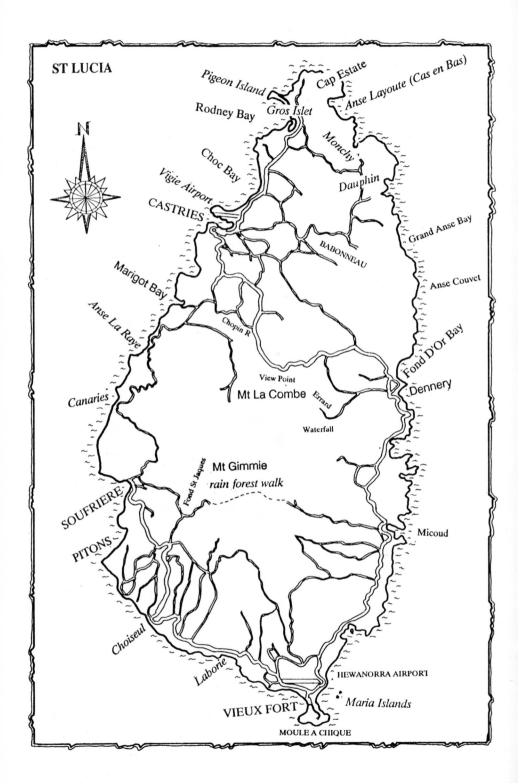

ST LUCIA

Pigeon Island
Cap Estate
Anse Layoute (Cas en Bas)
Rodney Bay
Gros Islet
Monchy
Choc Bay
Dauphin
Vigie Airport
CASTRIES
Grand Anse Bay
BABONNEAU
Marigot Bay
Anse Couvet
Anse La Raye
Chopin R
View Point
Fond D'Or Bay
Mt La Combe
Errard
Dennery
Canaries
Waterfall
Mt Gimmie
Fond St Jaques
rain forest walk
SOUFRIERE
Micoud
PITONS
Choiseul
Labone
HEWANORRA AIRPORT
VIEUX FORT
Maria Islands
MOULE A CHIQUE

120

EXPLORING PICTURESQUE PLACES

All St Lucia is scenic, and it is well worth exploring many of the smaller roads. Some of these can be rough, but if one drives slowly and carefully over the bad patches, most regular cars can make it. However, there are a few really bad roads, and anyone wanting to explore them should rent something suitable with four wheel drive.

Our map of St Lucia shows the places mentioned, but it is inadequate for serious exploration, as are the pretty little maps supplied by the car rental companies. Serious explorers should buy themselves an ordinance survey map. These can be bought from the Lands and Surveys department in Castries. It is on the opposite side of Jeremie street from Barclays Bank (down towards the Chausee Road). They come in various sizes, but the biggest is best, three huge sheets for about $20 E.C. and they will double as fine souvenirs when you get home! Smaller survey maps are sometimes available in boutiques.

NORTHERN TOUR

This is a drive that takes you through some varied country and then along a steep mountain ridge with sweeping views over the north of St Lucia. As you head towards Castries from Rodney Bay take the turning off to Monchy (sign post has currently disappeared but look for a turning to the left as you start down the first steep hill). From Monchy wind your way along to Babonneau. The trick here is to get a little south of Castries so that you pass Four Roads Junction where you will have bird's eye views over Castries and finish up along Victoria Road up on the Morne. The general state of the road on this drive is fair, but you will have to go easy over one or two bad patches.

CHOPIN RIDGE

After you pass the Hess Oil depot on the way from Castries to Marigot Bay the road gets somewhat rough. At one point you come to a sharp right bend in the road while opposite you a road leads off the to the left. Turn down this and keep going till you come to a small narrow road on your right which leads downhill. This road runs right over Chopin Ridge, from where you see the countyside spread out for miles on both sides. You will eventually rejoin the main highway that runs across the island. This is a short run, and the road is rough in places. It might be a nice detour if you were returning from Marigot Bay (see separate section) with plenty of daylight left.

SOUFRIERE ROAD

Unfortunately, the road from Castries to Soufriere down the West Coast is not in the best of repair, but nonetheless it is well worth seeing, not only in order to get to Soufriere (see separate section), but because the road itself offers a rich variety of landscapes. You pass through lush banana plantations, and wind along mountain roads with precipitous views out to sea and onto the fishing villages of Anse La Raye and Canaries, and then as you approach Soufriere comes the best bit of all. You drive through dramatic mountain scenery amid exotically dense vegetation, and for the last part of the road you get a fabulous view of the twin towering Pitons. If you are making an island tour, start with this road and then return via Vieux Fort, you will get the optimum views going round this way.

MAIN HIGHWAY, CASTRIES TO VIEUX FORT

This road goes through some very pleasant country, especially as you pass through the rain forest in the middle of the island and as you skirt the Windward coast (see also separate Vieux Fort section).

DENNERY RIVER

There is a narrow road that leads back along the Dennery river in Errard Estate. This road is rough in places but takes you up a beautiful lush valley. On your left you will eventually see the sparkling Errard waterfall. There is a rough trail to the river, and the dedicated explorer can find his way to the falls, but this is a scramble. The waterfall is photogenic, but while one can swim in the pool it can be rather muddy. Keep in mind this is a private estate with no right of way. Treat it with respect and ask permission if you can.

THE CITY OF CASTRIES

The City of Castries has been ravaged by fire some four times! It all started in 1795 after the French Revolution when agents of the new France went round inciting the slaves to join forces with them and rebel against the British. In return they would get freedom, equality and fraternity. This was a time of unrest throughout the Windwards, In St Vincent they had the Carib Wars, in Grenada Fedon's uprising and in St Lucia it was the "Brigands War". This lead to a period of destruction and terror. Many estates were destroyed, the Diamond Baths were knocked down, and the City of Castries was razed.

The other fires were, as far as one knows, accidental. There was one in 1812 and another in 1927, and the most recent in 1948. Well, I guess the government learned by experience and most of the city was rebuilt in concrete! However, some older very charming houses from an earlier age did escape the fire. "Rain" on Brazil Street is a good example. As you walk from Columbus Square towards the Chausee road, you find yourself in among fascinating hodge podge of old and the new buildings, many with balconies and gingerbread decoration; it has a very Creole feel.

SHOPPING

Castries offers a wealth of shops for the souvenir and bargain hunter. Everyone should pay a visit to the big colorful local market. In addition to the exotic array of tropical foods there is a huge selection of straw goods including mats and baskets in all shapes and sizes. Unfortunately one of the best buys is almost impossible to transport - for just a few E.C. dollars you can become the proud owner of a huge pottery coal pot (a sort of West Indian hibachi) made out of local clay and fired in an open fire!

Noah's Arkade, just off Bridge Street, is well worth looking for. They keep an enormous stock of every kind of souvenir, as well as locally made clothes and local books. Across the street, the Sea Island Cotton Shop sells vivid Batiks - designs of yachts, sunsets and wildlife, which can be bought as wall hangings or made up as clothes. If you want jewelry, perfumes and clothing accessories try Y de Lima, Images, and Cox and Co. You will find numerous little boutiques to explore, but don't miss the one hidden away in "Rain" restaurant. Book lovers will enjoy the Book Salon and the Sunshine Bookstore (near the B.W.I.A. and Eastern offices on Brazil Street). If you are short on film or want your color prints developed try Bryden's. After all that rushing around you may need somewhere for lunch!

RESTAURANTS

Rain is oldest and most important bar/ restaurant in town - everyone ends up meeting here because of the pleasant atmosphere - a charming old courtyard house complete with balconies, gingerbread, ceiling fans, and posters of the stars of the movie version of Somerset Maugham's turgid tale. You can sit outside in the courtyard below, or upstairs on the balcony overlooking Columbus Square. Light or full lunches depending on your appetite. At night they stage a magnificent dinner - you are whisked back a century and enjoy the re-creation of a champagne buffet served in 1885 to members of the Castries Philharmonic Society. There are 7 courses and four wines, appropriately served on Victorian china, by staff in 19th century uniforms (wine is sipped from French crystal glasses) - fully inclusive cost around $85 E.C. (a la carte menu also available).

There are numerous small Creole restaurants around town where you can buy

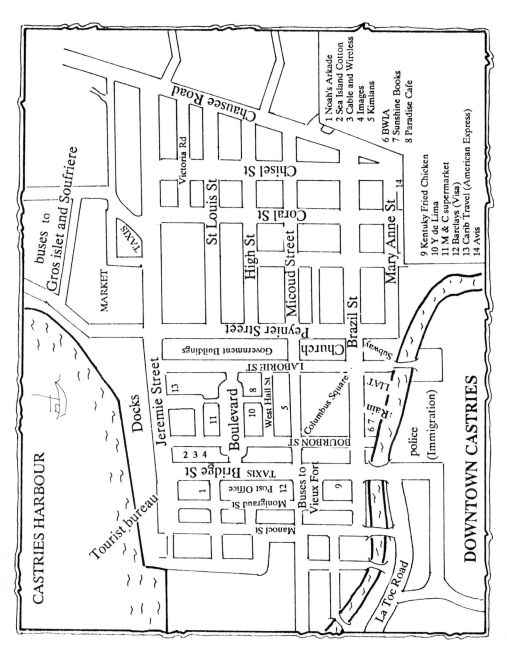

1 Noah's Arkade
2 Sea Island Cotton
3 Cable and Wireless
4 Images
5 Kimlans
6 BWIA
7 Sunshine Books
8 Paradise Cafe
9 Kentuky Fried Chicken
10 Y de Lima
11 M & C supermarket
12 Barclays (Visa)
13 Carib Travel (American Express)
14 Avis

tasty local snacks. Typical of these are E's, Kimlan's and The Subway (located in "The White House" on Brazil Street, just to the east of Columbus Square).

SHOPPING HOURS

Normal shopping hours are Monday to Friday, 8.00 a.m. to 12.30 p.m. and 1.30 p.m. to 4 p.m. Banks open Monday to Friday 8 a.m. to 1 p.m. with a little extra opening time on Friday afternoons between 3.00 p.m. and 5 p.m. If you get stuck for a supermarket on a Sunday, and you have a car, try Marche de France at Rodney Bay Marina, the Mini Market at Harmony Appartel, or Glace Mini Market at Marisule on the Gros Islet Highway all open on Sunday mornings from about 9.00 a.m. to 12.00 noon.

124

ON EITHER SIDE OF CASTRIES - VIGIE TO MORNE FORTUNE

Close by Castries one finds beautiful beaches, numerous views, an interesting harbor, good hotels and fascinating shops.

The main road going south of town winds up Morne Fortune (The Morne). From on top, around Fort Charlotte or along the Victoria Road, you can view Castries and the north of the Island spread out like a giant map.

North west of town, Vigie Creek with its marina and hauling facility (Castries Yacht Center) will please the boat lover, as will a glimpse of the quaint tall ship "Unicorn" anchored next to the Coal Pot.

Just over the water from Castries is "Pointe Seraphine" a duty free shopping haven especially designed for tourists.

LA TOC

Everyone has heard of the famous Cunard luxury liners: the Q.E.II, the Cunard Princess and Countess, and Saga Fjord and Vista Fjord. As one would expect from the owners of such illustrious ships, their St Lucia hotel, The Cunard La Toc, is something special.

Let us start with the grounds - 106 acres of beautiful gently sloping land that meets the sea in a half mile long golden beach. There is a private 9 hole golf course as well as a fitness center and five all weather tennis courts. There are two fresh water swimming pools, (one even has a "tropical island" in the middle complete with palm tree!), full water sports and of course such facilities as a beauty salon, boutiques, card rooms, lounges and conference halls.

With about 300 bedrooms it is one of St Lucia's larger hotels, but the accommodations are split into numerous different buildings and areas spread around the property, so they have managed to create a smaller more intimate atmosphere. The whole property has been completely renovated and they recently became members of the exclusive "Leading Hotels of the World".

There is no question that for those who can afford the luxury "La Toc Suites", this has to be the place to stay. Imagine a huge bedroom, a gorgeous living room (designed and furnished by Hirsch and Bedner), opening onto a balcony with a plunge pool in which you can sit and enjoy a tropical drink while admiring the view of the beach framed by bright red bougainvillaea! You will be met by the resident host and hostess who will introduce you to your personal maid. She will pamper you, starting on your arrival when you will be presented with your own kimono and slippers for lounging around. You have a library of both books and films to choose from and you have preferential treatment at the exclusive "Les Pitons" restaurant, where the food is prepared by a first rate French chef.

The three restaurants are open to the general public. Les Pitons is the best, and outside bookings are only available on a limited basis. The main Terrace dining room overlooks the pool and you can order both a la carte or from a fixed menu. There is nightly entertainment with music for dancing, and a cabaret on Tuesday, Thursdays and Saturdays. The Quarter Deck (open during the season only) is a smaller more intimate restaurant serving mainly Creole dishes.

Those who want more than a hotel can combine a week in the hotel with a week on one of the Cunard Line's cruise ships - how would that be for the best of both worlds!

Not far from La Toc one finds the Tapion Reef Hotel. This rather curious building started life designed as a hospital, but was converted to a hotel before being used. It has a good view over the sea, a small pleasant beach that would be excellent for snorkeling, and a pool for swimming. The rooms are self-contained and reasonably priced. Renting a car would be advantageous, but the rates are reasonable enough to let you do this. A good place for independent people who want to be away from the resort hotels.

UP ON THE MORNE

The Morne with its panoramic views and cool breeze was an obvious building spot, not only for the fort, but also for better class residences. All the establishments listed below have wonderful views! However, for the most part you will do better in this area if you rent a car, as it is hilly and you may have to walk a while to get a bus.

The Green Parrot is run by Chef Harry, and like many of the world's great chefs he is well padded. This is understandable, as is his broad welcoming smile, for Chef Harry has the enviable reputation of having been St Lucia's premiere chef for 15 years ever since he returned from London where he cooked at Claridges.

While Harry may be considered the top chef, his restaurant the Green Parrot is definitely the top of the hill restaurant. Perched way up the Morne, above government house, it has a view over Castries and the north of the island.

But perhaps Harry's greatest attribute is as an entertainer - the Green Parrot is the place to go to have a fun night out - and the best nights to go are on Wednesday and Saturday when Harry hosts his own floor show including limbo, fire-eating and famous local dancer Princess Tina. Harry has a knack of getting all his guests out of their seats and onto the floor dancing!

Monday is another special night called "Ladies night" If the lady comes with a flower in her hair, and the gentleman with a tie and a jacket, the lady gets her meal for free. Music is supplied by a local "shac shac" band.

Although known primarily for its restaurant, the Green Parrot is also a 40 room hotel. All rooms have a living area and a balcony overlooking the view. There is air conditioning, a swimming pool and a boutique.

San Antoine is a very special place, it oozes sumptuous charm and elegance in the best possible way, and just to walk in the door elevates ones mood and sets the tone for the evening. I regard it as one of St Lucia's special features that should on no account be missed.

San Antoine stands a little way up the

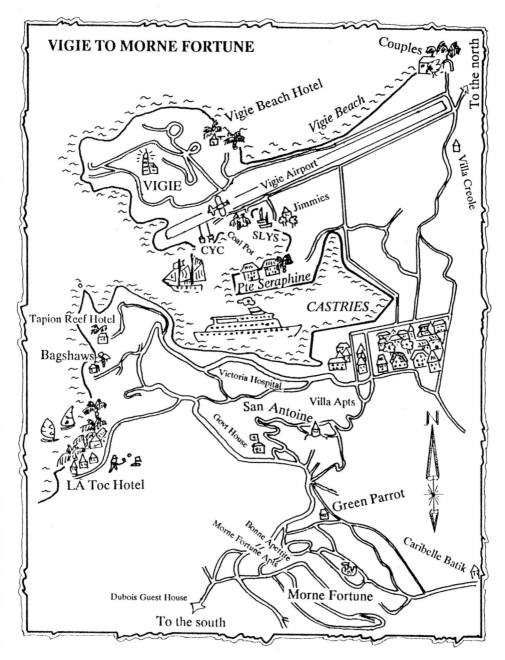

VIGIE TO MORNE FORTUNE

Morne with a commanding view of Castries and the harbor. It was built in the 1800's as a private great house. In the 1920's it was converted to become St Lucia's first hotel by Aubrey Davidson-Houston, a famous English portrait painter whose clientele included Somerset Maugham and Alec Waugh. In 1970 it was gutted by fire leaving only the heavy stone walls, arches and the lovely sweeping staircase.

After being derelict for 14 years, both the

127

building and its 12 acres of grounds have been magnificently restored regardless of cost. While one can read about the dark varnished wood, wrought iron and polished brass all gleaming by candle light, one really has to go there to appreciate it.

San Antoine is open for both lunch and dinner, The dinner menu is long and imaginative and browsing through it is part of the evening's pleasure. Owners Michael and Alison come from a family who have been in the catering business since the 1880's, and have included many showy main courses such as Filet of Beef Pont Cheval - medallions of beef sauteed in sweet sherry with raisins and peppercorns, thickened with cream and flambeed at your table.

While San Antoine will live up to the best outfit in your wardrobe, cool informal wear is perfectly OK.

At some point in the evening you should stroll around the grounds, which include a fish pool, floodlit paths and reproductions of Carib drawings.

GUEST HOUSES

There are several guest houses that take advantage of the Morne's views and breeze. Bon Apettite is an excellent guest house by any standards, the rooms are light, airy and nicely decorated; each has its own bathroom. Manager Ezra Charles is St Lucian, and his wife, born in the U.S.A., came to St Lucia in 1980. They have a bar and well recommended restaurant, but would appreciate an hour or two notice if you plan on coming to dinner.

DuBois Guest House is on the main road, which would make it O.K. if you wanted to travel by bus. Nice view from the lawn, smallish but clean rooms, sharing the bathrooms.

Twin Palms is a small and adequate guest house that was undergoing some renovations when I visited.

APARTMENTS

Morne Fortune Apartments (Top of the Morne), is a wonderful, old brick barracks, close by the fort, which have been very successfully converted to apartments - they are enormous, with vast rooms and an even larger private balcony overlooking the view. The interiors are tastefully furnished in Caribbean style - all wicker and rattan with suitable pictures on the walls. The one bedroom apartment would probably sleep 6, but the management limits it to 3 sharing, and the two bedroom apartments to 5, but this is in great style and comfort! There is a swimming pool and a reasonably priced car rental service available only to residents.

Villa Apartments are just out of town as you wind up the Morne, they are just far enough out to afford peace and a good view, while being within easy walking distance. The building dates from the 1930's when it was built as a judge's home. The apartments are luxuriously decorated in modern style and very comfortable. Many are taken on long term rentals, and they are often full, so book well in advance!

VIGIE

The Coal Pot, a cosy waterside restaurant, drums up images of a bygone century, with old chain, a cannon, a ship's wheel and a few spars stowed aloft. Just ahead looms the silhouette of the magnificent brig Unicorn. Palm trees, the water and candle lit tables all contribute to making this a very romantic atmosphere for that quiet meal out.

Jimmie's is the best seafood restaurant in St Lucia, and you will find it in the St Lucia Yacht Services complex overlooking the harbor. Popular with locals and visitors alike, it has an easy quiet atmosphere, it is the kind of place you can feel comfortable just eating a soup or desert if you do not want a complete meal. Some excellent sauces go with the seafoods, try the "Harbor Catch" with a spicy local sauce.

Couples is a special hotel for special people - couples. The idea is you should be able to relax and enjoy your holiday without having to worry about money, so everything is included in the price.

Everything in this case includes as much as you want to drink at the bar, as many cigarettes as you can smoke, all activities including waterskiing and scuba, horseriding and exercise classes and two tours a week - a day sail to Soufriere and a half day trip to Pigeon Island.

The only snag is you must be a couple (male and female that is). There is no age limit but the hotel is immensely popular with honeymooners and, the average age of clients is in the mid 20's.

The hotel itself is first rate, built right on a lovely beach with 70 double rooms, each with a balcony. There are a variety of accomodations including some with a private sitting room and patio overlooking the sea.

Couples staying elsewhere can give this special resort a try by coming for a half day (breakfast till lunch) for $30 U.S. or full day (breakfast till 6 P.M.) for $40 U.S. As for all you singles - eat your heart out!

The Vigie Beach hotel is conveniently situated within walking distance of the airport, and just a short ride to town or the the island's prosperous north. Set on the sweeping Vigie Beach, it is being completely re-modeled. There is a bar, restaurant, pool and entertainment on Mondays, Thursdays and Saturdays with a steel band over Sunday lunch.

The Creole Inn is small guest house located on a rise not far from the airport with a distant view to the sea. The main living room is quaint and full of character. Inside, rooms are adequate, the one with its own bathroom is definitely the most spacious and comfortable and worth the extra couple of dollars!

Below the Creole Inn is the workshop of artist Ron Savory. Ron was born in Guyana and has worked at every kind of job imaginable from broadcasting and theater to pledge clerk and civil servant.

He has lived and worked in remote areas such as the Guyana/Venezuela border. Ron has been painting since 1958, since when his work has been in great demand. He has lots of paintings on show, and art lovers should stop by.

SHOPPING

The area around Castries offers some unusually interesting shops and the huge "Pointe Seraphine" complex.

Pointe Seraphine is a duty free shopping village, built specifically with the visitor in mind. Visit when there are 4 or 5 cruise ships in the harbor, and you will come across a bustling scene - a band playing in the square, artisans working on handicrafts by the pavement, and many salesgirls in bright traditional costumes. It gives a feeling akin to an eastern bazaar.

One can just walk around and enjoy the atmosphere. The serious shopper will be in seventh heaven with about 20 shops in one small area. Visit them all, but among others keep in mind that Windjammer is a St Lucian company making cotton holiday wear exported all over the world. Close to home in Pointe Seraphine prices are better. The same is true of Bagshaws hand printed fabrics from original designs. There is much more; swimwear, handicrafts, china, crystal, jewelry, and electronics all at duty free prices. If you are not a cruise ship passenger, all you need is your airline ticket when you make your purchase. There is a double decker bus which shuttles between Pointe Seraphine and town.

Just a short ride from Castries are three

unusual shops which can be a lot of fun to visit, you could take in all three in a morning making it a sort of mini tour, and along the way you will be treated with some memorable views.

For years Bagshaws have been selling fabric, clothes and other items from material they silk screen themselves. The colors are bright and clear with the designs straight from nature; trees, birds, butterflies and fish, many so accurately reproduced one can learn a lot about the local wildlife just from looking! While there is a small "Bagshaws" in Pointe Seraphine, those with the time should treat themselves to a trip to the real Bagshaw's, which is a place of special interest and elegance.

To get there you take the road from Castries towards La Toc and follow the "Bagshaws" sign which takes you down an elegant tree lined lane to a huge garden overlooking the sea. You will be greeted by a brightly colored macaw as you walk in. It is a large spacious shop, open at the front with a broad balcony offering a sweeping view over La Toc Beach and out to sea. (If your husband is now bored with shopping he can relax here in a comfortable chair, or visit the refreshment bar.)

The shop has several rooms of different products including tote bags, place mats, cushions, wall hangings and pictures. Those who have despaired of finding a really artistic postcard, you will find several here, photographed by Alice Bagshaw herself.

Eudovic's studio is on the right side of the main road as you head south from Castries, and is on the far side of the Morne. It is in a delightful spot with views over the countryside.

Several artists work co-operatively to produce beautiful carvings from mahogany, cedar, eucalyptus and coconut. Some of the figures are representational - tall thin figures that have their roots in African folk art, but some of the most enthralling work is abstract - free flowing forms of great style and feeling. Some are too big to take in your suitcase, but shipping can always be arranged. There is also a small handicraft shop.

The Caribelle Batik factory is housed in an enchanting old house along Victoria road on the Morne overlooking Castries. It produces batik, and one is welcome to visit. A large selection of the their products on sale. There is also a bar.

CHOC BAY

The coast from Castries to Rodney Bay includes miles of perfect beach in the long sweeping "Choc Bay".

Halcyon Beach Club is a 180 room hotel situated right on Choc Beach. The double rooms are built amid a garden blooming with hibiscus and bougainvillaea. One of the main dining room is right beside the swimming pool, which is a stone's throw from the beach. There is a second "garden pool" with a built in bar to allow you to refresh yourself inside as well as out. The hotel offers two tennis courts as well as a full range of water sports. There are two boutiques and a "vendors market". Rooms are all comfortable air conditioned doubles with a big bathroom and outside patio.

For those with kids there is a playground complete with slides and swings. Halcyon Beach Club also boasts a pier which houses their "Fisherman's Wharf" restaurant, where you sit out over the water. Here you can choose from a big a la carte menu, with prime ribs their specialty. In the main dining room you will find a set four course dinner.

Drinkers will be delighted to know there are several happy hours daily. From 12.30-1.30 p.m. and from 5.30 to 6.30 p.m, and from 11.00 p.m. to half past midnight. There is live entertainment every night. Later at night the Pier comes alive with their disco which goes on until the early hours. Sunday lunch is a good time to visit when they offer a barbecue to the music of a steel band. Luckily it coincides with a happy hour!

Edgewater Beach Hotel and Restaurant, a tiny hotel tucked out off the main road, escapes many people's notice, however those in the know go for excellent seafood and the best pizzas. Look for the sign on your left as you drive from Vigie airport towards the north, it is not too far along on your left hand side. Edgewater is right on the lovely Vigie Beach, separated from it only by a small garden of exotic tropical plants. Manager Jane Tipson likes dogs and cats, who loll around under the shade of the trees. There are five clean and simple rooms (some air conditioned), at a fraction of the price you will find in any other similarly located beach hotel. Ideal for pizza fans and beach lovers on a budget.

In the same area, just across the road from the beach, is the Sundale Guest House. This is a superior guest house, and each room has its own bathroom. The rates are exceptionally reasonable when one considers they include a big breakfast. The house is well kept, and to stay here is much like being a guest in someone's pleasant and properly run personal home.

A short walk from Sundale one finds E's Serenity Lodge - with 5 double rooms and one self contained apartment. The building is brand new and everything is very clean - the rooms with balconies are a couple of dollars more expensive but well worth the difference!

Eastwinds Inn has just been taken over by experienced hotelier Peter Kouly who also happens to be the Danish consul. It is being completely rebuilt and the envisioned result is an exclusive, gastronomic, up market hotel that offers very personal service and has rates fully inclusive of everything. Unlike most other "all-inclusive establishments" at this one you can select from an elegant wine list, and those who so wish can breakfast, lunch and dinner on French champagne and lobster tails! (subject to legal season).

Those not staying here can test it out with a special lunch or dinner option.

The Modern Inn is a simple pleasant guest house with a good view over Choc Bay and Vigie. Rooms have private shower and some are air conditioned.

APARTMENTS

Right now the Windjammer Landings is a large worksite in Labrelotte Bay not far

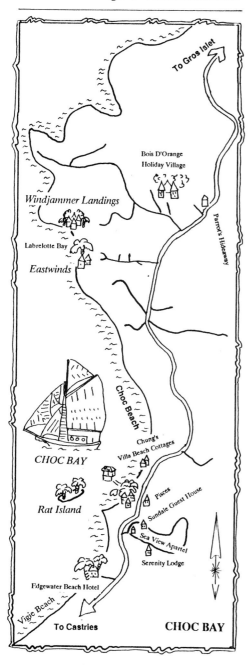

from Eastwinds. But, by the time this book reaches the stores, it is due to be St Lucia's newest, most luxurious, self-contained holiday resort, with accommodation in spacious villas, each with its own swimming pool, all close by a good bathing beach. All the usual resort facilities from water-sports and tennis to a babysitting service are planned.

Seaview Apartel is a brand new apartment block on the main road opposite the airport. (If you walk across the runway path you arrive right there.) The rooms are comfortable and air conditioned. For those not wanting to drive there is a bus route right outside.

Friendship Inn is a brand new complex of 10 self-contained rental rooms, just off the main road close by the Halcyon Beach Hotel.

Villa Beach Cottages are older, rather basic, self-contained cottages right on the beach just past the Halcyon Beach Club as you drive north. You have the convenience of Chung's Chinese restaurant next door.

Bois D'Orange Holiday Village is a collection of self-contained rooms and apartments up on a hill, with views of Rodney Bay. It is reasonably priced but far enough from the beach and other restaurants to make renting a car desirable.

Pisces is an upstairs restaurant which specializes in local food, situated right opposite the Halcyon Beach Club. They offer very reasonable lunch time specials.

Parrot's Hideaway (not to be mixed up with the Green Parrot.) This local establishment belongs to Soca Calypsonian "Lucian Parrot", a well known local musician who has several albums out as well as having played in the U.S.A and Canada. It is a basic and inexpensive guest house on the road between Castries and Gros Islet. There is also a restaurant downstairs offering local food and occasional jump ups on a Friday night.

THE NORTH END OF ST LUCIA, RODNEY BAY TO CAP ESTATE

Nowhere else in St Lucia has shown such intense recent development as the northern sector. Two man made feats of engineering have encouraged this phenomenon. One is the Causeway which links Pigeon Island to the mainland and helps shelter Rodney Bay. The other is the dredging of the lagoon which has created a huge, completely protected anchorage for the burgeoning yacht trade. The last few years has shown a vast increase in houses, hotels, bars, restaurants and yachts.

Places of interest include Reduit Beach, the big new Rodney Bay Marina, the Pigeon Island National Park, Gros Islet and Cap Estate.

IDEAS FOR A QUICK DRIVING TOUR

Take the main road round Rodney Bay Lagoon and drive past the turn off to Gros Islet Village. Take the next big road to your left which leads to Pigeon Island. This road runs along a narrow spit of land with the sea on both sides, the protected side being a good bathing beach. This is the man made causeway. In the old days Pigeon Island was a true island surrounded by sea and back in the 18th century it was Admiral Rodney's main base. He choose it for good reasons - to the north one could see Martinique, home of his traditional enemies, the French. It provided enough protection from the swells, but did not block the wind, so ships could be sailed out at a moment's notice. Although there are much more protected harbors to the south, they are subject to calms and fluky winds, which in a quick engagement could be critical.

In Rodney's time Pigeon Island was covered with buildings - storerooms, a hospital and a fort. It is well worth the climb up to the fort, where the battlements and cannons have been restored. The real treat is the view so remember your camera! You will be charged a small admission into the

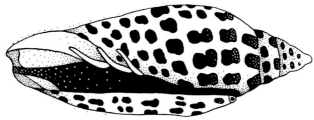
park but it is money well spent as it goes towards the National Trust. While in the park you may visit the small museum.

After Pigeon Island return to the main road and hang a left to Cap Estate. Drive into the Estate and keep going. You will pass a rather curious sign saying "Hump here". When you see Le Sport sign posted to your left, keep going straight ahead. Pass a round-about with a sign saying "Saline Point" and keep going till you arrive at a T-junction at the top of the hill. Here Saline Point is sign posted to the left and you go right. Follow the road; it is in terrible condition, but with great care even a normal car can make it to the very top by a little shelter. The view from here over the north end of the island is worth the journey, on a clear day you can see Martinique.

If you are in need of refreshment on the way back you can always visit Rodney Bay Marina where you will enjoy looking a their shops and the yachts. Finish up with a swim at Reduit Beach, it would be hard to find a better spot!

CAP ESTATE

Cap Estate covers over 1500 acres of attractive land leading right up to St Lucia's northern tip. There are two hotels, 7 beaches, a nine hole golf course, and numerous lovely homes, with ample space for more. Horse riding is available at Cas en Bas Beach (turning opposite Gros Islet).

HOTELS

Many people go on holiday not only to enjoy themselves but also to rest and recover from the daily routine. Le Sport is geared to help you make the experience not only thoroughly enjoyable, but healthy and theraputic as well. Firstly, forget worrying about money - once you have paid for your holiday everything is included in the price (except cigarettes which were considered a bit too degenerate to include in a health deal, but addicts needn't do without- they are on sale!). Then enjoy a program of active sports including all the water sports, tennis, archery, riding, bicycling, fencing (with foils, not repairing the perimiter...) and volleyball. In between these you can relax with Thalassotherapy - a wonderful rejuvinating therapy based on hot sea water baths with thermal jets and underwater massage - ideal for all those sore muscles! At night you can keep going with the nightly entertainment program and finish up at the disco. As is in keeping with a health oriented program, food is light French cuisine with plenty of healthy fresh food.

The hotel is large, modern, and well maintained right on the beach. There are boutiques, a swimming pool and three floodlit tennis courts. Those who are not staying there can a get a quick tone up by joining for a day or half day (call for details).

Club St Lucia is geared to offering a first rate all inclusive holiday at a reasonable price. They offer everything you would expect in a major resort - sailboarding, sunfish, paddle boats, waterskiing, horseback riding, golf, tennis and even a day trip - but all are included in the fixed price as are all your meals and drinks. There is

nightly entertainment, a fortnightly beach barbecue and three cabaret shows a week! Club St Lucia is based on the old "Smugglers" hotel - it was always pleasant and spacious but the beach in the old days was not that great for swimming. Now, as well as completely renovating the hotel, the new management have removed most of the reef so the beach is good for bathing and watersports.

The grounds around Club St Lucia have a lot of lawn and are well away from a main road. This makes it ideal for those with children, and to make the vacation fun for both of you there is a children's mini-club program.

For those staying elsewhere - especially those in smaller guest houses - the Club St Lucia offers really fantastic "Join Us" deals. For $40 U.S you can spend a full day at Club St Lucia - start at 7 am and finish at 1 a.m.! It includes all your meals, your drinks, you can go sailing and use all the facilities, as well as enjoy the evening entertainment - all at the price one meal will cost you in many establishments! If you

cannot make a whole day you can join from 2 p.m. to 1 a.m. for $35 U.S. Otherwise if you just want some evening entertainment there is an evening pass (inclusive of drinks and snacks but not dinner) for $35 E.C.

RODNEY BAY

Set around a huge lagoon, Rodney Bay is fast becoming St Lucia's main leisure center. All kinds of water sports and yachting activities are based here, as well as a dense configuration of bars and restaurants. This has become one of the most sought after home locations for middle class St Lucians and overseas visitors.

Rodney Bay Marina is the brain child of Arch Morez, it has taken several years and some millions of dollars to build. Everyone who likes to look at boats should come by and take a stroll. It is pleasantly laid out with lawns and palm trees, and there are numerous shops including an auto rental agency and yacht chandlery. Stop for a snack at Mrs Taylor's little home made bakeshop, and explore all the boutiques. You can return in the evening to try the "After Deck" restaurant (happy hour 7-8 p.m.). The food is good, the prices reasonable, and they have a pleasant waterfront

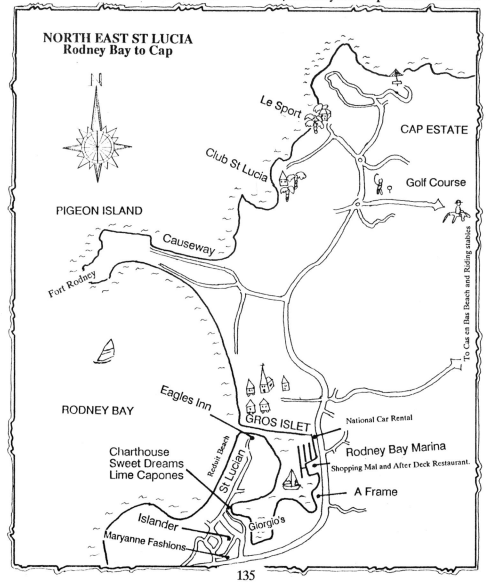

NORTH EAST ST LUCIA
Rodney Bay to Cap

Le Sport

CAP ESTATE

Club St Lucia

Golf Course

PIGEON ISLAND

Causeway

Fort Rodney

To Cas en Bas Beach and Riding stables

Eagles Inn

RODNEY BAY

GROS ISLET

National Car Rental

Charthouse
Sweet Dreams
Lime Capones

Reduit Beach

St Lucian

Rodney Bay Marina

Shopping Mal and After Deck Restaurant.

A Frame

Islander

Giorgio's

Maryanne Fashions

location.

Rodney Bay is the home of many of St Lucia's main charter companies -including Stevens Yachts and Tradewind Yacht charters. You can come here to charter a yacht or just to wander round them and dream.

Just down the road from Rodney Bay Marina, the Blue Lagoon Guest rooms are simple, clean, convenient and inexpensive. Some units have their own bathroom and some have kitchen facilities. Those that don't, get to share the communal bathrooms and big kitchen. There is also a completely self-contained two bedroom cottage available.

It would be hard to imagine a more perfect setting for a hotel than Reduit Beach. Over half a mile that could have been invented for a travel brochure - white sand, waving palms and water that goes from turquoise to aquamarine, in fact the lot! The St Lucian covers almost half this beach, all its 220 rooms a mere stone's throw from the water's edge. You will find here a very comprehensive water sports

facility, they are agents for Mistral sailboards and run a school. There are sailing dinghies, scuba and for high fliers it is the only place to go para-sailing. More earthbound people will enjoy the floodlit tennis courts, the complete boutique shopping center and the evening entertainment.

While your loved one is out there trying to stand up on a sail board you can watch from the comfort of the Surf Club Bar right over the water sports shop where you can get a splash by splash view.

Come evening you can choose between the Hummingbird set menu restaurant and the poolside a la carte restaurant and snack bar. Entertainment is one of the St Lucian's strong points. There is a dance band every night, floor shows on Saturday and Thursday, limbo on Tuesdays, and crab racing on Wednesdays. But perhaps the St Lucian's main claim to fame in entertainment, is the famous Splash Disco (open nightly except Sunday and Monday).

The St Lucian has a poolside bar where you can buy snacks. Sunday lunch is espe-

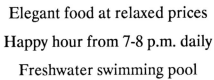

cially pleasant as they have a barbecue and steel band.

Right on the waterfront inside the Rodney Bay Lagoon, the Harmony Apartel is a moderately priced, self-contained apartment hotel, with clean rooms built round a swimming pool. The famous Reduit Beach is just a few minutes walk down the road. Their restaurant the "Mortar and Pestle" looks over the Lagoon and specializes in a wide range of famous Caribbean dishes from Jamaican Ackee and Saltfish to Antigua Baked Clams. They have a tiny mini market, conveniently open on Sundays when the big stores are closed.

Built leaning over the edge of Rodney Bay Lagoon, the A-Frame bar is a simple cheerful place that has become the local hang out for yachties, who have been known to get maudlin late at night and burst into song. The atmosphere is very informal; it is the one of the best places to go and meet people and it is a popular "warm up" spot on Friday nights before moving on to Gros Islet. There are occasional darts and backgammon contests. Happy hour is nightly between 6.30 and 7.30 and if you are having too much fun to go home and cook you can eat here. Fare varies from rotis to best steaks. A-Frame is open all day every day except Monday.

Capone's is painted in various shades of bright pink, iced with green, and sits, like an enormous Christmas Cake, close by the Lagoon. At night hundreds of bright lights proclaim its presence, and after the more conventional establishments one may be excused for blinking one's eye and asking if it is really there. Closer contact proves it

to be real - an art deco replica of a 1930's Miami Beach style Speakeasy. There is even a sign saying "To Enter, knock twice and say Al sent me". The outside cover is a pizza and ice cream parlor with brightly painted awnings and umbrellas. You can get pizza, milk shakes, hamburgers and excellent pita bread sandwiches.

Once you are admitted to the inside you will find gangster barmen complete with shoulder holsters, and if you are scared of a raid you can order Prohibition Punch, as

The Blue lagoon Guest Rooms and cottages

Box 637, St lucia. Tel 28453

*INEXPENSIVE *CLEAN *MODERN

Rooms with and without bath and cooking facilities.
2 bedroom guest cottage also available.

Near bus route. Close by Rodney Bay Marina, the beaches, the hotels and the nightlife.

tasty high proof drink that comes discreetly disguised in a coffee cup, which is yours to keep! Other delights include St Valentines Day Massacre (a real killer) Cosa Nostra Colada and Mafia Mai Tai. Come between 11 and 12 p.m. and you can join "Happy Hour". The food is Italian in the best American tradition. The service is excellent, and the bill comes in a violin case together with candy.

Shining even more brightly than Capone's, their new "Sweet Dreams" is an ice cream parlor straight from Disneyland.

Many flavors of ice creams and a whole range of cookies and baked goods. Perfect for dessert.

The Lime is one of the best local restaurants in the area, The atmosphere is informal, and for those on a budget they keep the snack menu available in the evening, Their rotis, fish and chicken snacks are first rate and plenty. Follow one with a dessert at "Sweet Dreams" and you have an inexpensive feast!

The Eagle's Inn is a local restaurant with an excellent location right on the canal

leading into Rodney Bay, giving one a good view of the yachts as they come and go. This is a good place to try local food at reasonable prices, service a bit slow but who's in a hurry?

The Islander is a convenient, modern, reasonably priced hotel, situated between Reduit Beach and the Lagoon, It is inward looking with all the rooms and the restaurant facing onto a well tended garden and swimming pool. The restaurant specializes in seafood and steaks as well as snacks (try their fishburger). They have live music on Friday nights in season, and a double happy hour nightly between 4.30 and 6.30

The Charthouse is an excellent choice for a middle priced restaurant. You can be assured of first class service and consistently good food. The secret to its success is that your host Nick keeps an eagle eye on proceedings at all times and personally greets you when your arrive. The Charthouse menu never varies: all kinds of steak, seafood and lobster, with local crayfish when it is available, along with a selection of starters and deserts. The Charthouse is on the waterfront and one can sit looking out over the lagoon. Inside a mass of climbing and hanging plants gives a pleasing greenhouse atmosphere. As might be expected, the tables are all covered in charts. At the bar you can select from Nick's extraordinary selection of rums (70 at the last count).

Cheap and cheerful, The Rib Shak is just the place to go when you start to feel terminal hamburger deprivation. They sell spare ribs, fried chicken and barbecued meat on a bun.

SHOPPING IN THE NORTH

As can be expected in a fast growing tourist area, new little shops sprout up all the time. Each of the large hotels has its own boutiques, and both Rodney Bay Marina and the St Lucian hotel have small shopping centers. Just outside the St Lucian is a large "Noah's Arkade" brimming with souvenirs.

On to the main road to town you will come to "Mary Anne's Fashions", mainly casual clothes. If you want something al-

tered or made up, or if you are an unusual size, Mary Anne is the one to see.

FRIDAY NIGHT AT
GROS ISLET

At first glance Gros Islet is like any other sleepy Caribbean village. It is built on a flat stretch of land that runs down to the sea. A large Catholic church dominates the other buildings which are for the most part built of wood. Many are humble, little houses of broad planks held a foot or two off the ground by wonky posts or uneven heaps of stones, and capped with a few sheets of galvanised iron. But others are more elaborate; handsome two story structures with balconies, all the woodwork being elaborately carved into intricate patterns in typical "Gingerbread" style. Gros Islet was recently upgraded from a village to a town, but it is still the kind of place where breadfruit trees and flowers grow between houses and goats wander freely along the streets.

A few years ago, Friday would be like any other night at Gros Islet, cars would be parked along the streets, and a few residents would wander around drinking "white-lightning" and playing dominoes in the local rum shops. But then some of the bars started putting loud speakers out on the streets to attract customers and the residents decided to close the main road to traffic to give them a little space to mingle and dance. Word soon spread that Gros Islet was a fun place to be on a Friday night and locals and the occasional tourist would come by to enjoy the atmosphere. All that is long ago - today it is an institution - a joyful festival that blends the atmosphere of a carnival with a street fair, but which is none-the-less something unique - its "Friday night at Gros Islet"!

People start to arrive at about 9 p.m. All along the streets smoke rises from a hundred little roadside stalls, where one can buy a wonderful variety of local delicacies - tender juicy conch served on homemade skewers, fish cakes, chicken, crispy fried fish, roast corn, baked goods, fresh fruit, and peanuts are all available. It is a wonderful way to sample local food and very inexpensive. For those who do not like to eat standing up, many of the bars have put chairs and tables out on the street where one can sit and enjoy a beer with one's food.

Youths push ice cream carts along, ringing their bicycle bells in time with the music which blares out from a dozen different bars.

Although tourists arrive by the mini-bus load, they do not outnumber the locals and the special Gros Islet atmosphere remains. People wander from bar to bar, drinking beers, talking, dancing in the streets, and generally enjoying the scene. If it all gets to be too much one can wander down past "The Wall" and sit by the water's edge and listen to the rhythm of the surf and look up at the moon through the waving palms. By 10.30 the action is swinging, and it will keep going well into the early hours of Saturday morning - a party not to be missed!

A FEW OF GROS ISLET BARS AND RESTAURANTS

As Gros Islet inhabitants have realized the value of tourism, restaurants have proliferated, and Gros Islet has become the place to get an inexpensive local meal. This is a good place to try creole dishes - lambi, fish and chicken are the staples. The following list of restaurants is by no means exhaustive!

Marine House just at the entrance to the turn off for Gros Islet offers typical local food such as chicken stew and creole fish. Food is good and a lunch plate will cost around $10 E.C., snacks are also available. Dinners are by advance order only.

Lilly's (ask anyone the way), has a small, quiet and pleasant dining room, where you can get good fresh seafood.

Coco's restaurant is in Gros islet not far from Rodney Bay Lagoon. They cook local food to order.

The Wall. A rough and ready restaurant built round a little garden. You can probably order something to eat here, but their main efforts have gone into becoming a kind of Friday night disco - they call themselves the "Pscyadelic (sic) Garden".

The Banana Split on the water front in Gros Islet, is a large modern building, with the the atmosphere of a village hall, but serves some of the better food in Gros Islet.

The Golden Apple, a somewhat New Orleans atmosphere in quite an attractive dining room.

O'Reilly's makes a great haven away from the bustle of Friday night - a nice quiet spot to buy and beer or get a snack.

Love and Paradise Bar is Rasta run, local food and loud music.

Scottie's, right in the middle of town is the most attractive of the old buildings with balconies and gingerbread. On Friday nights they put tables out on the street so people can have somewhere to sit down. If Gros Islet is your kind of scene you can rent a basic, inexpensive room at Scotties.

When It Comes To The Finest Sailing, The Moorings Covers All The Bases. Including All The Bases.

The Moorings is, unquestionably, the finest sailing organization in the world.

It's a position we have earned — and *continue* to earn — by making sure that all the bases are covered.

ALL THE BASES: The Moorings offers more worldwide charter bases: The British Virgin Islands, St. Lucia, Mexico's Sea of Cortez, Tahiti, the South Pacific Kingdom of Tonga, the Mediterranean (Yugoslavia, Turkey and Greece).

ALL THE BOATS: Choose superb Moorings-designed sailing yachts from 35' to 60', and a new turbo diesel power yacht, The Moorings

370. Bareboat or crewed. Always impeccably maintained.

ALL THE SERVICE: We handle *every* detail of your sailing vacation — from plane to hotel reservations to provisioning to selecting the ideal crew (if you wish) to everything in-between.

ALL THE BEST: The best food. The best anchorages. The best crews. The best restaurants. The best hotels. The Moorings offers it all.

For more information, contact The Moorings, USA., Suite 402, 1305 U.S. 19 South, Clearwater, FL 34624. 813-535-1446; outside Florida toll-free **1-800-535-7289.**

⚄ The Moorings

The Finest Sailing Organization In The World.

St. Lucia • Virgin Islands • Mexico • Tahiti • Tonga • Greece • Turkey • Yugoslavia • St. Martin

BAGSHAWS
"Stands on its own anywhere in the world of quality fashion."
With studios at La Toc and Pointe Seraphine.

The Pitons, photograph courtesy of Alice Bagshaw, Bagshaws' Studios

MARIGOT BAY

Marigot Bay is a hidden lagoon encircled by steep green hills. Just a narrow channel leads back out to the sea. Legend has it that a small English fleet, pursued by a stronger French one, sought refuge here. They hid themselves by tying branches from palm trees among their rigging, so that their ships would merge with the surrounding land. The French fleet sailed right on by, totally unaware that their enemy was hiding a short distance away!

Today Marigot is a special resort area, and if you are staying elsewhere on the island, it makes an excellent destination for a day trip. If are not renting a car, and cannot afford a taxi, you will be able to get a bus which goes in that direction and negotiate an extra fee to have it take you all the way there. You may have to walk about a mile back to the main road for your return journey. There are also guided tours by sea and land that go to Marigot.

Just before you get to Marigot Bay, you find yourself looking down on it from a steep hill - it is worth stopping, the bay looks enticing with blue water, green trees and a dozen or so yachts peacefully at anchor. If you follow the road down to the waterfront it comes to a stop by a small dock and wooden office that houses the customs. To your right through a garden of palms and bright red bouganvillaea is the Hurricane Hole Hotel and restaurant. Opposite you, across the bay are the Marigot Bay Inn, Doolittle's Bar and Restaurant, and Marigot De Roseaux, some holiday cottages. All together, these are known as Marigot Bay Resort.

Hurricane Hole Hotel is the home base of the Moorings, a large international charter company known for their first class yacht and hotel management. Outside the hotel they keep a fine fleet of yachts.

The far shore is accessible only by boat, and there is a delightful system whereby everything is linked by a little ferry which meanders all day between the hotels and the dock according to the whim of the visitors. This service is free and adds to the nautical atmosphere.

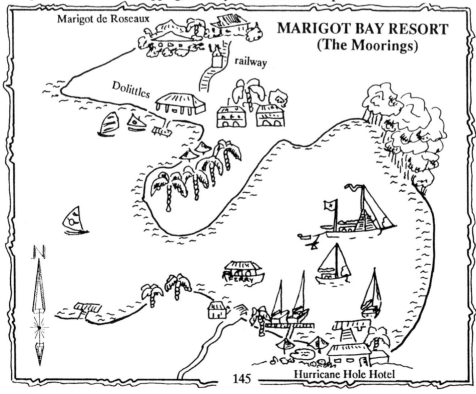

Marigot de Roseaux

MARIGOT BAY RESORT
(The Moorings)

railway

Dolittles

N

Hurricane Hole Hotel

For day visitors, Marigot is a great place to come for a leisurely lunch. Most people will be quite content to sit back and watch the comings and goings of the yachts, or maybe take a swim in the pool or the sea. More energetic souls can arrange to sail dinghies, or go scuba diving or sailboarding. Being a protected area it is quite good for beginners. It is also a delightful spot to come for a romantic evening. The stars, palm trees and yachts all add up to a special atmosphere.

As a place to stay it will appeal to those interested in boats and watersports, and is ideal for some days ashore before starting on a sailing cruise. It is also good for those who want a very quiet relaxed hideaway to get away from it all.

SOUFRIERE AND THE PITONS

The area around Soufriere is a scenic wonderland, steep mountain ridges, incredibly lush valleys, flowers that grow wild along the roadside, and the amazing towering Pitons - steep conical mountains that rise up out of the sea to about 2500 feet. In addition to this there is an area of unusual sulphur springs known as the Drive-In-Volcano, the lovely Diamond Mineral baths, and if you go inland a few miles, you come to St Lucia's dense tropical rain forest. All this adds up to an area of almost magical natural beauty, that will more than reward any visitor interested in nature. You can visit Soufriere on a day sail, or tour, which will give a glimpse of it, and for some this will be enough. But those who like to explore will want to return here, ideally in a self-drive rental car and spend at least another whole day looking around. Those on a tight budget could think about taking a bus down here and spending a night or two in one of the inexpensive guest houses. For those that really want to immerse themselves in nature, there are good hotels, and one could stay here for one's whole holiday.

PLACES OF INTEREST

The beauty of Soufriere becomes apparent even before you arrive; the views over Soufriere and the Pitons as you approach on the main road from Castries are fabulous. The view from hotel Dasheene is absolutely breathtaking, and a visit there for a drink so you can admire it should be given top priority (but see our "Dasheene" write up). Other attractions include:

THE TOWN OF SOUFRIERE

Soufriere is a picturesque old town with many elegant and typically Caribbean buildings. For a while it had a bad name because every time a tourist arrived he found himself surrounded by kids scrambing to make a dollar. It was like a scene from the Pied Piper. All this has mercifully changed as a first step to making Soufriere one of St Lucia's major attractions. There is already a handsome new tourist center, and there are plans to rebuild the waterfront, restore many of the historical houses and turn some to museums. Some of the work is slated for November 1988, when the main dock will be rebuilt, along with a brand new waterfront walkway which will provide a place for yachts to tie up. In town you will find a variety of little souvenir shops.

THE SULPHUR SPRINGS

You get your first glimpse of these on the hills above Soufriere. From a distance it looks like a giant steaming slag heap, what one imagines our world might become in our worst nightmares of out-of-control industrial waste. The sulphur springs are overseen by the tourist board; there is a small admission charge and official guides are available to tell you the fascinating geological facts.

They are certainly an amazing sight, acres of barren earth and gravel are brightly colored in lilacs, yellows, browns and reds. There are hundreds of gurgling, bubbling pools which belch forth steam up to 100 feet in the air. Even the paths you walk on sigh and hiss as the strongly sulphurous malodorous gases escape from the inner depths. If one added a few little men with pitch forks, one might believe one had died and gone to the wrong side of the fence! It is not everyone's idea of beauty, but you should visit it as you are unlikely to see anything like it again!

THE RAIN FOREST

Most of the rain forest is now maintained as a nature reserve, and you are asked not to wander into it without first getting permission from the Forestry Division (tel:23231) (see also our seperate section on the rain forest walk).

However, even without getting into the reserve, you can have a fabulous walk to its edge along the feeder road that leads to it from Fond St Jaques. At the moment this road has deteriorated beyond use for normal cars, though you will probably be able to drive some of the way up. You could make it to the end in a four wheel drive jeep, but either way walking is going to give

you the most satisfaction, and with the present state of the road you are unlikely to meet any traffic.

When we went the air was filled with the sweet perfume from what are sometimes called wild orchids - delicate white flowers that grow along the roadside. As in any self-repecting rain forest you may get some good showers, and from time to time heavy misty clouds may swirl around. The sunny spells in between offer panoramic views over the hills back to the Pitons.

The vegetation is dense and comes in bewildering variety. We left the road to go down a very steep and difficult trail that led to a river. Being a muddy wet day, it was somewhat surprising to meet almost a dozen people coming up the track at different times, carrying on their heads sacks of produce they had cultivated deep in the valley. Tall trees decorated with lush creeping vines grew along the trail, though at times the cover was so dense little grew

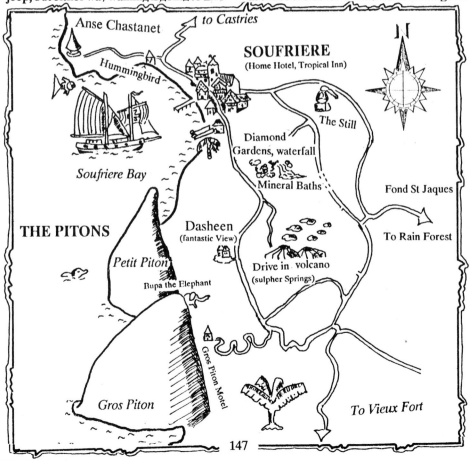

below except air plants which clung tenaciously to tree trunks. There were several small rapids at the river which formed a sort of natural swirl bath. The water was sparkling clear and cold.

DIAMOND BOTANICAL GARDEN, MINERAL BATHS, AND WATERFALL

This delightful place is a great favorite of mine, not to rush through on a five minute tour with 20 others, but to savor with a few friends for an hour or two. The setting is a large and lovely garden rich in all kinds of tropical flowers, shrubs and trees. At the head of the garden is the photogenic Diamond Waterfall that tumbles down a hill and forms a river which flows through the grounds.

The baths themselves were originally built in the 1786 by Baron de Micoud to help protect and fortify the troops against the tropical climate. They were destroyed during the French Revolution and only recently renovated. They are fed by an underground flow of hot water. It is fed via huge pipes to a series of baths and one can choose water at different temperatures, and finish up by relaxing outside in one of their warm bathing pools, enjoying the view. The baths are said to be highly theraputic for arthritis and many other complaints, but for the healthy they are a delightfully relaxing and invigorating experience!

There is a small fee for the baths of $5 E.C. - bring your own towel. If you just want to walk round the garden it is $3.50. Fresh iced lime juice and fruit are on sale.

SOUFRIERE ESTATE

Offers a short estate tour including a mini zoo of local fauna (agouti, manicou, boa constrictors, birds etc), cocoa and copra works, and the oldest running water wheel in St Lucia. It is eventually hoped to link the estate to the Diamond Botanical Gardens with a nature trail. This whole estate is steeped in history. Originally granted to the Devaux family by Louis 14th in 1713, it was first exploited by 3 Devaux brothers in 1740. As a result of the French revolution

there was a slave uprising known as the Brigands War. A guillotine was set up in Soufriere and heads rolled! The Devaux brothers escaped that fate by being hidden by faithful slaves. Shortly after, Soufriere estate became the property of Baron de Micoud. He was reputedly killed in a duel, and as the church refused him burial on sanctified ground he was buried on the estate - it is thought at a spot known as "En Tombeau". The estate became the property of the du Boulay family and has remained so since. They imported the old water wheel in the early part of the 19th century. It was originally used to crush cane, then when the sugar market crashed it crushed limes and not so very long ago it supplied all the electricty to Soufriere.

ANSE CHASTANET REEF

Perhaps because the countryside around Soufriere is some of the prettiest in the island, it is only fitting they should have the prettiest reef and the best scuba diving. This is to be found under the cliffs between Anse Chastanet Hotel and Soufriere as well as between the Pitons. The water's edge shelves steeply in these areas and one can wade in and quickly swim down to 130 feet. There is abundant coral and fish life, and divers come here from all over the world. Scuba St Lucia, St Lucia's most active diving organization is part of the Anse Chastanet Hotel, and one can arrange one's diving through them.

BUPA

Soufriere has its own elephant who lives between the Pitons. He was brought here by Colin Tenant who owns the land as a sort of publicity stunt. Although access is easy by boat (you can find a boatman on Soufriere's waterfront) it is a long way by land and there is no road. If you do visit Bupa take some nuts or fruit and he will be your instant buddy.

RESTAURANTS AND HOTELS

For the right kind of traveler, Soufriere offers a variety of restaurants and hotels. One has to keep in mind that Soufriere is a good one and a half hours drive from

anse chastanet

somewhere you can still escape to....

ANSE CHASTANET - a romantic holiday setting amidst a 400 acre secluded estate with two of the most beautiful beaches on the island and surrounded by St.Lucia's finest virgin coral reefs - ideal for honymooners, snorkelers, nature lovers, scuba divers, bird watchers and all those who want to get away from it all....

37 delightful octagonal gazebos with magnificent views of the Pitons and the Caribbean Sea nestled into a lush hillside above the beach, spacious beachside rooms and 1 and 2 bedroom suites are awaiting the discriminating traveller.

If doing nothing is not enough, Anse Chastanet's professional PADI 5 star Scuba Facility, complimentary water sports, tennis and personalised excursions such as daysailing, exploring Anse Chastanet's old French Colonial Plantation, visiting the Sulphur Springs, the Rain Forest and the Louis XVI Mineral Baths will keep the active going.

ANSE CHASTANET HOTEL
P.O.BOX 216,
SOUFRIERE, ST.LUCIA,
TELEPHONE:
809 454 7355
809 454 7354
809 454 7350
809 454 7000
TELEX: 0398/6370 ANCHASTA LC.

Castries down a winding road, whose surface leaves quite a lot to be desired. But for anyone looking for a hideaway, in an area of outstanding natural beauty staying in Soufriere is perfect.

Anse Chastanet Hotel is built right on the best beach in the area. It rises up a steep hill and is set in the middle of a 400 acre estate. The gardens are always pleasant to the eyes, but in early summer when the bright red flamboyant trees bloom, they set the whole hill ablaze with color. The hotel rooms are built up the hill, and all have a patio with a view - either out to sea or back over the hills to the Pitons which loom in the background. Anse Chastanet prides itself on being a real hideaway, well away from the main crowd of tourists. With only 40 rooms it never gets over crowded.

The waters off Anse Chastanet offer the best diving in St Lucia and the hotel is well equipped for divers. They also have sailboards, sunfish, and a 37ft O'Day sloop; one may go deep sea fishing or learn how to sail. Trips and picnics can be arranged by sea or land, and there are tennis and table tennis at the hotel.

At Anse Chastanet, dinner is served in the dining room which is perched on the hill overlooking the sea. Lunch on the other hand is taken down at the comfortable bar/restaurant right on the beach. Snacks are also available.

The Still restaurant is part of a working estate; its name comes from the huge copper still mounted just in front. About 100 years ago it was producing rum, but when the sugar beet was introduced the bottom fell out of the sugar cane market, limes replaced sugar cane and the still was converted to producing lime oil. Now it is purely decorative, but the estate continues with acres of coconuts and cocoa as well as some chickens. There is a little waterfall and some interesting old farm buildings. You can get inexpensive creole food and snacks. It is open daily for lunch but dinners are available by appointment only. They also rent a three bedroom beach house and a two room apartment on the estate (more rooms are being built). Beside the restaurant, they have a boutique selling pottery, clothing, straw goods and many other souvenirs. If you need to cool off there is a swimming pool.

At the time of writing Dasheene is closed down, but I am including a description as it is one of my favorite spots and hopefully it will soon open again. However, before rushing down there telephone first and make sure!

Are you the kind of person who only feels at home securely bounded by four square walls into which a smoothly running air conditioner is placed? Well if you are do not even consider staying at Dasheene, for not only is the air conditioner missing, one whole wall has gone. One whole wall has what? Well perhaps we had better start again.

What we start with is the Pitons - St Lucia's world famous twin towering peaks, a spectacular feat of nature that dominates the whole south east part of the island. Just behind them is a steep ridge that affords a breathtaking view, so fantastic it is unmatched not only in St Lucia but probably in the whole of the Caribbean.

Now comes the architect, and unfettered by strict cost controls or bureaucratic regulations he goes wild. Roofs sprout a dozen peaks, each room is handsculpted out of cedar with sunken flower gardens, and what about a window with a view? "Yes, well, I was thinking of rather a big window" - "sounds good how big?" - "Well, the whole wall actually" - "The whole wall! how would you close it?" - "Why would you want to, the rain comes from the other way".

If this sounds strange, well it is a strange hotel, but outstandingly beautiful and imaginative as well, not for the fainthearted, but certainly for the romantic. Can you imagine lying there at night watching the moon over the Pitons? Maybe that is why they attracted so many honeymooners, artists and writers. Dasheene is not of course on the beach, though it has a pool, and there is a twice daily bus service to the beach. Many rooms have their own dip pools and there are some three bedroom units.

If you do not stay here you must at least visit Dasheene and sip an exotic drink as you admire the view. In fact if you only sightsee to one place then this should be it.

The Hummingbird is Soufriere's most popular restaurant, an ideal spot for a long relaxing meal, where you can enjoy the surroundings and perhaps take a swim in the pool. It has been artistically created out of rock and stone, with a clever use of different textures (one whole wall is made out of clay coal pots!). The dining room looks out over the pool across the bay to the Pitons. A garden rambles down to the beach, and yachts often anchor just outside. The range of the menu is broad enough to appeal to anyone and includes well known local dishes. Joyce, your proprietess, not only runs the restaurant but makes batiks which are offered on sale. There are also two double guest rooms available, and another 10 under construction.

Right on the town square, Home Inn is a good little guest house for those who want reasonably priced accommodation,

Cheap and basic, the Tropical Inn will suit the traveling backpacker on a budget.

I always thought a motel was somewhere on a road you stopped in for the night. Not around Soufriere. We followed a sign saying "Gros Piton Motel just 20 minutes walk" and drove for what seemed like at least half an hour down the roughest track imaginable. It took us through luxuriant farm land, we forded two rivers and passed a lovely old water wheel. We finally made it to the end of the road and the motel was still nowhere in sight - but it was in fact just a short walk away. The views are superb, and the hiking would be excellent, but while you are just a short hike from Bupa, you are miles from anywhere else. Make sure they are expecting you, or walk with provisions!

151

St Lucia's southern tip, the area around Vieux Fort, offers some long beaches, several hotels and restaurants, the Maria Islands, and St Lucia's large airport, Hewanorra.

Anyone passing though this area should at least take the narrow winding road back up to Moule A Chique lighthouse. They will be rewarded with sweeping views back over St Lucia, and south to St Vincent. Beach lovers can have a ball on the miles of gorgeous windward beach that stretches all the way from Moule A Chique to beyond Club Med. There are also pleasant beaches on the leeward side, in the area of Il Pirata restaurant.

MARIA ISLANDS

The Maria Islands lie in the Atlantic ocean just a cannon's shot from the mainland. While the rest of St Lucia has been modified to suit man, the Maria Islands remain essentially untouched. In order to keep them that way, they are a strict nature reserve and part of the national trust. They are mainly of interest to naturalists and wild life photographers. They are famous for two species of animal unknown anywhere else in the world! One of these is a small harmless snake known as "Kouwes" and the other is the Maria Island Ground Lizard (Cnemidophorus Vanzol). There are of course many other less rare reptiles and quite a number of birds. If you want to visit you could ask around one of the Vieux Fort hotels or restaurants, or go to their base on the main road by the east end of the airport. But remember the ecology of these islands is very fragile, and the little snake is already a threatened species. If you go, tread lightly, take nothing but photos, and under no circumstances light a fire or let your guide do so!

HOTELS AND RESTAURANTS

The Cloud's Nest is an unusual little restaurant of great charm. The walls are

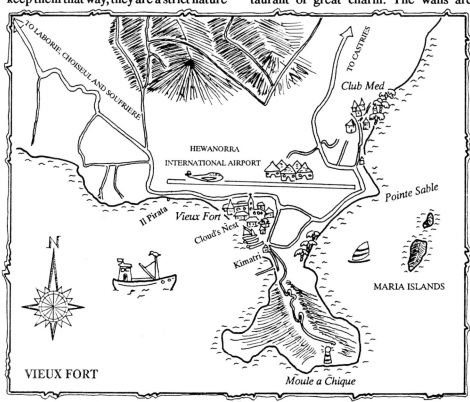

covered with bric-a-brac gathered over the years. There is a comfortable lounge area to sit and enjoy a drink or cup of coffee, the food has a local flavor and is good, the service wonderfully attentive. If you do not stop by at meal time, at least take a look at their little boutique. Cloud's Nest is also a hotel with single, double and three room suites.

The Kimatri is built on a hill just beside Vieux Fort with a commanding view over the bay, probably the perfect place to watch the sun set! They offer both hotel rooms and self-contained apartments. They have a very inexpensive restaurant serving mainly fish, chicken and spaghetti.

There is something very incongruous about Il Pirata. You drive along way out in what seems like the wilderness beyond Vieux Fort and suddenly there is is a real genuine, completely Italian restaurant. Since it is run by people with names like Ezio and Rosalba Nelli and Gherardo Gualeiri, there has to be a story. No it is not a family on the run from the Mafia, it is more romantic. It concerns a pretty young air hostess who fell in love with St Lucia and a St Lucian. The marriage to the man did not work out, but the love of the country stayed, so she decided to start a real Italian restaurant.

For this enterprise it just so happened she had the perfect family. Her father was a professor of cookery who had even won an award for his rissoto. So they came out and started a perfect restaurant, as genuinely Italian as any you will find in Italy. All the pasta is made right on the premises, and to add atmosphere the waiters are all dressed up as pirates. Open for lunch and dinner daily except Monday.

Since it is a long way from town, many people visit Il Pirata on the day their flight leaves Hewanorra. They arrive at the aiport in good time (somewhat over the two hour minimum), check in their bags, then leave for a great Italian meal, returning just in time to catch the plane!

I guess everyone has heard of the Club Med., the resort that pushes active sports - water-skiing, sailing, scuba, tennis etc., all taught by a bunch of good looking pareo-clad G.O's. Fantastic buffet lunches, delightful dinners, entertainment where everyone takes part, and for the party goers, a late night disco.

No money is used in the Club Med., rather one uses beads for the bar, decoratively worn round the neck so pockets are obsolete! Club Med is the kind of resort where is it almost impossible to avoid making a bunch of new friends and having a good time. They are immensely popular with active couples and singles.

There are branches of the Club Med in every desirable spot in the world - the Mediterranean shores of France and Spain, Tahiti, Guadaloupe, Martinique, and now for the first time a 500 person complex in St Lucia. The Club Med stands on a long windward beach, a short drive from the airport. People not staying there who would like to check it out can visit for lunch or dinner, but reservations a day in advance are essential.

St Lucia, although a small island, offers a variety of activities that should keep even the most restless traveler satisfied. The island has two golf courses (one at Cap and one at La Toc), every sizable hotel has tennis courts and a range of watersports, one can go parasailing at the St Lucian hotel, or take a helicopter ride from Pointe Seraphine. For those who don't want to explore on their own, the range of activities available through the tour desks at the hotels or the travel representatives in town is wide ranging and includes:

SHOPPING TOURS

Which not only take you to town, but include those special out of town places such as Bagshaws, Tapion Craft and Eudovics, sometimes they can offer you a discount card valid in most of the shops.

ISLAND TOURS

Both full and half day tours are available. The full day tours include all St Lucia's famous attractions such as the sulphur springs and the mineral baths, and they usually include a good lunch somewhere.

SEA TRIPS

A variety of day sailing trips are available, mainly between the north of St Lucia and Soufriere. You can choose between going on a 40ft yacht or St Lucia's magnificent "flagship" the Unicorn, or the Buccaneer (see section "Day Sail to Soufriere"). Combined land and sea trips, where you go one way and come back another are also available.

PIGEON ISLAND

Half day picnic tours are available to this charming historic site.

SPORTS FISHING

How about a day out after the big ones? Jump aboard and you will soon be heading out to sea with trolling lines set. Relax in the shade and wait for the action. Its pleasant out there with the sea breeze and the motion of the boat. You'll probably be lulled into a tranquil dream when "ZZZZing", a line starts screaming. Time to sit in the fighting chair and follow the directions of the captain - maybe it will be an easy catch - barracuda, tuna or kingfish. But if you are looking for a battle, a blue marlin, sailfish or mako shark will surely oblige, and keep you fighting for hours on end. Most of the available sports fishing boats are between 20 and 40 feet long. Typical cost for 4 persons would be in the region of $200 U.S.for half a day. There are a variety of operators to choose from. Captain Mako is perhaps the most experienced. He has been fishing since he was knee high, he has caught many thousands of pounds of fish all over the world and knows just where to look for them.

AN EVENING IN MARIGOT

This starts with a romantic cocktail cruise down the coast from Vigie to pic-

If you only take one day trip, make sure you do it right. Insist on a:

Day Charter with

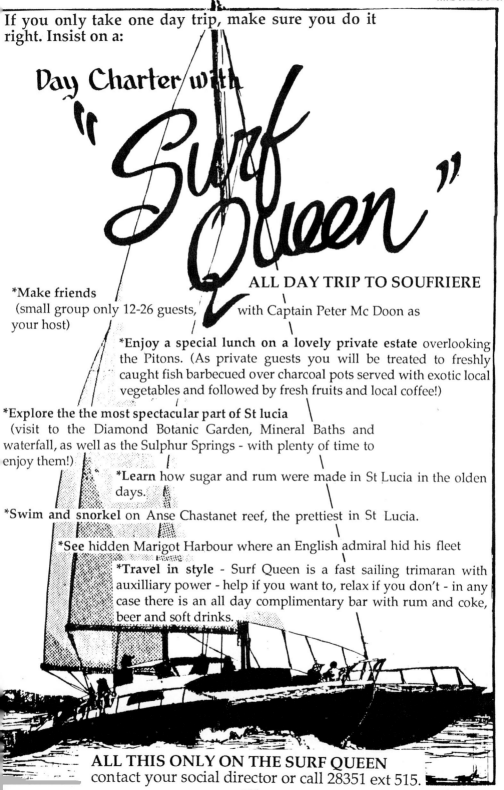

"Surf Queen"

ALL DAY TRIP TO SOUFRIERE

*Make friends
(small group only 12-26 guests, with Captain Peter Mc Doon as your host)

*Enjoy a special lunch on a lovely private estate overlooking the Pitons. (As private guests you will be treated to freshly caught fish barbecued over charcoal pots served with exotic local vegetables and followed by fresh fruits and local coffee!)

*Explore the the most spectacular part of St lucia
(visit to the Diamond Botanic Garden, Mineral Baths and waterfall, as well as the Sulphur Springs - with plenty of time to enjoy them!)

*Learn how sugar and rum were made in St Lucia in the olden days.

*Swim and snorkel on Anse Chastanet reef, the prettiest in St Lucia.

*See hidden Marigot Harbour where an English admiral hid his fleet

*Travel in style - Surf Queen is a fast sailing trimaran with auxilliary power - help if you want to, relax if you don't - in any case there is an all day complimentary bar with rum and coke, beer and soft drinks.

ALL THIS ONLY ON THE SURF QUEEN
contact your social director or call 28351 ext 515.

turesque Marigot harbor. You stay there for some dinner and entertainment before heading back.

ANSE JAMBETTE

What nicer way to spend a day in the Caribbean than by taking a boat or car ride down to a secluded beach, firing up as drink or two and taking a swim or a snorkel followed by a good barbecue lunch? Well you can do just this by going on one of the tours arranged by chef Harry to his beach-side restaurant at Anse Jambette. Snorkeling gear and changing rooms are available and sea trips can also be arranged. (if your tour rep cannot help call 23399)

FRIDAY NIGHT AT GROS ISLET

One can arrange a visit as part of a group (see our section "Friday Night at Gros Islet" under "North St Lucia").

OUT OF ISLAND TOURS

Some of the most popular tours involve a day trip to another island. The most famous is the Grenadines tour. You fly from St Lucia to the heart of the Grenadines and join Captain Yannis on his yacht for a day to explore some of the islands (see our section on St Vincent and the Grenadines,). You can also fly to Martinique for a shopping tour or further north to Dominica to visit their rugged rain forest.

RAIN FOREST TOURS

Both the rain forest tour and the day sailing tours deserve further mention, but before we get onto this a word about the tour agents. In general each tour operator designs his own tours. Therefore although two tour operators might be offering what seems like the same trip, they may vary with regard to exact itinerary, where you eat your lunch, etc. It pays to shop around among the different agents, pick up their brochures and decide which one is the best for you. The big hotels have social desks, but if you need more information consult the listings section in the back of this book.

ST LUCIA'S RAIN FOREST

Before Europeans came to St Lucia, most of the island was a dense forest with huge ferns, tall trees, orchids, and a wide variety of wild life including the St Lucia Parrot (Amazona Versicolor). The cool greenery attracted the rain, forming many rivers which ran playfully to the sea. Along their banks trailing vines hung from the trees, an open invitation to any aspiring Tarzan looking for a quick way across the river!

While today civilization has changed the picture, about 11 % of the island is still covered by rain forest, most of which is now protected as a nature preserve. Visitors are welcome to visit the reserve, either taking a quick walk along the marked path towards Mt La Combe, or by taking one of the much longer organized walking tours which lead right to the heart of the island. You will be rewarded by entering a world that is in complete contrast to the hot sun and open beaches along the coast. The rain forest is cool, damp and overflowing with life. You will get far away from cars and the normal sounds of human activity, and instead you will be treated to a symphony of birds and tree frogs and the air will be fragrant with the smells of the earth and the trees.

On the longer walk you will also have a chance of seeing or hearing the almost extinct St Lucia Parrot, considered one of the most endangered parrot species in the world. This bird mates for life and lays only two eggs a year. It lives in the St Lucia's rain forest and exists nowhere else. There are only about 100 left alive today.

RAIN FOREST WALKS

Most tour agents organize rain forest walks in conjunction with the forestry department. You set off in the morning and drive by coach through St Lucia's pretty countryside down the East Coast then as far as the road goes into the interior. There follows a walk right through the island (about 3 hours) until you emerge on the other side behind Soufriere. The bus

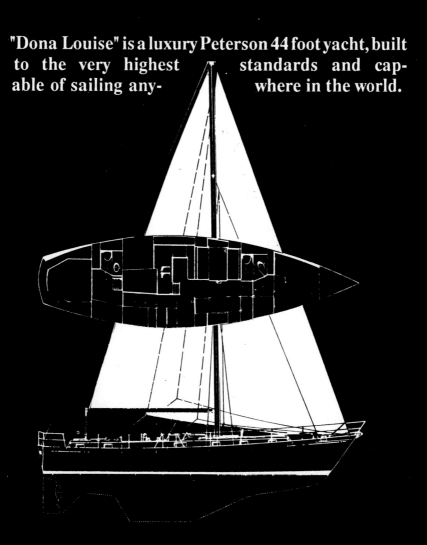
157

vegetables. You have plenty of time for a visit to both the Diamond Botanic Gardens and the Sulphur Springs. On the way back you get to snorkel at Anse Chastanet and pass through Marigot Bay. Best of all since the group is small you will make plenty of friends.

Power boat Vigie Cove gives you a coastal cruise and lunch at the excellent Hummingbird restaurant.

Moorings and Marigot Bay offer two day sailing yachts. Celtic Charterer, a 37 foot yacht sets out five days a week and heads north to Rodney Bay or south to the Pitons depending on the whim of the guests. The limit on this yacht is 6 guests, so you will never feel crowded, but book early!

Marigot Connection is a cute 21 foot Beneteau which can be chartered for 1 to 4 passengers with or without skipper. Call Marigot Bay Resort (34357) and ask for the "Watersports Center".

Egon (La Mauny), has a wonderful sailing boat "Lone Star" (Carib 41 class). It is very fast, spacious, comfortable, stable, unsinkable and a real gentlewoman on the high seas. I could be biased; it just so happens I own the same kind of boat myself! Egon has been around here for years and he offers a most personal kind of day charter (average number of guests 6-8). On most day trips some rum punch and soft drinks are thrown in, but Egon goes the whole way - you can drink what you like - champagne if it takes your fancy! and all at a very competitive rate. Egon also goes on weekend trips to Martinique, or longer trips down the Grenadines (max 4 guests,) all at an inclusive rate much lower than staying in a hotel. He gets lots of repeats so he must do something right and regulars include Shirley McLaine and former New york City Mayor Lindsay.

Dona Louise is a classy yacht - 44 feet of fiberglass and teak handcrafted in Taiwan. For years she sailed in the Steven's charter fleet. Then the owner lost interest and she lay at the dock. The teak turned grey, the mechanics ceased to work, rust started to form. Happily, Dona Louise was found by Jeff and Lorraine an enthusiastic young couple who saw her potential. At the time of writing, they were both working long hours sharing the tasks; you can find Lorraine welding and Jeff cooking! By the end of 1988 she will be back in tip top shape and you will be able to join a small group for that day trip on a real yacht with congenial hosts.

ENTERTAINMENT

In St Lucia nightly entertainment is to be found in all the big hotels. Here one can dance to a steel band or combo, and watch floor shows including limbo, local dancing and Princess Tina. Chef Harry up at the Green Parrot puts on one of the best shows on Wednesdays and Saturdays.

Later you can dance at the discos - Splash at the St Lucian takes the prize for decor, but try also the Halcyon Beach Club where you can dance right out over the water on the pier.

Friday night is Gros Islet night followed by "heavy action" in such places as the Banana Split and Parrot's Hideaway.

Sunday lunch is a good time to relax on the beach, eat good food and enjoy a steel band. Check out the St Lucian and Halcyon Beach Club.

If you happen to be here in February, carnival runs for about a week before Ash Wednesday. Big bands in wonderful costumes compete with each other, a Calypso King and Carnival Queen are chosen, and everyone "jumps up" for days. In the early hours of Monday morning (J'Ouvert) the streets come alive to music and dancing. On Tuesdays the costumed bands parade around town.

At Whitsun you can join in "Aqua Action" - lots of fun centered around Reduit Beach (by the St Lucian hotel). Local boat races, yacht races, "anything that floats races", tugs of war and a hundred other games!

LAST WORD

St Lucia was supposed to have been discovered by Christopher Columbus on St Lucy's Day (December 13th) in 1502. This is St Lucia's national holiday (Discovery Day). However, recent research shows that not only was Columbus nowhere near St Lucia on this particular date, he never even landed here! So just which European made the discovery and when remains a mystery.

St Lucia is named after St Lucy, saint of light and patron saint of spectacle makers (so when you are here you can make a spectacle of yourself!) St Lucy died horribly in A.D. 304 when being persecuted for refusing to deny her Christian faith and worship pagan gods. In an attempt to persuade her they blinded her, but miraculously her sight returned. An attempt at burning her similarly failed. Eventually her persecutor said "No more Mr Nice Guy" and ran her through with a sword.

Early visitors in St Lucia were not as welcome as they are today. In 1605 a ship called "Olive Branch" put in en route from England to Guyana carrying settlers. It had been a nightmare trip. A storm had blown them off course, they had run out of food, water and toilet paper and were arguing among themselves.

Land was such a welcome sight that 67 of them decided to leave the Olive Branch and stay in the Vieux Fort area. The Caribs who lived there sold them some houses and they settled in. However, they soon wished they were back on the Olive Branch. First a 15 man expedition went out looking for gold and never returned, then an 18 man group, invited to the Carib camp for a feast were ambushed and became dinner, instead of guests for dinner. Finally the camp was surrounded and all but 19 wiped out. These were given a dug out canoe and set back out to sea. We can guarantee you a better welcome today!

In June 1988, a gentleman saw a huge turtle lay some eggs not far from the bar at the Carib Blue Hotel (now "Le Sport").

The next day he told people what he saw and it seemed a good idea to have a "Turtle Watch" to make sure the no one stole the eggs, and give the little critters a good start in life. Enthusiasm mounted, the area was fenced off, people came to see the sacred spot; business in the bar had never been better. Even after the bar closed valiant individuals stood long night watches to guard their safety. For some 60 plus days this went on, and the excitment mounted - when would the big day come? As it approached more and more people came down to watch - would they be the lucky ones to see the little turtles make their dash to the sea?

As time went on people began to get worried, and at last it was decided to make a small dig in the spot to see what was going on. Well they dug and they dug, and not an egg did they find! Where they ever there? Did someone manage to steal them? No one knows, but for sure never have so many people spent so long looking at an empty patch of sand!

It is worth knowing that there is a well-produced, very informative booklet on St Lucia given out free, called "Paradise St Lucia", ask in any major hotel, or in the larger shops in town..

MARTINIQUE

Martinique is the largest of the Windwards and by far the most populous. Her 3 to 4 hundred thousand people are more than can be found in the rest of the Windwards put together. It is part of France in the same sense as Hawaii is part of the U.S.A.

Not suprisingly then, it is the most sophisticated and civilized of the Windwards - wonderful roads sweep the length and breadth of the island to reveal well tended fields, flowers adorn round-a-bouts. The Caribs called Martinique "Madinina" - Island of Flowers, which is apt as even today it brings to mind the feel of a well tended garden.

Martinique hosts a mixture of residents; there are the Martiniquais, born and bred here, whose families have been here for years, and then there are many French businessmen, who have come from the mainland for a change of pace and climate. Probably the loveliest people are the elderly who live in little villages far from the beaten track. They have wonderful manners and it is quite usual when you go into a bar or restaurant in quiet corners of the island to greet everyone individually and shake their hand. In the more bustling places such as Fort de France and Anse Mitan, the atmosphere is much more international, and as in any such area, you will meet all kinds of people from the delightfully polite and kind to the brusque and offhand.

The language and ambience is naturally French, which provides much of the pleasure of being here - to sit in a cafe and watch the world go by - a world of smartly dressed people with chic hair styles and fashionable clothes. Good French coffee - looking for a restaurant where a meal is going to be an exciting gastronomic experience - and a wonderful array of shops and boutiques which bring you the latest Paris fashions. Martinique is naturally a very popular destination, especially with the French - it is like a little part of the Riviera tucked in the more exotic Caribbean.

In order to get the full benefit of Martinique one has to travel around - there are many roadside attractions. The south end (from Fort de France southwards) hosts most of the large hotels and activities, it is cultivated, rolling and gently picturesque. Flowering trees are planted along many road sides, affording welcome shade. As you get to Trinite and venture further north, the topography changes - the island becomes more rugged with exquisite views and far fewer people; this goes on all the way to St Pierre. Hotels in this area are off the beaten track, and therefore both less expensive and easier to reservations for than those further south, and most have both charm and individuality.

Accommodations vary from huge multi-story hotels to tiny little "auberges". The price range is vast, the larger hotels with more facilities generally being more expensive. The smaller less expensive hotels are often more personal, and many people find excellent deals in self-catering apartments.

Since Martinique is quite big, about 50 miles long and 20 wide, you have to consider far more than you would in a smaller island, just what you are looking for. Many holiday makers will be content to stay in one of the large resorts or resort areas, spending their time on the beach and relaxing, using the excellent tour and recreational facilities available to see the island. For these people Anse Mitan offers the most benefits.

Others who prefer less organization will want to rent a car or motorbike. Once this decision is made it considerably frees up your idea of where to stay. If you like being near the action on holiday, then definitely stay in the southern, more populated, area. If you prefer to be a little more away from bustle, then think about the east coast, Trinite, the north or St Pierre. If beaches are important, here is what you need to know: most of the large hotels have their

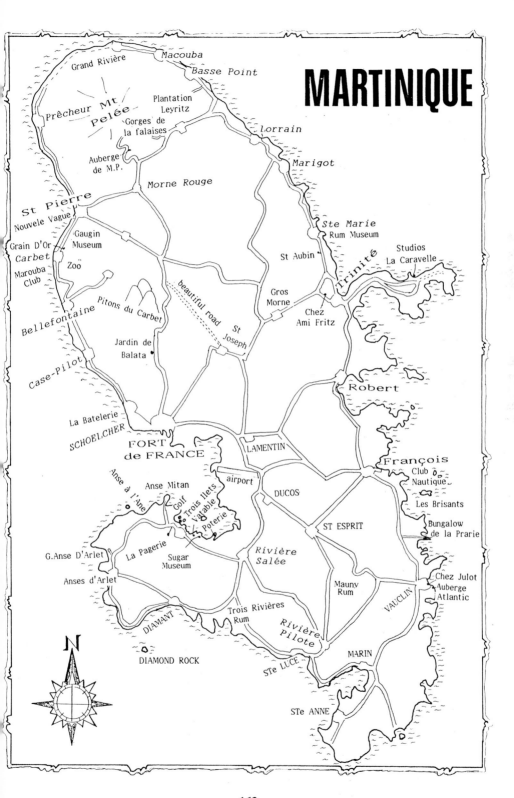

MARTINIQUE

own small beaches "Riviera" style - with rows of neatly laid out beach chairs for sunning.

There are quite a few accessible public beaches in the south - at Anse Mitan, Anse A L'Ane, Grand Anse D'Arlet, and St Luce; these are very pleasant but also sometimes crowded. Some of the best beaches are in the area of St Anne - the best known being Plages des Salines which is magnificent, but the whole south east coast has numerous hidden bays and beaches, many of which you have to hike to and which are therefore less frequented. The Tartanne peninsula (Presque Ile) east of Trinite also has a number of attractive and quite secluded little beaches you can walk to. The west coast is endowed with numerous beaches, of the darker (and hotter) volcanic sand.

ANTHURIUM

TRANSPORT

Martinique is a relatively prosperous country and many people have cars. But there is both a suburban bus system and a system of communal taxis (taxi collectif) that can get you around the island inexpensively. For the most part this is designed to get people to and from Fort de France, so anyone wishing to see the island this way might do well to use the town as the base of their operations. Nearly all the communal taxis have their station over near the Abri Cotier restaurant on the water front, as do the buses to Schoelcher. Many other buses start along Avenue General de Gaulle. Their destinations are Didier, Balata, and Dillon. Buses and communal taxis all have the name of their destination writ-

ten on them, so with a map it is easy to find the one you want. For the airport take the Ducos communal taxi, it passes right outside.

There are plenty of regular taxis available at the hotels or along La Savanne. Always negotiate fees in advance.

Martinique is large enough to make renting a car or motor bike a worthwhile idea. There is a wide range, but in the height of the season there are sometimes none left, so you may want to book in advance.

There are fast ferry systems linking Fort de France, Anse Mitan and Anse A L'Ane. These are discussed in that section.

FORT DE FRANCE AND SCHOELCHER

Fort de France is a bustling French town, and the center of all commercial activity on the island. The streets are so well lined with little boutiques, it is possible to go into a complete shopping frenzy here! An easy landmark is La Savanne park. At the south end there is a handicraft market, and across the road the ferries go to Anse Mitan and Anse A L'Ane. The main post office is on Rue de la Liberte about half way up the park. If you have to make an overseas phone call and it is not possible from your hotel, go into the post office and buy a little telephone card (they come in different values), which is usable in some of the phone boxes (the best ones are by the "parking" on Rue Ernest Deproge). They take some patience, and you have to get the sequence right - lift the phone, insert the card, close the window when it tells you to, then dial the number. (19 gets you out of Martinique, then 1 for the U.S.A., 44 for England). A meter on the telephone tells you how many francs worth of calls you still have left.

On the next block south of the post office is a well organized little museum of pre-Columbian life in the islands. The Library at the end of Ave Des Caraibes is a rather elaborate piece of architecture and fun to look at. The main shopping streets run back into town from Rue de La Liberte away from the park. Banks sometimes have horrendous lines in them. It is worth knowing that down the tiny "Galerie Flibustiers" which runs between Rue Ernest Deproge and Rue Victor Hugo there is an efficient little change place that gives a fair rate of exchange. You can also get a 20% discount if you shop with your U.S. travellers checks in the large jewelry store Roger Albert.

You should as soon as possible visit the tourist office. They are very helpful and will give you a stack of maps, books, newspapers and brochures with all the latest information.

WHERE TO STAY

Most people on holiday prefer to be by a beach rather than in town, however there are a lot of hotels in Fort de France since many people do business here. Someone wanting to see Martinique "on the cheap" might in fact do well to stay in Fort de France as all the inexpensive transport fans out from here. Traditionally the cheapest place to staying town has been Chez Anna, which is at the moment changing hands but hopefully it will remain reasonable.

Lafayette, Malmaison and Imperatrice are handsome hotels overlooking La Savanne. The Victoria is built on a hill just outside town and is spacious and pleasant, with an excellent restaurant (L'Arc En Ciel, see below). At Schoelcher, just five minutes from town by car, there is La Batelerie, a large 200 room resort hotel with beach, pool, disco, and complete water sports including a branch of Tropicasud diving.

EATING OUT

In general local residents lunch in Fort de France but dine out in the residential areas. There are plenty of touristy little restaurants, close by La Savanne, on Rue de La Liberte and the roads leading back. Getting away from these, one of the best restaurants at a reasonable price is The Crew on Rue Ernest Deproge. It tends to get very crowded at lunch, but much less so in the evenings. If you want to try something very local and Creole, there is a little restaurant called La Terrace, upstairs over a fishmonger on the junction between Bvd Allegre and Rue Moreau de Jonnes. Knowing the name won't help as it there is no sign, you just have to look for the doorway with a menu on Blvd Allegre. Upstairs it is cool clean, and breezy. Another quiet place to take a lunch break from shopping is Aux Pates Fraiches, an Italian restaurant on Rue Victor Hugo.

Restaurants are not always stable in Martinique. It is not unusual to have a really superb meal somewhere, then go back with all your friends a year later having built up an elaborate description of the wonderful gastronomic delights in store, only to be served an expensive, badly cooked meal, which your friends don't let you forget for years! Restaurants often change hands and some really expensive ones go in cycles depending on who they manage to get as chef for the season. Keeping this in mind, all the following restaurants have remained top notch for some time and look like continuing that way!

Most of the best (non-tourist) restaurants are in the suburbs, a minimum taxi ride out of town. They are all open for lunch, but will be rather livelier in the evening. Mme Yenel, who runs L'Arc en Ciel, is Vietnamese, but not so her cuisine which is gastronomic French and Creole - the restaurant is at Rond Pt Didier, part of the Victoria Hotel. Tiffany's is in a fine old Caribbean building in Schoelcher, and Claude Pradines is not only an excellent restauranteur, he is a magician, and will occasionally take your mind off your filet mignon by pulling a rabbit from a hat. Full magic shows are given with dinner on Wednesday and Friday nights. Other top class restaurants not far away include Mme Zamie's La Fontane (Rue de Balata) and Joseph Rosso's La Belle Epoch.

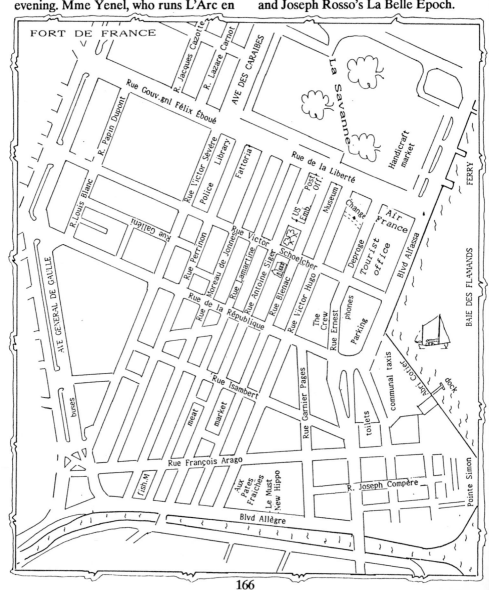

ANSE MITAN

Opposite Fort de France, on the far side of the bay, a peninsula juts out from the land. It is made up of a large bay, Anse Mitan, and the head of the peninsula, Pointe du Bout. In general the whole area is known as Anse Mitan. Just to make things more confusing it is part of a larger area known as Trois Ilets, and is also referred to by this name. Anse Mitan is linked to Fort de France by two excellent ferry services, each taking about half an hour. The journey is pleasant with good views of Fort de France and the bay. One runs from the marina, the other higher speed ferry between town and the "Langouste" dock on Anse Mitan main public beach and Anse A L'Ane.

> ### Marina ferry times
> ### from Marina Point de Bout:
> AM: 6:10, 7:15, 8:30, 9:30, 10:30, 11:30, 12:45
> PM 2:30, 3:30, 4:30, 5:30, 6:30, 7:30, 10:45, 11:45.
> ### From Fort de France:
> AM: 7:00, 8:00, 9:00, 10:00, 11:00
> PM: 12:15, 1:15, 2:00, 3:00, 4:00, 5:00, 6:00, 7:00, 8:00, 10:45 and the last one at ten past midnight.
>
> ### Langouste dock - Anse A L'Ane
> ### ferry times:
> These start from town every half hour (except 1330 when everyone is at lunch) and leave Anse Mitan at either 10 to, or on the hour (this varies). They continue till about 6.00 p.m. The round trip is about 16 francs. (All ferry times may be subject to change).

Anse Mitan is Martinique's most important tourist area - it holds over 9 hotels with about 700 hotel rooms wrapped up in the four largest ones alone. The main hotels have their own small beaches which are neatly laid out with deck chairs Mediterranean style. The longest beach is public and popular - facing a large bay that usually has upwards of 100 yachts anchored off. Here you can enjoy browsing in the smart boutiques that line the sidewalks, and sit in the cafes and watch other people walk by. Tourists are catered to by a wide range of activities from going up in a helicopter to going down in a semi-submersible. During the busy winter season it bustles with activity and the hotels are all full. It is a very civilized area where you can feel very safe, and there is plenty to do.

WHERE TO STAY

The largest (and one of the most expensive) hotel is the Meridian, a huge multi-story affair of around 300 bedrooms. It has its own casino (you need a passport and if you are not a guest there is an entrance charge) and disco. The next largest at about half the price is the Carayou, on the eastern side of the peninsula. The Bakoua, which is built on a hill leading up from the sea, has the nicest view overlooking the bay. The less expensive large hotels include La Pagerie, which is situated around the main shopping area, and the Bambou, which works with Nouvelle Frontieres. (Nouvelle Frontieres is a very large French travel agency specializing in package holidays).

Apart from these there are numerous small hotels many of which have self-contained rooms with cooking facilities. Auberge de L'Anse Mitan, and Alamanda (with Caraibe Auberge) have pleasant locations overlooking the bay a short walk from the beach. They are quiet and pleasant. Some of the rooms are self contained. The Auberge de Anse Mitan is slightly smaller and more personal.

Rivage Hotel is brand new, set a bit back from the beach with a small garden and swimming pool.

La Bonne Auberge, and Le Matador are both back down the road from the beach a ways, with simple adequate rooms.

Eden Beach is inexpensive, older and right on the beach.

Madinina is right on the Marina front,

with a style and location comparable to La Pagerie.

EATING OUT

It is fun to start the evening by taking a beer or aperitif. Le Langouste, right on the water by the dock, has a sunset view over the bay. If you prefer more "action" you can wander over to the marina where the Madinina or Marine offer ringside seats to watch all the early evening activity as the charter boats return home to roost.

If you want to eat well and very inexpensively you go to "Fanny's", which is next to the Creperie, and called "Bar de la Plage". It is not in the least a tourist place - you line up to order and pay at the same time, then go sit down outside in the pleasant dining room and a good meal comes to you. This little place offers best value and is often full of French yachtsmen.

If you want to be more elegant try La Matador, L'Amphore or Villa Creole, all of which will present a tasty meal. Aux Poisson D'Or, just down the road from the Matador, is small with a pleasing intimate atmosphere. Aux Regal de La Mer and La Langouste are both close by the waterfront and specialize in seafood. Over in the Marina the Madinina and Marine are popular eating spots.

If you are looking for entertainment as you eat, you can find it in the large hotels. The best known floor show is a kind of lively dance routine depicting local life. You can find such a show at the Hotel Carayou on Wednesdays, the Meridian on Thursdays and the Bakoua on Fridays. You can also hear a steel band at the Bakoua on Wednesdays and Thursdays and with limbo on Saturdays, or at the Carayou on Sundays. The Bambou offers entertainment most nights; it is a rough and ready place but everyone has fun. No big cover charges, and if you want to eat, the dinner price is reasonable. Late at night you will be limited to the discos in the Meridien and Carayou. These carry about a 100 franc cover charge. Entertainment plans can change, so to get the latest update you buy Choubouloute, a 4 franc advertising guide available everywhere.

WHAT TO DO

One of the pleasures of Anse Mitan is to wander around all the chic little boutiques that line the roads around the Marina. For those doing their own cooking there is Mme Riveti's complete Bora Bora supermarket. If you are staying on a "bed only" plan then visit Delifrance for breakfast; they have wonderful fresh coffee, croissants and a seating area to enjoy them. It is pleasant to stroll around the Marina and watch the activities on the boats, or sit and take a drink in one of the Marina side restaurants.

The main beach is a popular place to soak up some sun; sailboards and pedalos are available for rent. The large hotels also have their own little beaches. When you want a change of scene take the 10 minute ferry ride over to Anse A L'Ane.

You can embark on just about any kind of activity from Anse Mitan. Many start at the Marina or the hotels, and you just walk up and book. Others such as helicopter rides, or a tour round the bay in an ultra-light aircraft, have to be arranged, which you can do through Alize Plus. If you want to join a group tour to see the island, or even to visit another island then you visit Caribtours (at the junction where the road goes up to the Bakoua) or Jet Tours in the Marina (see our tours section).

One of the marina attractions is George Voisin's "Aquascope", a strange looking trimaran berthed opposite Madinina. His billboard tells you the time of the next trip. You step aboard and go below into a glass sided spherical chamber which gives you an interesting view, half above water, half below. As you set off, the two views get divided by the swirling churning and bubbly waves that flow along the side. Below you watch the bottom glide by, looking far away as if you were viewing it from a huge airplane window. Fish traps, bits of wrecks, coral heads and sand flow by in steady stream - there is a strange swinging motion, a bit like one imagines being in a balloon. As the aquascope reaches the reef it descends - now the whole bubble is under water, electronic music comes on, and you hover over the reef as schools of colorful

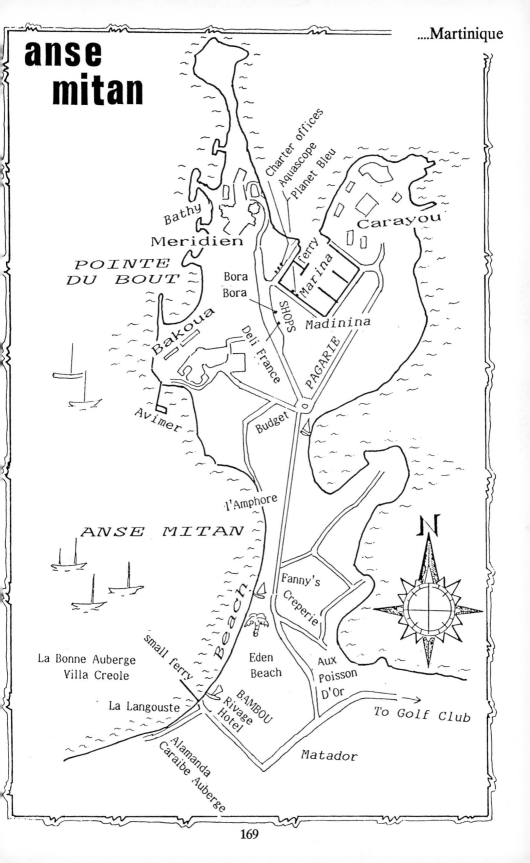

fish suround the bubble, peering in - you move gently around, through canyons and over rocks. The atmosphere is straight out of 20,000 Leagues Under The Sea and one expects Captain Nemo to make his entrance any time! Lots of fun for the family.

There are many day charter yachts lining the marina, any one of which will give you a memorable day's outing. Absent among them is the 42 foot Baraka, which anchors offshore. To book this one, there are no agents and no telephone - you wander down to La Langouste restaurant and take a beer at about 6 in the evening (if La Langouste is closed go to Bambou beach bar). You cannot miss owner Yves Jacquesson - he has thick white hair, a bushy white beard and smiling eyes. He will be accompanied by one of his crew, "Lof", a big shaggy brown dog that looks like a bundle of wool with a nose sticking out. Yves, his wife and Lof crossed the Atlantic on Baraka some 10 years ago, when Yves retired from his job as a doctor. Baraka only operates in the winter season (summers are spent in Venezuela). For around 500 francs per head, you make a leisurely mid-morning start and sail to Anse D'Arlet, a peaceful bay with a pretty beach. Here you can swim or snorkel while Yves' cook Francois prepares a sumptuous full French lunch, which is going to give you a much better idea of French cooking than many restaurants. All drinks and lunch with wines are included in the price. You return around 6.p.m. (Yves speaks English).

There are two dive stations - Bathy's in the Meridien hotel goes out daily at 2 p.m. The shop is on your left as you go down the steps from the pool to the beach. If you've never dived before, go in the morning for a complimentary resort course. Christine at Bathy's also does sports fishing trips before breakfast. The other dive station is Planet Bleu - a power yacht which goes out daily from the Marina. You can book on board or at Alize Plus. Planet Bleu also offers all-day trips to such places as St Pierre, which include a couple of dives and lunch.

If you want to head offshore there are 3 yacht charter companies in the Marina (see our chartering section).

If you have hired a motor car or scooter, then there are several roadside attractions a short ride away. The first of these is the golf course which unfolds below you as you descend the hill to the main road. The 18 hole course lies along the water's edge and is perfectly maintained. You can rent equipment and there is a restaurant.

Opposite the golf course is the Pagerie Museum - this was the home of Empress Josephine until she moved to France when she was 16. Not much remains by way of the original buildings, but there is a kitchen, and pictures depicting life in the days of slavery. The grounds are quiet and pleasant.

As you head on eastwards down the main road, you pass through the town of Trois Ilets. This picturesque little town has a good Creole restaurant called La Reine Hortense. Not long afer there is a public park called "Foret de Vatables" a wooded area suitable for a walk. As you continue you come to "La Maison de Cane" a picturesque museum which shows the equipment and way of life in the old days of sugar cane. The last of the nearby attractions is the old pottery - you have to go down a long winding drive, but you can watch the potters at work and buy something unique to take home.

THE SOUTH
FROM TROIS ILETS TO ST LUCE

ANSE A L'ANE

As you wind westwards from Anse Mitan, the next bay along is Anse A L'Ane. This bay has an attractive beach which is backed by a large camp site. There is one good hotel; Le Calalou which is right on the beach, and which has a unique hand carved merry-go-round in the garden. There are some other inexpensive restaurants; Le Nid Tropical, Chez Jo Jo, and Reflet de la Mer (which also has a few rooms available). Although popular, this is a much quieter place than Anse Mitan. You might want to look at the small shell museum, and if you like to ride horses there is a stable up the hill (68 63 97).

GRAND ANSE D'ARLET

Further down the road you come to Grand Anse D'Arlet, the first of two delightful bays. This is a small picturesque fishing village, with brightly painted "Gommiers" (dug-out canoes) pulled up under the palms. A perfect beach extends well beyond the village, and this makes a pleasant place to spend a day. Take lunch at "Chez Gaby" just behind the dock. This inexpensive little place is run by Gabriel who is German and her husband who is French.

PETIT ANSES D'ARLET

In the next bay along "Anses D'Arlet" is a somewhat larger village with a handsome church. There is a fun restaurant here called the California Saloon, which is inexpensive and has a lot of atmosphere - well worth driving over to for dinner one night

if you are staying in Anse Mitan or Anse A L'Ane.

If you drive right through the village (turn left along the shore) and keep going you will find yourself on a dramatically scenic road that winds its way steeply around the south coast.

DIAMANT

Diamant looks out over Roche du Diamond (Diamond Rock). Alluring from afar, this rock is not very hospitable, being very steep and infested by poisonous snakes. In 1804 the British, who had their main base in St Lucia, sailed over and commissioned the rock as a "ship" (it went down in the books as "H.M.S. Diamond Rock"). They hauled cannons to the top and kept a full crew on board, playing havoc with the unsuspecting French ships sailing into Martinique. It was liberated 18 months later by Admiral Villeneuf acting under express orders from Napoleon who was more than a little peaked about this insult to the home of his beloved Josephine.

Just on the edge of town, Diamant Les Bains spans from the road down to the sea. Rooms are cottage style round a swimming pool. They have a dinner dance here every Tuesday night. A little way out of town is the huge 173 room Novotel with two restaurants, a disco, diving and sailboarding. Not far from Novotel, back from the sea, Diamant Bleu is a new little cottage residence set in a very quiet garden, with a swimming pool. It would be suitable

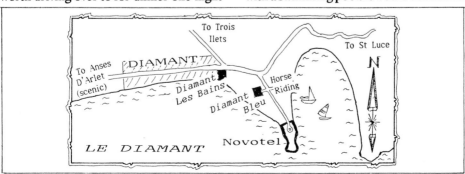

for kids, who could run around without fearing for their lives from passing traffic. The rooms are self contained, smallish but adequate with a small patio area. The rates are inexpensive, which would leave you plenty of money for renting a car which would be essential here.

Right opposite Diamant Bleu is a riding stable (76 22 94); they ride between 8 and 10 in the morning and 4 and 6 in the afternoon.

ST LUCE

St Luce is a small fishing town just off the big new highway that sweeps from Fort de France all the way to Marin. All along the shore boats are pulled up under shady trees. If you hit here at lunchtime, Vagues de Sud is one of the better Creole restaurants, situated upstairs on the waterfront (you will find a parking spot in the square next to Ets Aglae). There are several small but O.K. beaches west of town, and there are several places to stay. La Petit Auberge is reasonably priced and full of quaint character. It has a well situated restaurant, overlooking the sea. Brises Marine is an attractive and reasonably priced cottage residence right by the sea. It offers excellent value and tends to be full. If you are prepared to live in close quarters with five people "French style", in the larger units, the price would be unbeatable. Douces Vagues offers a block of self contained rooms close by the beach, and Residence Grand Large has rooms in a large apartment building.

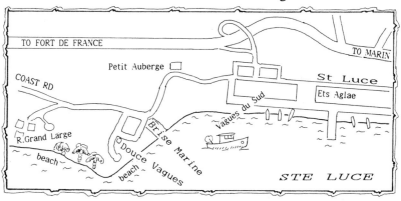

SOUTH EAST CORNER

The south east corner of Martinique is a very attractive area for a holiday, and would suit those who like things to be a little on the quiet side. It is linked to Fort de France (and Anse Mitan) by an excellent highway which makes it easily accessible. Although you can get to town easily on a communal taxi, a small motor bike or car would be of great help in getting to the beaches and exploring.

WHERE TO STAY

There are two large hotels for those that enjoy close proximity to others. The Club Med is on a beach lined peninsula. The majority of the clients are American, and the style of the place is famous - you are just not allowed to have a bad time, with activities and festivities from morning to night. The other large hotel is the Villa Club Anse Caritan, on its own small beach just outside St Anne.

The little town of St Anne is very quiet, clean and picturesque. There is a square, a church, just about two streets and a wonderful waterfront with a superb view looking up the south coast to Diamond Rock. La Dunette is a small but charming looking hotel right on the waterfront. It would be well worth paying the extra money for a front room with a balcony overlooking the view, and provided you did this, it would be harder to imagine a more pleasant or romantic spot. Just out of town Manoir de

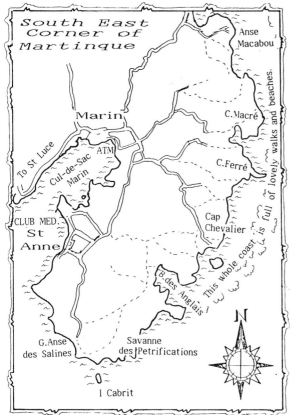

South East Corner of Martinique

Anse Macabou

C.Macré

C.Ferré

Cap Chevalier

This whole coast is full of lovely walks and beaches.

Marin

ATM

Cul-de-Sac Marin

To St Luce

CLUB MED.
St Anne

B. des Anglais

G.Anse des Salines

Savanne des Petrifications

N

I Cabrit

on your dinner - on a glass covered lobster tank! In addition to these, all the hotels have their own restaurants.

WHAT TO DO

St Anne is one of Martinique's best areas for walks and beaches. Grand Anse des Salines is one of those "dream" beaches backed by palms, though very popular, especially in the season and on weekends. Walking further along there is Savanne des Petrifications - an area where there used to be a petrified forest, but I think many of the best bits have now "walked" as souvenirs although this is forbidden. As you continue northwards the whole coastline to Anse Macabou is full of hidden bays and beaches, some of them somewhat secluded. Baie des Anglais, Cap Chevalier, Cap Ferre, and Cap Macre are all worth exploring.

There is another Aquascope at St Anne, and Marin is the home of ATM, Martinique's largest yacht

Beauregard is a recreated old "great house". The restoration has been well done and the hall and communal rooms are very impressive. The bedrooms are acceptable, but even the offer of an antique cupboard and bed wouldn't lure me away from a seaview elsewhere!

EATING OUT

Despite its small size, St Anne offers several promising places to eat out. Les Tamerindiers is very sweet, the exterior being covered in flowers. Inside, Jean Claude Edmond produces good French and Creole food at a very reasonable price, and he adds artful touches like serving his more expensive plates decorated with blossoms.

Poi et Virginie is a little more expensive and also highly thought of, and right on the water front. On the beach just to the north of St Anne, on the first part of the "Club Med" peninsula, Le Filet Bleu offers you a unique opportunity to dance

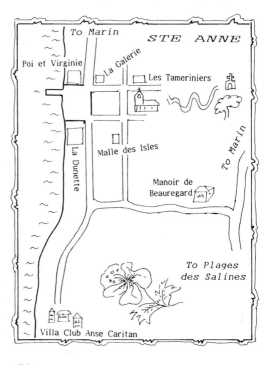

To Marin

STE ANNE

Poi et Virginie

La Galerie

Les Tameriniers

Malle des Isles

La Dunette

Manoir de Beauregard

To Marin

To Plages des Salines

Villa Club Anse Caritan

charter company. Scuba diving might be arranged at the Club Nautique next door.

For nightlife you will have to make do with periodic entertainment at Villa Club Anse Cariton, and dancing on the fish tank at Filet Bleu. You can in fact also join in the activities at Club Med if you want. For a fee you can stay a half day there, either taking in the morning and lunch, or dinner and the evening activities.

EAST COAST - VAUCLIN TO TRINITE

Much of this stretch of coast is deeply indented, the shoreline being protected from the sea by a barrier reef. There are beaches up near Trinite but not many along the rest of the coast. There are several traditional fishing towns. At Vauclin you are still just a short run from St Anne. There are two small hotels - Chez Julot an acceptable hostelerie with a typical Creole restaurant in town, and Auberge Atlantic overlooking the fishing port. Auberge Atlantic is basic, but the cheapest place I found to stay in Martinique. Suitable for back-packing students on a budget.

Further up the coast Bungalow de La Prairie lies down a long quiet backroad on a small hill overlooking the sea. These ten cottage units are really attractive, set in a very well tended garden. Access to the water is on the property, though there is no beach. You would need a car here, but for those who like to be a little bit apart, this would be a choice place to stay. There is plenty of space in the cottages, though not a lot of privacy - they would take two in luxury, up to 5 "French style".

Francois offers a day tour with a bit of a difference - you go through the town down to the Club Nautique, next to the Club Nautique is the small Marina de Francois (tel:54 45 03). From here you can hire pirogues to take you for trips to the off-shore islands, some of which have small beaches that would make great picnic spots. The round trip is about 300 francs for the boat, which will take up 7. (In the height of the season it might be an idea to get your hotel to call and book for you in advance).

The peninsula to the east of Trinite is lovely. There is one small village, Tartane, for the rest you have several beaches and hikes. The road has two branches - the main coastal bit and another that winds through the hills - this upper road is well worth exploring for its magnificent views. One of the beaches lies at the end of the very rough road that goes to the end of the peninsula. You have to hike down southwards. If you are staying elsewhere on the island come here for a picnic one day. If you like this kind of area, there are a couple of places to stay. Studios La Caravelle are built on a very steep hill and negotiating the steps will keep you fit. There is a beach below, and although the units are rather basic they are very reasonable.

Up in the hills behind Trinite, Chez Ami Fritz is something rather special. The building is not at its most impressive from the road, but the lush garden immediately catches your attention, and inside Daniel Rebert has done a superb job of creating a house of class and distinction in traditional style, reminiscent of a miniature "Stately Home". Chez Ami Fritz is one of the best restaurants in Martinique, and wherever you are staying you should come one night for dinner. A lesser known fact is that he has five elegant guest rooms. If you are staying somewhere else in Martinique, try this for an idea - Take your spouse or lover to Chez Ami Fritz for dinner, pack a toothbrush and arrange to stay the night - if that doesn't turn out to be one of your best and most romantic evenings, better buy someone else's guide next time!

THE NORTH

The north end of Martinique is truly beautiful. Along the coast - richly cultivated land set between mountain and sea; in the center - rain forest. The north is a real haven for people who find the southern end of the island too populated. Once you leave Trinite, there is not much in the way of beaches till you get round to the lee coast again, as conditions tend to be too rough for swimming.

The north east coast road offers sweeping vistas. St Aubin's Hotel is an absolutely gorgeous old traditional Caribbean manor house converted to a small hotel. The buildings, the garden and the view are magnificent. The rooms themselves are nothing special, but the ambience in such a classic old house makes up for it. You are still in easy reach of Trinite and Tartanne for beaches, and right at the beginning of the dramtic northern terrain. St Aubin's is an excellent spot for people who want something very quiet in picture book sur-

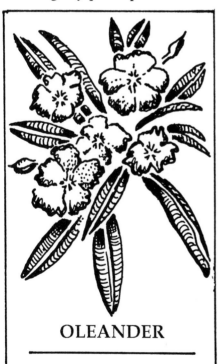

OLEANDER

roundings at a reasonable price. (Restaurant is open to guests only).

Le Gibsy is a brand new hotel just outside Lorrain. The outlook is back into the hills, not out to sea. At the moment there are 7 rooms, 30 more are planned. One room had a large balcony, and if I was staying there that is the one I would ask for!

St James Distillery has a rum museum at Ste Marie. The coast road is worth following all the way to Grand Riviere, in some places you will pass fields of pineapples.

When they say "Plantation Leyritz" they mean it; you wind down a tiny dirt track sandwiched between bananas and citrus, and when I passed, you had to ford a stream before you arrived. This is a popular place for visitors to come for a lunch stop during their stay - the dining room has plenty of atmosphere, being made out of an old barn. The food is well prepared and the prices reasonable, and as an added roadside attraction they have a tiny doll museum, all the dolls being made out of various kinds of dried leaf and plant. The property is dotted with little guest cottages, many of them being converted from old farm buildings. They offer a health spa with mud baths and massage. With 53 rooms, a swimming pool and a tiny disco you do not need to feel too cut off from civilization, but you are a long way from anywhere else!

On the road that skirts Mt Pelee you come to a sidetrack leading to the Gorges de Falaises. These are closed during the heaviest of the rainy season (September to Christmas) because of the danger of falling rocks. Here you can follow a footpath way up in a beautiful gorge till you come to a waterfall. There are pools to swim in lower down. Guides are advisable and available at the gate.

French engineers are something else; they have not only built the best Caribbean road system I have come across, they think nothing of taking it most of the way up the volcano. Your only problem here is to go on a day clear enough so that you will get the views, as Mt Pelee does spend quite a lot of time with its head stuck in clouds. Auberge de Mt Pelee is built on this road, and has heavenly views all around. It is cool up here and sometimes misty, a completely different atmosphere from the coast. I would make this a definite lunch destination on a clear day, and if conditions changed head to St Pierre or Plantation Leyritz. If you like mountains you may want to stay here, they have little cottage style rooms. You can climb Mt Pelee; a guide is advisable. Guides can be arranged through the parks commission, though it would be easier just to ask at the Auberge.

St Pierre used to be the cultural and spiritual capital of Martinique, with handsome houses, a theater, and an elegantly dressed population. In 1902 the volcano erupted and the whole town was destroyed in seconds by a cloud of superheated gas. 30,000 people perished, the sole survivor being the inmate of the local dungeon. Today it is a small and pleasant seaside town, with an interesting museum depicting those earlier, more glorious days. Anyone interested in diving should give serious consideration to staying up at this end of the island. There are 12 wrecks that were sunk during the tragedy, and going further north there are exciting wall dives with big fish.

St Pierre's only small hotel, Nouvelle Vague is well situated on the water front. As of this writing, the rooms were just going to be renovated, and it is inexpensive. The Nouvelle Vague also has a good restaurant, as does La Guinguette, further down the beach. La Guinguette is also the home of Tripicasud diving station, where Dominique will take you on all those wrecks. There is also a pizzeria in town that uses an old wood fired oven.

Not far down the road lies Carbet, offering a Gaugin Museum and small zoo. Grain D'Or is a sweet little auberge with a pleasant small restaurant, beside the road. It is inexpensive, and for divers, the base of Michel Metery who discovered all those wrecks in the first place and produced a superb color book about his work called "Tamaya" (unfortunately only available in

French). Michel takes people diving and his rates are slightly less than most of the other establishments.

The Marouba Club is a large (100 rooms) hotel owned by Nouvelle Frontieres. It is quite pleasant, accommodation is in chalets in a large garden that leads to the sea. Tropicasud also has a diving station here.

THE RAIN FOREST AND JARDINS DE BALATA

The rain forest is bisected by four roads, all of them scenic. There is a fifth, tiny road that sometimes joins the main road to St Joseph. This road is barely the width of a car and very exotic, unfortunately it is not always open all the way. Still, explore it as far as you can from either end!

The rain forest is dominated by the dramatic "Pitons du Carbet" that rise majestically out of the forest. Just below them, with a clear view to the south, Jean-Philippe Those has created a magnificent masterpiece of a garden. Those's family has been in the island since about 1750, and one of their properties was a small mountain retreat. Jean has created his Jardin de Balata on this piece of property. He has worked for 20 years, slowly and painstakingly, with the eye of an artist. His creation includes an artificial river with several ponds. There is an entrance charge of 30 francs, and it is worth it. It would be a shame to rush, it is the kind of place you could profitably spend an hour or two. Behind, the Pitons of Carbet tower upwards, and ahead on a clear day you can see all the way to St Lucia and St Vincent. The gardens are only a short drive from Fort de France and if you do not have a car you could take the Balata bus from Avenue General de Gaulle. If you want to avoid crowds, do not come on Mondays as this is when most of the tour operators bring their groups. (tel:64 48 73).

OTHER ATTRACTIONS

MARTINIQUE RHUM.

The rum of Martinique is something unique. English style rum is a byproduct of sugar, made from molasses - a process that involves heating up the sugar cane juice. The resulting liquor is high proof, but not very tasty. In Martinique they crush the cane, and then without heating it they ferment all the juice with yeast before distilling. The result is a much "fruitier" rum. This rum is naturally white. The traditional way to drink Martinique rum is in a "Petit Punch". You mix a little rum with sugar cane syrup, add a slice of lime and sip slowly! Brown rum is made by aging white rum for 3 to 12 years in oak casks, till it takes on a golden-brown color from the wood. The Martiniquais are very proud of their rum and nearly all the distilleries are open to visitors. We went on a tour of La Mauny, the largest. We watched as the cane was loaded, cut, crushed and fermented, the whole operation being powered by steam engines that used the dried left over sugar cane husks as fuel. The tour was very informative (all the guides speak English) and followed by a tasting session. The sugar cane season is only for the first three months of the year, when the factories go into production, but they are open to guests year round.

MATNIK GASTRO

Starting around the third week in March and running into April, Matnik Gastro is a Creole food festival and competition. Each night another restaurant is highlighted with a special creative menu that costs around 150 francs. Courses in creole cooking are available, details from the tourist office.

CARNIVAL

Just before Lent, days of fun and partying, with colorful street parades. Traditionally, red clothes are worn for Mardi Gras, black and white for Ash Wednesday. Ask for details at the tourist office.

LES GOMMIERS

The boats used today for fishing are direct descendants of the old "dug out" canoe used by the pre-Columbian indians. Many of them are still built by hollowing out a huge "Gommier" tree. In the old days they would sew planks to the side for added freeboard, today they nail them in on frames. No one sails them any more for fishing - they all use outboards. However, quite a few villages run sailing races in these old dug out canoes - no holds barred and about ten people hang onto outriggers to keep them upright under their enormous sails. Ask in the tourist office for details.

TOURS

Martinique is well serviced by the tour industry, and most of the larger hotels have tour desks where you can book. You can join in nearly every activity on a tour, and for those who don't want to rent a car this is the alternative. Each of the main tour operators designs their own tours and markets them. If you want to really get a review of what is available you will go to all four main agents and compare brochures. However, there is a lot of overlap in general scope. For an example we took the program offered by Caribtours of Anse Mitan. Their northern tour takes you to the Jardins de Balata, through the rain forest, gives you lunch at Plantation Leyritz and visits a rum factory on the way back. Their southern tour offers you the Pagerie Museum, a lobster barbecue on Plages des Salines, a visit to La Mauny distillery, a cock fight and a trip along the scenic south road.

They do a trip to the offshore islands at Francois which includes lunch in a Creole restaurant. They offer a trip to Mt Pelee by helicopter, and a variety of day charter trips by sail or power, half or full day. They also offer day excursions to Dominica, St Lucia, and the Grenadines by plane.

SAILBOARDING (Windsurfing)

These days everyone is doing it, even Grandma! They are flying about, jumping the waves, hanging onto a giant sail. It's not quite surfing, nor exactly sailing or flying - It's sailboarding - the craze that offers the thrills, spills and excitement of all three. It gives plenty of exercise and a whole new vista on life. If you have never done it before, why not give it a go? and if you are an old hand conditions in the Windwards will offer a real treat.

Most learners' early attempts are characterized by an ungraceful wobbly stance followed by a swift unintentional plunge. The warmth of air and sea make this more pleasurable in the Windwards than elsewhere, but the healthy trade winds which delight the expert, all too often leave the beginner clinging to the board with his head bobbing above the surface wondering "What happened?" If one can possibly get a toe hold, so to speak, in the sport before coming, so much the better. If not, try to find a sailboarding school here that offers training boards with small sails or a beach simulator. These are much easier to learn on than the standard model. Also it is worth noting that the calmest conditions are along the western (lee) shores, or in deeply indented bays. Many places that rent sailboards are also accredited schools, and it does help to have lessons.

Experienced sailboaders can take their pick of locations. Eastern (windward) shores are often very rough, and on the large islands the tall mountains can "back up" the wind enough to create dead spots, though elsewhere there will be plenty of breeze. Those that want not only thrills, but also to see their families again, would probably do best to choose a protected bay either along the south coast or towards the north of a large island from where they can venture out into the rough stuff as far as they feel able. It should be kept in mind that once you get away from an island there is a strong current which usually runs westwards across open water all the way to Panama. Gear can break, so it is crazy to get out of protected water on your own without someone keeping an eye on you. I found the best way of limping back is to take the sail off the mast and hold the mast (or the longest piece if it has broken) in the middle using it as a long kayak-style paddle.

SAILBOARDING LOCATIONS

Martinique
Anse Mitan is an ideal spot with good learning conditions close to the main beach, and plenty of wind and little waves out in Fort de France Bay.

St Lucia
Carib Blue offers exciting conditions for the experienced. Reduit Beach (The St Lucian Hotel) offers conditions which vary from being good for beginners to good for experts depending on the strength of wind. As you go further down the coast to La Toc, Marigot and Anse Chastenet, the lee conditions are generally best for beginners and intermediate learners.

St Vincent
Young Island cut provides a place calm enough to be O.K. for beginners with quick access to the open sea which will provide conditions to match the best. Sometimes "jumpable" waves off Blue Lagoon, but mind the reef!

The Grenadines
Since the Grenadines are lower-lying they are usually breezy and offer excellent conditions for experienced people. In addition one could learn in such places as Admiralty or Friendship Bays in Bequia, if in Mustique at Grand Bay, or in the islands of Canouan, Mayreau, Palm, P.S.V. and Carriacou. Admiralty Bay, the Tobago Cays and the open water between PSV and P.M. can provide great speed runs - lots of wind, not much waves.

Grenada
Grenada has good conditions for both

beginners and intermediates in both Grand Anse and along the south coast. More experienced sailboarders might favor the south coast where they can sail out into good waves.

Those going on a yachting holiday who know how to sailboard should ask to have a sailboard put aboard, as nearly all the anchorages offer a good breeze.

SAILBOARDING AVAILABILITY

GRENADA
PRICKLY BAY
Virgo Water sports, Horseshoe Bay Hotel, has school.
Geoffrey Thompson (private) call 444 4475/ 440 2198 board rental one day or longer.
MT HARTMAN BAY: Secret Harbor Hotel: 444 4548
GRAND ANSE: HMC with sations at Coyaba, Ramada Renaissance and Spice Island Inn. (includes school and training boards):444 4334/4371/4432
LOWER GRENADINES
Most of the hotels have sailboards for the use of their guests only.
Anchorage Yacht Club in Union has boards for hire:88221.
Dennis Hideaway, Saline Bay, Mayreau (VHF CH 68) offers boards for hire and instruction.
BEQUIA
ADMIRALTY BAY
Sunsports. (Clubhouse) call 83577. Board rental, school, beach simulator. training boards.
FRIENDSHIP BAY
Friendship Bay Hotel call 83222. board rentals, school.
Bequia Beach Club call:83248 .board rentals.

MUSTIQUE
Basil's Bar call 84621 ext 350, Board rentals.
Cotton House call 64777. Board rentals.
ST VINCENT
YOUNG ISLAND CUT
Mariners Scuba shop call 84228. long and short term board rental.
Liston Phillips International Windsurfing School call 84287/ 84157. board rentals, teaching, training boards.
BLUE LAGOON
CSY. call 84308. long term board rentals.
ST LUCIA
St Lucian hotel call: board rentals and sailboard school.
Marigot Bay Resort. call: board rentals and sailboard school.
All major hotels have both sailboards and training facilities for their guests.
MARTINIQUE
ANSE MITAN
Matos. call 66 02 22/ 66 04 30. Shop on the road, stand on the beach. long and short term board rental, training boards.
Beside La Langouste. call 66 02 19 (evenings only). On the beach by the dock. board rentals by the hour. training boards.
PLAGES DES SALINES.
A stand on the beach.

For anyone with a yen to sail, the Windwards are a dream; 120 miles dotted with islands, consistent winds and just enough distance between landfalls to ensure open sea sailing at its best. So if you feel the call of the distant horizon, the rhythm of the sea and the captain's cogent cry of "who's for rum punch?" why not charter? One does not have to be a gung-ho sailor, complete with eye patch, parrot and a store of oaths that would make a harlot blush. In fact one does not even know the difference between bow and beam, all one needs is the romantic dream of silent travel with nights at anchor under the stars. You can get a group together and charter a yacht, or you can join a cruise. Below we will outline the various types of charter and tell you who to contact.

TYPES OF CHARTER

With a fully crewed charter you take a yacht which carries its own permanent crew: captain, cook and sometimes extra hands. This is the best kind of charter for inexperienced people as well as those who wish to have a break from housework. The captain has all the headaches, all you have to do is sit back and enjoy. The meals are prepared by the cook and the standard of food is generally excellent. The guests may sail the yacht as much as they want, or leave it to the crew. The captain should be happy to teach a novice how to sail. The crew normally lives on board, giving the yacht a warm, lived-in feel with a good library of books and tapes.

The bareboat is at the other end of the scale. Here the charterer and his party rent the yacht fully equipped and use it as their own, sailing where and when the inclination takes them. They must be expert sailors, and they have the full responsibility for the yacht while it is their care.

The semi-bareboat is half way between these two. It is a bareboat to which is added a captain who knows how to navigate. The customers need have no experience, but they are expected to help run the ship and to take full responsibility for the cooking (including the captain's meals) and cleaning.

Chartering can in fact be a very economical proposition for groups of 4 or more. Fully crewed charters often represent excellent value. Food is generally included and drinks are normally either thrown in as well or sold at cost, so there are none of those expensive bar bills which can double the price of a hotel room.

Every kind of yacht is available from huge "gin palaces" where the captain wears gold stripes and the steward serves breakfast in white gloves, to little 35 footers where you all share the main cabin and Granny has to sleep on the saloon table. The wonderful thing is there are enough styles to suit anyone, and what the Lord Parsley-Parsons thinks is "bang up" Joe Blogs would no doubt find unbearably snooty. The trick is to choose the right yacht for you. There are a number of places to look.

CHARTER COMPANY, AGENT OR DEAL DIRECT?

There are several charter companies that have fleets of yachts under their management, some bareboat, others professionally crewed by a captain and cook. Most of these yachts are fairly new, 40 to 60 feet long, specifically designed for the average charter group of 2 to 6 people, the crew are generally very good. If the price and style suits, it is a good way to charter.

For a larger selection try a charter agent. This is an excellent way to go because they usually represents many of the charter companies as well as a wide selection of individually owned and run yachts. Agents vary from huge multi-million dollar companies to little old ladies operating out of a back room. Any one of them can do a great job, but the choice you are offered will depend on their idea of a "good yacht". Some go for acres of teak deck, polished brass and all mod-cons. Others go for less "yachty" boats which offer more of a spirit of adventure. You can choose a modern

NIRVANA

The comfortable way to see the Caribbean

Over 100 square of feet of deck space for sunbathing. Complete privacy with 3 separate double cabins, each with its own head, in the outriggers and aft.

Nirvana's large size (50' by 28') and complete stability, gives a wonderful sense of security and a real "big ship" feel. Women and children love her.

Kurt Bartz the licenced owner and skipper has chartered in the Caribbean for more than 19 years. The professional chef produces first class Caribbean cuisine. A large proportion of charters on Nirvana are repeat customers, what better recommendation could we have?

Airmail: Kurt Bartz, Box 826, St Vincent, West Indies, or contact your nearest charter agent. Charter during the winter season only.

racing boat, or a vintage old-time classic. It is your holiday, and the right boat for you is out there, all you need is the right agent to help. We give a selection below.

Another way to charter a yacht is by dealing directly with the owner. This is usually more trouble, and no less expensive, though one sometimes finds a good yacht whose owner prefers to deal direct. It is an especially good way to charter if you have had a reliable private recommendation. If not, best ask for the telephone numbers of a couple of previous clients so you can call them up and ask how they enjoyed their trip.

WHAT KIND OF BOAT

What kind of boat to charter? If it is a sailing holiday you are interested in, here are a few points to consider. If you will not be wanting to spend much time below, choose a yacht with a large comfortable cockpit where you can lounge around, take cocktails and maybe eat. It should be possible to sit in the shade, even under sail.

This can be provided with a "Bimini hood", "hard top" or maybe a permanently set mizzen awning. Wherever you sleep down below, there needs to be a large hatch facing forward to the breeze. Do not expect air-conditioning. If you want to sail, ask for a boat which sails reasonably well, and a skipper who enjoys sailing. If peace and quiet is important to you, a generator is not necessarily a plus. Despite manufacturers' claims, there is no such thing as a really quiet generator on a small boat in a peaceful anchorage! Ask how many hours a day it (or the main engine) needs to be run - two to three hours is acceptable; you can arrange to be ashore when it is going. Some yachts offer hair dryers, videos, quadraphonic disc players and microwave ovens. My feeling is, if these things are really important to you, you may be better off on a large power yacht or cruise ship. Be realistic about the amount of space and privacy you require - does "sleeps 9" mean that five of you will be snoring together in the main saloon?

WHERE TO GO?

One of the best things about chartering a fully crewed yacht is that you can normally start at one destination and finish at another without paying an extra fee. This enables you to venture further afield and have more time to relax. It may involve a short extra plane ride, but it is well worth this trouble and expense. It is best not to try and overdo the sailing. If you like the idea of a couple of fairly long open sea passages (6 hours) then I would recommend Martinique to Grenada as a two week trip, or St Lucia to Grenada as a ten day trip. If you are not sure how you are going to like sailing, or prefer short hauls, then the easiest is to go from St Vincent to Union, though for the extra few hours St Vincent to Grenada would be more exciting. St Vincent is close enough to the Grenadines that one can also enjoy a trip both starting and finishing there.

THE CREW

Most charter crew are easy company and love what they do, and really enjoy their guests, but nonetheless there are strains to this style of life, as the crew must always be on their best behavior. Screaming at one's help-mate and throwing plates around just isn't on! Guests can help a lot by making sure they leave the yacht for a couple of hours a day - they can explore, swim, hike and shop - and it gives the crew a chance to clean up the boat and have a few private moments together if they need it.

Discuss with your skipper what you would like to see and do, he will do his best taking into account weather, safety etc. If you have any food allergies, special diets or dislikes let the cook know well in advance of the charter; provisioning is planned well ahead!

It has become a tradition to ask the crew out to a meal once during the charter, and if you feel like giving your cook an extra break, you could always have a roti ashore for lunch one day. I'll tell you a secret about cooks - they will never say so, but they hate being watched when they cook. You will get better food and a happier crew if you keep well away from the galley!

SHORT CHARTERS

If you want to give chartering a go, but are nervous about spending a week on a boat, then it may be possible to arrange for a two or three day trip. Few boats will book less than a week in advance, but you may be lucky enough to find a yacht with a few blank days when you get there. Suitable 2-3 day trips include weekend trips to Martinique from St Lucia, a few days in Mustique, Bequia or the lower Grenadines out of St Vincent, Bequia or Union; a trip to Carriacou from Grenada, or a couple of days on Grenada's south coast. You would book by going to one of the companies, agents or yachts on the spot. You do of course take the chance there may be nothing available.

JOINING A CRUISE

If you cannot get a suitable group together to charter a yacht, but want to go anyway, then you get in touch with Mary Crowley at Ocean Voyages, who does a wonderful job of selling sailing holidays on an individual basis at reasonable rates. She offers one and two week packages on board yachts in the Grenadines.

From time to time the charter companies also offer cruises on a "per head" basis, usually to fill time in the summer.

Then there are "head boats" - bigger than yachts, but smaller than cruise ships - that carry passengers up and down the islands. This is an inexpensive way to see the islands, and can be exciting socially. One of these is the Carib Islander. She is a 120 foot power boat with 16 cabins, and will carry you around in a style reminiscent of Somerset Maugham's short stories. She does three day charters from St Lucia to Union Island or from Union to St Lucia via Martinique - You can also do the whole trip as a 7 day cruise. You can book before you come or join when you are already in the islands (space permitting).

Our other regular is the huge sailing ship the Mandalay. She is 236 feet long and was built in Denmark in 1923. Her career includes being owned by E F Hutton, and logging over a million miles as an oceanographic research ship. She does 13 day cruises between Antigua and Grenada, but it is quite possible to join for just part of a cruise.

A new-comer to the field is the 112 ft Vela Star with 17 air conditioned cabins which does one week cruises out of St Lucia.

Another regular visitor is the sailing cruise ship the Wind Star.

WHAT TO BRING

Yachts don't have enough room for hard suitcases, golf clubs and Granny's spinning wheel. Gather up what you think you might want, leave half behind and bring the rest in a couple of soft hold-alls. If something is really important to you, call up and ask - I have for example taken along a radio ham complete with all his gear! You will need shorts, T-shirts, a hat and plenty of sun protection. Use a block out with a protection factor of 10 to 15 or more, and buy it as a cream or milk type lotion - many gels have a nasty habit of chemically reacting with paint and fiberglass to turn them a grunge brown, and if anything is going to put your skipper's back up, that will! Oil type lotions are similarly taboo - they make walking on the deck look like ameteur night at the skating rink! You will also need a a pair of clean rubber soled shoes to be worn only on the boat (grit picked up ashore plays havoc with the decks). Remember to bring ample supplies of film and if you need any prescription medication pack it in your hand baggage.

TIPPING

Unless a service fee has been specifically added, it is customary to tip around 10% of the charter fee. This is important as many crew are poorly paid and depend on tips to supplement their income, and in the case of captains who own their own boats, with the high cost of maintenance, they are probably even more in need!

WHERE TO BOOK - CHARTER COMPANIES AND YACHTS
MARTINIQUE

ATM, Marina Du Marin, 97290 Le Marin, Martinique. call:74 98 17/ 87 88. Etienne Julien. telex::912763. Also: ATM, 8 rue Sedillot, 75007 Paris, FRANCE. tel:16 (1) 47 05 63 86. telex:200 437. 73 bareboats available, and three 50ft semi-bareboat catamarans. skipper, cooks and one way charters available.

Chimere Yachting, Marina Pointe du Boute, Trois Ilets, Martinique. Call 66 03 85. Michel Lance. Also: 20 Rue Victor Bart Versailles. 20 bareboats available including catamarans 30 to 45 feet. Jeanneau, Sun Light, Sun Magic etc.

Soleil et Voile, Marina Pointe du Bout, 97229 Trois Ilets, Martinique, tel:(596) 66 09 14. telex:912 344 MR. Selection of 34 yachts available (but not all stationed in Martinique) between 29 and 34 ft including 40 to 45 foot catamarans.

Star Voyage, (ex Voile et Vent), Marina Pointe du Boute,Trois Ilets, Martinique. call:66 00 72. Christian Bouffaro, telex:912 476 NR. also: Star Voyage, 5 Rue Lincoln, 75008 Paris. Call 42 56 15 62. telex:643738. 40 yachts from 28 to 44 feet and 8 motor boats from 20 to 33 feet. Skipper and one way charters available.

ST LUCIA.

Steven's Yachts base their yachts in Rodney Bay Marina, St Lucia. They have a large fleet of bareboats, and a smaller fleet of skippered yachts, these include Stevens custom 40's, 47's and new Moodies. Booking is normally done through their U.S. office. but if you arrive in St Lucia you can always try them. Weekend and day trips can be arranged.50 Water St., South Norwalk, Ct 06854. Call:800 638 7044/ 203 866 8989 telex:643914 PNI STEVENS. Also Ian Cowen, Box 928, Rodney Bay, St Lucia. Tel:(809 45) 28848 or 28648

Tradewind Yachts, Rodney Bay Marina. They keep a fleet of about 20 bareboats and act as agents for some skippered yachts, including some in the lower price range. Tradewind Yachts, 778, Wimborne Rd., Bournemouth, BH9 2DX, U.K. tel:0202-520105. Telex:41377. Or: 35th floor, 475 Park Avenue South, New York 10016. tel:800 222 6656/212-5326282. Locally Box 152, Castries, St Lucia WI. call Seth or Ted (809 45) 28424. Telex 6417 LC Fax:809-452-8442. Weekend trips often arranged.

The Moorings keep a large fleet of bareboats, and a smaller one of skippered yachts in their own resort at Marigot Bay St Lucia. They also have a day charter boat and can arrange weekend trips. 1305 U.S. 19 South, Suite 402, Clearwater, Fla 33546 Telephone 800 535 7289 or at Marigot Bay, call (809 45) 34246 or 34256

Austro Yachting, Hans Donee Box 1538, Rodney Bay Marina. In Austria call:0 22 36-85 5 10/82 6 45. Telex 79285. Small fleet of bareboats.

ST VINCENT

Caribbean Sailing Yachts (C.S.Y) Have a fleet of 15 - 20 bareboats in Blue Lagoon, St Vincent. These include CSY Gulf Star 42's and 50's, CSY Morgan 44.5 ft, and 50.5ft, old style 44's also available. Bareboat, Semi-

bareboat and one way charters available. BOX 491, Tenafly, NJ 07670 call 800 631 1593/ 201 568 0390. In St Vincent:Box 133, St Vincent W.I. (809 45) 84308. St Vincent manager:Ken Guynes

Bimini Yacht Charters are based in Blue Lagoon, St Vincent. 6 yachts Jeanneau 41's and 45's and CS 36's. Skippers and cooks available, No one way charters. Bimini Yachts, 431 Richmond St East, Toronto M5A1R1, Canada tel:(416) 366 1777. telex:065 24 754 or Box 39, St Vincent W,I, Tel: (809 45) 69324. St Vincent manager: Mary Barnard.

INDIVIDUAL YACHTS.

Amizade, halfway between a trimaran and a ship, about 16 double cabins. Inexpensive for large groups. Ken Guynes, Box 133, Blue Lagoon, St Vincent, West Indies. call:(809 45) 84308

Apogee, Carib 41. Bob Berlinghoff, Bequia, St Vincent, W.I. call:(809) 45 83615 semi-bareboat and fully crewed charters.

Danocha, a Cheoy Lee 40 footer. Based in G.Y.S. Dave Simons, 2 Cleaver Roat, Arima, Trinidad. or c/o GYS, Box 183, St George's Grenada. Call (809) 440 2508/ 2883 Semi Bareboat and fully crewed charters.

Damosel, a Pearson 43 and Samantha a Whitby 42. Semi Bareboat. Selwyn Guthrie, Grenada Sailing School, Box 220, St George's Grenada. Call (809) 444 4342.

Fredag, 50 ft Colin Archer type, good for adventurous groups. Peter and Marianne, c/o Frangipani (below).

Maiden Light, varnished 47 foot long sloop, fully crewed. Andy and Brigit, c/o Scuba Shop Box 639, St Vincent, WI. Call:809 45 84228

Nirvana (also available through agents), Immensely spacious 50 ft trimaran, very stable and comfortable, for fully crewed charters. Kurt Bartz, Box 826, St Vincent W.I.

Secondo (O'Day 37). Johnny Olliviere, Bequia, St Vincent, tel: (809 45) 83695. Crewed or semi-bareboat.

Tjaldur, 50 foot steel yacht takes 8, rates from $2100 per week. Bjorn, C/O Dolphin, St Vincent, W.I. tel:84238. telex: 7500 CW AGENCY VQ TJALDUR

Waltz, a slipper 42 ft ketch 2 guests only. John Williams, or Touch of Time, Edson Hazell, both c/o Nicholsons, English Harbor, Antigua, W.I. Based Antigua but both know Windwards well.

LOCAL AGENTS

Alize Plus, Marina de la Pointe du Boute, Martinique. M. Morand. Call:66 04 81. - About 20 Martinique yachts listed plus day charter boats, scuba, helicopter flights, ultra light flights and aquascope rides.

Aquasail Yacht Charters. St Lucia - Can arrange "on the spot" charters - call (809 45) 28234 weekend or longer charters at short notice.

Sue Halbich, Mariners Scuba Shop, Villa, St Vincent. Agent for several boats including a Bowman 46, a Freedom 33 and a Gulf Star 43 - semi bareboat charters a speciality, a cook can be arranged. Box 639 St Vincent, West Indies. Tel (809 45) 84228.

Barefoot Holidays, Blue Lagoon, St vincent. Agents for about 15 yachts. Box 39, St Vincent. tel: (809 45) 69334. telex:7506. Or through JRC travel, suite 1200, Toronto, Ontario, Canada M5B 2EC call 800 387 2647. telex:065 24228. Or BMIT, 149 Main st., Medway, Mass 02053. 800 343 6472/982 2299/ 617 533 6683. telex:710 346 6520.

Frangipani Yacht Services, Box 1, Bequia, St Vincent. Agents for boats from 25 to 70 feet semi- bareboat and skippered.

Anchorage Hotel, Union Island, St Vincent, W.I. Call: (809 45) 88221/ 84848/ 88328. telex: 7595 AYC VQ. Can arrange short term or longer charters on yachts out of Union Island.

Spice Island Marine, Box 449, St George's Grenada. Tel: (809 444) 4342, Can arrange day, weekend or longer charters. Yachts include Whistler a CT 47, semi bareboat.

Grenada Yacht Services (G.Y.S.) Box 183, St George's, Grenada. Telephone (809 440) 2883 or 2508. day and term charters on boats in Grenada.

U.K. AGENTS.

Camper and Nicholsons, 16 Regency Street, Westminster, SW1P4DD
Tel: 01 821 1641, telex 918078 NICLON G. Speak to Jennifer Brewis. About 200 boats in the Caribbean.
Caribcrewz, 98 Star Street, London W2 1QF Tel: 01 724 6582

Castlemain Marine, 71,Pavilion Road, Knightsbridge, London SW10ET.Tel: 01 235 9988. Telex 8955287 Castle G. Speak to Judith Hambridge. About 200 boats in the Caribbean.

Liz Fenner, World Wide Yachting Holidays, 35 Fairfax Place, London NW64EJ Tel 01-328-1033. Telex 262284 REF2641 attn Fenner. Small, personal agency, with about 50 carefully selected yachts in the Caribbean.

Halsey Marine Ltd., 22 Boston Place, Dorset Square, London NW1 6HZ. Tel:01 727 1303, telex:265131. About 200 yachts in the Caribbean.

U.S.A. AGENTS

Anne-Wallis White, 326 First Street, Annapolis, Maryland 21403, Tel:301 263 6366. Small personal agent, large range of skippered yachts all prices.

Bob Smith, Box 512, Larchmont, New York. NY 10538. Call: 914 834 1123. Small personal agent, large range crewed and bareboats.

Joanne Russell, Ste 15, 2750 Black Rock Turnpike, Fairfield, Ct.06430. Tel: 203 372 6633. Small personal

agent. Good range of middle priced yachts - has a fondness for the Windwards.
Lynne Jachney Charters inc., 1 Townhouse Square, 2nd floor, Marblehead, MA 01945. tel:617 639 0787 or 800 223 2050. telex:928013. fax:617 639 0216. 85 Boats ranging from 42 to 271 feet, $2400 to $84,000 per week. also bareboats.
Mary Crowley, Ocean Voyages, 1709 Bridgeway, Sausalito Ca.94965. Tel: 415 332 4681. Telex: 470-561 SAIL UI. Larger agency, very wide range of yachts, Mary has a fondness for old wooden boats as well as the new ones.

JOINING A CRUISE

Carib Islander. Caribbean Safari Tours Ltd., Beckwith Mall, Bridgetown, Barbados. Call: (809) 427 5100. tlex: WB. In Europe: Transatlantic Wings, 70 Pembroke Rd, London W8 6NX call: 01 602 4021 telex: 888788 CARIB G. In U.S.A. Donal Copeland, 535 5th Ave., suite 1604, New York 10017. call:800 223 1682/ 212 661 8900. In Canada: Air Canada Touram 350 Bloor Street, East Suite 403, Toronto, Ontario, Canada M4W 1H4. Call: 416 975 8000. telex:06218336. Or through St Lucia tour agents. 7 Day cruise $495-795.
Mary Crowley, Ocean Voyages, 1709 Bridgeway, Sausalito Ca.94965.
Tel: 415 332 4681. Telex: 470-561 SAIL UI. 7 and 14 day trips in the Grenadines on yachts.
Windjammer barefoot cruises (For Mandalay), Box 120, Miami Beach, Florida 33119. Call 305 534 7447. Or 800 432 3364 or 800 327 2601. 13 day cruise from $1300. 6 day from $750.
Peter Kouly (Vela Star).Box388, Castries, St Lucia. tel:25331-4 telex:6343LC

BOAT SHOW!
Sample accomodation plans of typical sailboats 39 to 47 feet for charter in the Windwards

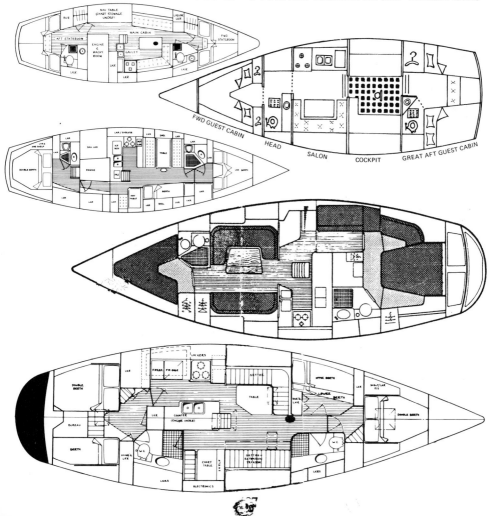

SCUBA DIVING

"It's fantastic - I could breathe underwater just like a fish, and they swam up and looked at me - what an incredible feeling".

"It's the greatest sensation I've ever felt - when we swam back with the current it was just like gliding through a beautiful garden!"

These are typical comments from first-time divers who usually agree diving is the most exciting thing they have ever done. No wonder, it is probably the closest most of us will ever come to visiting a strange planet, but not only that, underwater we are weightless, and actually seem to fly. Rather like birds we can soar, hover and dive down to see anything of interest - with a scooter it is even better; we can loop the loop or silently swoop through a rock arch.

The underwater world is full of wonders, tall soft waving plants that are really colonies of tiny animals, sponges looking like ancient urns in colors ranging from yellow to a psychedelic luminous blue. Huge schools of fish swim by unconcerned about one's presence. Little squids move by a kind of jet propulsion, turtles and gentle giant rays glide with elegant ease.

Yet many people are put off diving because they are under the impression it is complicated and difficult. Nothing could be further from the truth. With modern equipment diving is very simple, and with one of the popular "resort courses" you can be diving in half a day. In fact the only problem most divers have is to avoid boring their non-diving friends to distraction with tales of undersea adventure!

EQUIPMENT

Experienced divers will want to bring their own mask, fins, and possibly their own regulator. If one happens to have a really good comfortable B.C. (buoyancy compensator) it might just be worth bringing; as for the rest, forget it. There is no point in humping tanks and weight belts - far better to rent them here. Those with no equipment don't need to worry, the dive shops will supply all, and for the most part it is excellent, up-to-date gear. In many parts of the world one has to wear a protective "wet suit" against the cold - but in the Windwards the water is warm enough that for most of us this isn't necessary.

COURSES FOR LEARNERS

Anyone who just wants to give diving a go, can do so very quickly with a "resort course". It will only take one whole morning or afternoon. Firstly you get about a one hour talk which tells you in simple language what it is all about. Then, you get to try out the equipment in shallow water, and lastly you go for your first dive. A resort course only qualifies you to dive under the close supervision of an instructor. If you are staying in the same place, you will be able to keep going on dives with the instructor without further training, and if you keep a log book of your dives then you may find another instructor in another island willing to take you down. But once you go home and stop diving, you would have to take another course before you could start again. If you take to diving it is much better to become fully qualified.

CERTIFICATION

If you've ever thought about getting certified, or if you try a dive and like it, then it makes sense to get certified on your holiday. If you get certified at home the chances are that it will be in a swimming pool with nothing more interesting to look at than white walls, and if you can find open water experience it is unlikely to compare with the Caribbean. Furthermore you will probably have to buy or rent equipment which makes it unnecessarily expensive. In the Caribbean you can train at a cost not much greater than the dives alone. The course includes all equipment, you do everything in open water, the dives are fantastic, and you can take home a diving certificate as well as your memories. There are several diving associations who have accredited diving instructors who can train you and give you a certificate. These include P.A.D.I. and N.A.U.I. and they are equally good. A full diving course in the islands takes about 4 or 5 days, with a couple of hours instruction followed by a dive during which you increase your practical skills daily.

If you are staying in a hotel then check out the nearest dive shop. For those headed for the Grenadines either by yacht or ferry there is good news. You can learn as you go. Try a resort course in Bequia. You will almost certainly find yourself at Devils Table - an easy dive, but interesting enough to attract even aficionados. The rocks and coral start at 12 feet and roll down a hill to about 35 feet deep. You enter the water and feel a bit nervous, you breathe out and gently sink. Soon your attention turns outwards. Large pillar corals rise from among the rocks - they look fuzzy but as you brush them ever so lightly with your hand the tentacles withdraw leaving them rocklike. You stop to examine some pretty shells clinging to a waving sea fan, to your surprise a tiny damsel fish shoots up and tries to chase you away - he's protecting his patch, and you don't scare him - you find you can even laugh through your regulator! There is plenty more to see - brightly colored parrot fish and angel fish, Moray eels staring at you from the their holes, strange looking arrow crabs and brightly banded coral shrimp. You enjoyed it? Good! It can count as your first day towards full certification. Bequia by night is pleasant and the bars are fun, so maybe you stay for another dive or two there. Then new horizons call - over to Mustique and a different dive site, before sailing down to the Tobago Cays or Union to take a look at their brightly colored reefs. Finally, you could finish your training in St Vincent, whose spectacular wall, wreck and cave dives will send you back loaded with memories. You get the added bonus of different instructors and new dive sites all at the same cost. This is possible because DIVE BEQUIA, DIVE MUSTIQUE, SCUBA SAFARI (UNION,) and DIVE ST VINCENT work together so that for the customer they are just like one dive shop. You can select your own route and which dive areas you prefer.

FOR QUALIFIED DIVERS.

Some people, especially those chartering yachts, prefer to rent gear and go off diving by themselves. Others prefer to join a dive with the professional instructors. I recommend going with the dive instructors. They know all the good sites, the hidden caves, the special ledge where angel fish live, and maybe they know where there is a tame octopus, seahorse or frog fish. A good instructor is also a good guide and can often point out many things that would otherwise be missed and can greatly add interest to your dive. But perhaps the most important reason is that the good dive sites are often in places that you need a powerful dive boat rather than a dinghy to reach. I have worked with many charterers who have tried it both ways and noticed that those who went with dive instructors had a much better time then those who went on their own. If you plan a few dives, then nearly all dive shops offer economical "dive packages" and those yachting or ferrying around, can buy a "dive package" which can be spread out between Dive St Vincent, Dive Bequia, Dive Mustique and Scuba Safari.

Further north in Anse La Raye one finds the wreck of Lesleen M, a 165 foot freighter sunk in 1986 as a marine park dive site. It is already well encrusted with corals and supports many fish. (30-65 feet.). These are just a few of the many St Lucia dives.

MARTINIQUE

All along the coast from Grand Anse D'Arlet to Diamond Rock. Plenty of coral and small fish, Diamond Rock is an exciting wall dive. St Pierre offers very exciting diving with the wrecks of 12 ships that sunk during the volcanic eruption in 1902 that completely destroyed the town. Further north there are several good dives with plenty of big fish.

I feel diving in Martinique needs special mention, as many people who have learned in England or the States have anxieties about the gear - as the French sometimes do things a bit differently. The French often learn to dive without pressure gauges, using instead an air reserve. This is safe enough if you learn this way, however they realise it is unacceptable to most Americans and ALL the dive stations below have pressure gauges either as a matter of course or on demand. Instead of B.C.'s the French often use a separate life jacket, which, like a B.C. is attached to the tank and can be inflated on demand. Some keep B.C.'s for U.S. clients. The French do not use double regulators, which are now becoming standard further south, but gear is so reliable this is really not all that important. All the gear I looked at was in good condition. If you have never dived before in Martinique initial lessons and pool training are often provided free. I have occasionally heard "know it all" dive masters further south making derogatory comments about French diving - don't take them too seriously. The French invented scuba and they are still pretty good at it!

I went with "Bathy's" at the Meridien hotel - they dive every day at 2 p.m. going to different sites each day. I joined their large power cruiser and we went out towards Cap Salomon and anchored close to shore. The visibility was clear, and there were many canyons and large rocks interwoven with sand. We explored a little cave, surfacing deep in the rock hidden from shore. Back outside we visited giant sponges, and played with the largest variety of sea urchins I've ever seen, including one huge white one who ran around in a positively speedy fashion! There were plenty of fish from small brightly coloured reef fish to schools of ballyhoo. This was their "initiation" dive site - a very suitable and pretty place. As we motored back we all got to know each other over a little "Petit Punch".

The French certainly know how to enjoy themselves! Large comfortable cabin cruisers are often used as dive boats, and Planet Bleu for example, offers whole day trips which include lunch, maybe some shore activity (if diving at St Pierre, a visit to the museum), and a couple of dives. Then after a good day, out comes the bottle of Martinique white rum and you toast the day's activities!

DIVE STATIONS

(Prices are in $U.S., rentals daily unless otherwise stated. Dive prices include equipment unless otherwise specified.

GRENADA

HMC DIVING CENTER. With 4 locations: Ramada Renaissance. tel:444 4371-4 (fax444 4800). Coyaba. tel:444 4129. Spice Island Inn tel:444 4528. GYS. tel: 440 2508. also vhf ch 16. directors: Hamilton Mosden Cumberbatch and Jim Concannon. resort course:$75. single dive:$35. two tank dive:$50. night dive:$40. full certification:$250. scuba gear:$30. tank only:$10. refill:$5. cc:VISA, AM.EX.

VIRGO WATER SPORTS. location: Horseshoe Beach Hotel. tel:444 4410/4244. also vhf ch 16. manager:Hans Dijkman. resort course:$65. single dive:$30. two tank dive:$45. night dive:$35. full certification:$325. scuba gear:30. tank only:$10 refill:$5. package holidays from $499 inclusive accommodation. contact I.T.R. cc:VISA, AM.EX.

UNION ISLAND

ANCHORAGE YACHT CLUB. location:Clifton Union, at hotel. manager:Glenroy Adams. tel:(809 45) 88221/84848/88328. VHF ch 68 resort course:$60. single dive:$40. two tank dive:$65. night dive:$50. full certification:$300. scuba gear rental:NO. tank only:$10. refill$5. .cc:VISA, AM.EX.

SCUBA SAFARI. location: Clifton, Union, on the beach. manager:Derek Posner and Marie La Mare. tel:(809 45) 88313. VHF ch 68 resort course:$60. single dive:$40. two tank dive:$65. night dive:$50. full certification:$300. scuba gear rental:NO. tank only:$10. refill$5. cc:VISA

CANOUAN

CANOUAN DIVING CLUB. location:Canouan Beach Hotel. manager:Frank Augustin. tel:(809 45) 84413 VHF ch 68. resort course:$45. single dive:$45. two tank dive:$67. night dive:OA. full certification:NO. scuba gear rental:NO. tank only:$10. refill:$5

ADMIRALTY BAY, BEQUIA

DIVE BEQUIA. manager:Bob Sachs. location:Sunny Caribbee Plantation House Hotel, tel:(809 45) 83504. VHF ch 16, 68 resort course:$60. single dive:$40. two tank dive:$65. night dive:$50. full certification:$300. scuba gear rental:$125 Per Week. tank only:$10. refill:$5. Combined diving holidays on application to Sunny Caribbee Plantation House Hotel.cc:VISA

SUNSPORTS. manager:Nancy Boake. location: Frangipani Clubhouse, Admiralty Bay, Bequia. tel:(809 45) 83577 VHF ch68. resort course:$60. single dive:$40. two tank dive:$65. night dive:$50. full certification:$300. scuba gear rental:$25. tank only:$10. refill:$5. combined diving holidays on application to Frangipani Hotel. cc:VISA

FRIENDSHIP BAY, BEQUIA

BEQUIA BEACH CLUB. manager:Tomas Hess. location: Freindship Bay, tel:(809 45) 83248. resort course:$165(Includes 4 Dives). single dive:$35. two tank dive:$65. night dive:$35. full certification:$300. scuba gear rental:$40 Per Day. tank only:$10. refill:$5

FRIENDSHIP BAY HOTEL. location:Friendship Bay, tel:(809 45) 83222. Plan new dive shop For Comming Year.

MUSTIQUE

DIVE MUSTIQUE. manager:Lesley Dunning. location: Cotton House, tel:(809 45) 64777 EXT426 VHF ch 16, 68. resort course:$60. single dive:$40. two tank dive:$65. night dive:$50. full certification:$300. scuba gear rental:$125 per week. tank only:$10. refill:$5

ST VINCENT

DIVE ST VINCENT. manager:Bill Tewes. tel:74714. resort course:$60. single dive:$40. two tank dive:$65. night dive:$45. full certification:$300. scuba gear:$24. tank only:$7. refill:$5. cc:VISA, AM.EX. package holidays from $450 inclusive of accomodation. contact:Bill Tewes.

MARINERS SCUBA SHOP, BOX 639, STV. manager:Sue Halbich. tel:84228. resort course:$OA. single dive:$OA. two tank dive:$OA. night dive:$OA. full certification:$OA. scuba gear:$125 per week. tank only:$10. refill:$5. cc:VISA, AM.EX

ST LUCIA

ANSE CHASTANET. manager:Nick Troobitscoff. location:Anse Chastanet, Soufriere. tel:47354/5. resort course:$50. single dive:$25 (regulator and BC extra $16). two tank dive:$50 (+$16 reg and BC). night dive:$50. full certif-ication:$325(includes 4 open water dives). scuba gear rental:about $20 a day. tank only:$6. refill:$5. cc:VISA, AM.EX. DINERS.

MARIGOT BAY RESORT, location Marigot Bay tel:34246, to re-open before the 88-89 season.

MARTINIQUE

(Prices in French francs) - Some English spoken in all dive stations

BATHY'S, Meridien Hotel, Trois Ilets. manager:Christine Formanino. location:Meridien Hotel. tel:66 00 00. resort course:ff:250. single dive:ff:250. two tank dive:NO. night dive:NO. full certification:NO. scuba gear rental:NO. tank only:NO. refill:ff:40. cc:VISA, CB, M.CARD.

CARIB SCUBA CLUB. manager:Michel Metery. location:Grain D'Or, Carbet. tel:78 02 27. resort course:ff:200. single dive:ff:150. night dive:ff:150. full certification:ff:800. scuba gear rental:ff:OA. tank only:ff:OA. refill:ff:30. cc:NO.

PLANET BLEU, Trois Ilets. location:Power Yacht in the marina. tel:66 08 79. resort course:ff:200. single dive:ff200. night dive:ff:200. full certification:OA. scuba gear rental:NO. tank only:NO. refill ff:40. cc:NO. English spoken. Dive price reduction after the first two. Special excursion to St Pierre etc, includes twin tank dive, lunch etc. ff:470.

TROPICASUD, 97233 Schoelcher. manager:Dominique. 3 Locations. St Pierre tel:77 15 02. Hotel La Batelerie (Scheoelcher) tel:77 15 02 ext 188 (Gilbart Prevot). Club Marouba (Le Carbet) tel: 78 01 88 (Ronald). resort course:ff:200. single dive:ff200. night dive:ff:200. full certification:ff:1150. scuba gear rental:ff:250. tank only:ff:130. refill:ff:40. cc:NO

Also **Polymar** (Quaie Ouest, tel:70 62 88 and Ship Shop (Rue Joseph Compere, Fort de France, tel:71 43 40) and Marina Ship (Marina Pte du Bout tel:66 04 25) are Scubapro agents and can fill tanks as does Accastillage Diffusion (Rue Ernest Deproge, 70 26 69).

HOUSE RENTALS IN THE WINDWARDS

Hotels are not for everyone - there are those who prefer the independence, economy and privacy of renting a house -this can be particularly good for family groups, and the only way for people wanting to stay a long time. However, as your travel agent is unlikely to have a list of prospective houses, you will have to make some calls on your own account!

Caribbean renting can in fact offer as much service as a hotel. Many properties come complete with staff, and if they don't it can be arranged. You can have someone to clean, cook do the laundry, and some of the more luxurious properties even have chauffeurs and butlers! Baby sitters can be arranged which makes it great for those with young children. There are all kinds of different properties available from small holiday villas to huge mansions.

In many islands now one is beginning to see hotel/villa complexes, where you rent a villa but have the amenities of a hotel - examples include Cinnamon Hill in Grenada, Marigot de Roseaux and the new Windjammer Landings in St Lucia. Most rental properties are rented by the week or month and a week is really the minimum time to think of when going this route - the choice is enormous, and all you have to get the ball rolling is call some of the numbers listed below!

BUYING IN THE WINDWARDS

It happens to all of us sometime, we go off on holiday, fall in love with a country, and start dreaming about having that second home or retiring there - everyone back home thinks we are crazy, but then how do they know, they have never seen just how wonderful it all is! Buying in the Windwards is not really all that hard.

Martinique is like buying in France. This means that for anyone from the EEC it is easy, and for others, buying the property may be easy, but there will be legal requirements for permenant residence (best arranged through a local lawyer).

Although St Lucia, St Vincent and Grenada are all seperate and independent at the moment (integration may come), they share similar attitudes towards foreign ownership. Basically ownership of personal property is encouraged, but speculation is discouraged. This is done as follows; in order to own property you must get a land holding license. This usually takes a few months and is best done by a local lawyer. There are various purchase taxes on buying real estate which run from about 5 -10%. If you buy land you will be expected to build on it within a reasonable time (up to about 3 years). Finally there will be annual property taxes which are generally reasonable.

Land values have fluctuated in the different islands - Grenada's have bounced up down the most along with her political fortunes, both St Vincent and St Lucia have shown a steady increase in value that has at least kept up with inflation. However, the thing to keep in mind is that the market in any island is small and while a good sale can usually be arranged, this may take years rather than weeks or months, depending on the state of the market, so you would not want to be in a position where you might have to sell in a hurry! While some property has leapfrogged in value, buying in the Windwards is best entered in a spirit of fun rather than profit.

The choice between buying land and

building, or buying ready built, is a difficult one. When you build yourself you can build your own dreams, on the other hand a second hand house is ready and you know how much it costs. There is no question building can be either fun or a real headache depending on your attitude! I built in Grenada, acted as my own amateur architect and master builder with two men to help with the labor. It was a lot of fun - though the resultant house, while interesting, took me some 15 years to sell! Local labor can be really excellent, but it is much better to work through a proper builder as one needs to know how to get on with the local people, as the the following story illustrates. A friend of mine called Tyson is a first rate carpenter. He was employed on a project, but to earn extra money he had outside work running at the same time. Each time his boss left the site he would whip out the extra job he was doing and put as much time as he dared into it, making sure the boss never saw him. One day the boss called out "Come here Tyson". He went up to the boss and stood a respectful distance away. "No, come closer Tyson" He took a few hesitant steps forward. "Kiss me Tyson". Tyson begun to wonder whether his boss was quite sane - "how do you mean sir?". "I said kiss me Tyson - everyone likes to be kissed when they are getting screwed, and you are screwing me royally!"

There is endless desirable property in the Windwards, and it is quite possible to buy a deserted bay or mountainside off the beaten track. However, phones and electricity could be a problem, and unless you are going to live there all the time, you may prefer somewhere that can be easily looked after while you are away, and perhaps rented out, which could cover your running costs.

If this is a consideration then it is best to buy in the areas where rental property is in high demand and there is someone who can look after it for you. Areas that fall into this category include L'Anse Aux Epines,

True Blue, Fort Jeudy and Westerhall in Grenada, In St Vincent and the Grenadines, the south coast of St Vincent Mustique or Bequia, and in St Lucia such areas as Cap Estate and Rodney Bay in the north, some areas around La Toc and Marigot on the west coast, and Anse Chastanet down in Soufriere.

The hassle free way is to buy in one of the managed holiday villa projects, which are geared to renting the property in your absence - examples include the Marigot de Roseaux project in Marigot and the brand new Windjammer Landings project in Labrolette Bay (both in St Lucia).

How do you go about looking? There are quite a number of lawyers who handle property for clients and there are the large development estates, such as Fort Jeudy in Grenada, The Mustique Company in Mustique and Cap Estate or Rodney Bay in St Lucia. There are also many independent agents who have a broad idea of what is available from houses to private land, to the lands held by development companies.

REAL ESTATE AGENTS
GRENADA (AREA CODE 809)

BAIN AND BETRAND, Lagoon Road, Box 262, St George's, Grenada tel:440 2848. Sale, management and rental of property.

BYER'S REAL ESTATE AGENCY, Morne Jaloux, Grenada. tel:443 5205. property sales.

PROPERTY MANAGEMENT, Box 218, St George's, . tel:440 1896/ 444 4462. telex:3431 CWBURGA. Registered International Real Estate Institute. Sells and rents properties.

SMITH ENTERPRISES, Box 247, Grenada. tel:444 4519/4199. telex:GA3431SMITH ENT. Sale and rental of all types of property.

THOMPSON, Box 188, Grenada. tel:440 2198/3422. telex:4342GA GRENTHOM. Sale of land overlooking Westerhall, Fort Jeudy and Calivigny.

WESTERHALL FORT JEUDY DEVELOPMENT CO, Box 263, Grenada. tel:440 2883. Sale and rental of land and houses mainly in Westerhall Fort Jeudy.

ST.VINCENT (AREA CODE 809 45)

A.C. HILLOCK AGENCIES, Box 63, St Vincent. tel:71181/ 61242. Property sales and rentals.

BERTRAM A ARTHUR, Box 264, St Vincent. tel:71228. Property sales.

JOACHIM HOME SERVICES, Box 600, St Vincent. tel:72797. Property rental, sales and management.

JOAN STOWE, Box 5, Bequia, St Vincent, tel:83223. Cottage and house rentals in Bequia.

LAVINIA GUNN, Box 126, St Vincent tel:71513. rental of private house in Bequia.

THE MUSTIQUE CO. Box 349, St Vincent tel:84621. Sale and rentals in Mustique.

REAL ESTATE INTERNATIONAL, Box 569, St Vincent tel:84284. Sale of property and some apartments to rent.

ST VINCENT AND GRENADINES REALTY CO., Box 599 St Vincent, or Box 33, Bequia St Vincent tel:83594/71513. sales and rental in St Vincent and Bequia.

SPROTT REAL ESTATE AGENCIES, Box 82, St Vincent tel:61647/ 84037. Sale of property.

SPRING PLANTATION, Bequia tel:83414. sale of land in Spring

ST LUCIA (AREA CODE 809-45)

CAP ESTATE, Box 328, castries, St Lucia. tel:28522. sale of preperty in Cap Estate.

HOME SERVICES LTD, Box 262, Castries, St Lucia. tel:20450. Sale, rental and management all types of property, and valuations. (fax 20071).

JULIEN HUNTE AND CO, Box 64 Castries, St Lucia. tel:22239. Property sale and rental.

RODNEY BAY LTD, Box 372, Castries, St Lucia. tel:28444. Sale of property in Rodney Bay

RODNEY BAY MARINA, Box 1538, Castries, St Lucia. tel:23024. Sale of property in Rodney Bay south of the marina

THE LANDING, Box 1504, Castries, St Lucia. tel:21041. sale of villas in the Landing Resort

TROPICAL RESORTS LTD., Castries St Lucia. tel:20460/28658. Rental of villas in the landing development.

TROPICAL VILLAS, Box 189 Castries, St Lucia. tel:28240. Rental of houses, emphasis on the large luxurious ones.

MARTINIQUE (AREA CODE 596)

MARCEL BOULLANGER, 10 Rue Joseph Compere, 97200 Fort de France, Martinique. tel:71 74 79

IMMOBILIERE ANTILLAISE, 9 Lotisment Bardinet, 97200 Fort de France, Martinique. tel;63 34 30

SOLUTION IMMOBILIERE, 32 Rue Shoelcher, 97200 Fort de France, Martinique. tel:63 09 77. Sales, rentals.

SARL MIG. 97200 Fort de France, Martinique. tel:63 15 22. Sales, rentals, property management.

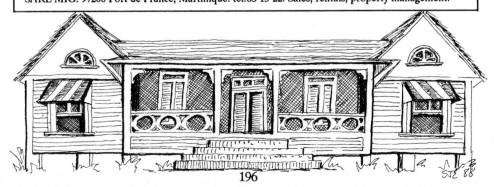

EXOTIC TROPICAL FOOD

One of the best ways to experience local foods is to eat out. This way you don't have to slave over the stove and best of all - no dishes to wash up. In this section we are going to introduce you to some of the wonderful local fruits and vegetables, as well as some ideas about sea food and locally obtainable meat. Those who cook for themselves will find recipes, for those who prefer to eat out, we will make some suggestions. But we cannot start without a drink in our hand, so why not make:

SKIPPERS RUM PUNCH. Mix: the juice from 3 limes, 1/4 cup of Grenadine syrup, 1 cup of brown rum with one liter of juice (orange, pineapple, or maybe local passion fruit). Serve with a lot of ice and liberally grate some fresh nutmeg on top.

We are not really going to be delving much into drinks, but for those who have a blender we should mention "smoothies". These are made by taking the flesh of any suitable local fruit (try mango, banana, guava, pawpaw, pineapple or soursop,) adding a good slosh of rum, a good measure of ice then blend. You can add lime or orange juice for flavor, and you can try combinations. An evening of research should produce your favorite concoction, and leave you so contented and full of fruit you will probably be able to skip dinner!

We should also mention the Caribbean's very own natural soft drink: Coconut water. If you are driving around the countryside, or even wandering around town you will probably see a home made barrow by the side of the road stocked high with green coconuts. These are "water-nuts" - young coconuts that have not yet developed a hard inner brown husk or firm white flesh, but are full of a delicious tasting liquid. The vendor will slice off the top of the nut for you - it now ready for you to drink, straight from the shell. As with any other soft drink, coconut water works as a "mixer" and can be spiced with a squeeze of lime.

COMMENTS ON EATING OUT

Eating out anywhere, even in the most international of restaurants will give you some idea of local food, because they will almost certainly use the local vegetables, seafood and fruits. But it is also worth trying some of the inexpensive local restaurants. You can be offered amazing fare - my favorite to date is "Chair broiled SirLion steak"! It would be a terrible mistake to eat steak in such a restaurant, though they often do excellent curries and creole style specialties, and Pepper Pot. I usually go for Lambi (Conch). This is firm white flesh from a large sea shell, and absolutely delicious. Soups are generally excellent in all restaurants, desserts better in the more expensive ones.

Those who go down to the Windwards and eat hamburgers deserve whatever they get. Much better to eat as the locals do and have a "roti" which is the ideal lunch-time snack.

A roti is curry wrapped in a wheat flour tortilla-like shell. It usually comes in three flavors: beef, chicken and conch. The chicken roti is often made from "back and neck" and full of bones; locals love to chew on them, but for others this can be an acquired taste. In the more expensive restaurants chicken rotis may be "boneless".

Mountain streams produce wonderful fresh water crayfish. These will occasionally appear in an inexpensive restaurant, but more often in a really good one. Nearly everyone offers lobster in season. Lobster is delicious, delicate and easy to ruin. The practice of many restaurants to "parboil" lobster, freeze it, then broil to serve, all too often produces something dry, chewy and tasteless. To be on the safe side only eat lobster at a restaurant where you can "select your own" alive and fresh from a pool.

A FEW THINGS TO KNOW

Grenada is the world's second largest nutmeg producer. Buy some fresh nutmegs as soon as possible. You will find them in the market and in boutiques, not only in Grenada but also in the other Windwards. If possible buy them as a "kit" with a little grater. The outer hard dark brown husk must be removed before grating! Nutmeg is not only essential for rum punch but excellent at spicing up deserts, pancakes, french toast and some vegetables...

In the market and the supermarket you can buy something locally called "Saffron", it is in fact TURMERIC - a root which can be brought fresh or grated. It is good in curries and for colouring rice. True Saffron

(made from crocus) is expensive and only to be found in the bigger supermarkets.

If you are in St Vincent and the Grenadines, look out for their wonderful peanuts, which are dry roasted and packed in old beer bottles! In Grenada you will find similarly packed local cashew nuts, also delicious.

Grenada's Spice Island Coffee is a superb, dark roast, freshly ground coffee.

EXOTIC TROPICAL VEGETABLES AND STAPLES.

(We do not mention the many vegetables - e.g. tomatoes, sweet pepper, cucumbers and beans - you will be familiar with from home. Cooking suggestions and recipes assume basic cooking knowledge).

COCONUTS are nutritious and cheap - coconut milk (not be confused with the water) is used in a lot of Caribbean cooking, much as one would use cream where cows are more plentiful than palm trees. *To make coconut milk, you need an older "flesh nut" - one of the brown ones you buy in the market. Grate the flesh, add any water from the nut, and add ordinary water till it is covered. Leave it for a few minutes, then squeeze the flesh into the water. Throw out the flesh, and the liquid you are now left with is the milk.*

BREADFRUIT, plentiful and inexpensive year round, is a savior to the cruiser or traveller man on a budget. It is green, balloon sized, pocked and hard. Originally from the Pacific it was imported here by Captain Bligh, but arrived late because of the mutiny. Watch it carefully or it will cause you grief too - It remains nice and firm for a day or two, but when it decides to go soft and rotten it can do so almost as quickly as Bligh could order a keel hauling. Best to cook it first and store after. Boil it (40 minutes in an ordinary pot or pressure cook for 10), or bake it in the oven (about 40 minutes). It will now store for quite some days in an ice box or fridge. Treat it like potato - mash it, cut slices off and fry it, use it in salad or stews. Mash it together with an egg and some cooked fish, season then fry to make wonderful fish cakes. Buy one for a barbecue, and cook it on the embers of a dying fire till you can slide a thin sliver of wood from opposite the stem up into the center. Cut it open and serve with salt, pepper and lashings of butter. Try making it like mashed potato, but mash with coconut milk instead of ordinary milk, cover with grated cheese and brown.

CALALOU - an 'elephant ear' shaped green leaf, grows on wet ground such as the banks of a small stream. Plentiful year round and inexpensive, available as bundles of leaves or in bags chopped and prepared for cooking. If you get the leaves it is necessary to remove the skin from the stem and off the center vein. Always boil Calalou for 35 minutes. Eating it raw, under-cooked, or badly prepared has much the same effect on your mouth and throat as one imagines chewing on raw fiberglass would. The discomfort is temporary. Calalou makes a wonderful soup and if you do not cook it for yourself, eat it in a restaurant at the first available opportunity. To use Calalou as a vegetable just boil it with a little salt for at least 30 minutes, it boils down to very little.

CALALOU SOUP - 1/2 lb chopped bacon, 1 pint of water, 1/4 lb peeled shrimp, 2 bunches of prepared calalou (about 1 lb). 5 sliced okras, 1 sliced onion, 1/2oz butter, salt, pepper, garlic, thyme and hot sauce to taste.

Fry the bacon and onion in butter, drain off excess fat. Add Calalou, okras, water and seasoning. Boil for 40 minutes then add peeled shrimp. Cook a little longer and serve. For thicker soup, blend then serve.

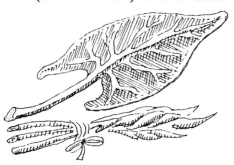

PLANTAINS. To the uninitiated these look just like bananas, but try putting one in a banana daquiari and you will soon know the difference! - Ask the market ladies to make sure you are getting what you want! Plantains have less sugar than bananas, and taste awful raw, but when ripe, split down the middle and fried (a couple of minutes on each side) or baked whole (about half an hour), they are delicious. Plantains perfectly complement any kind of fish.

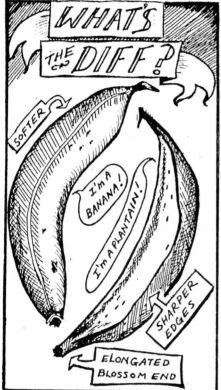

PUMPKIN. The local pumpkin is green streaked with white, and has an orange red pulp that is more akin to butter nut squash than the "halloween" pumpkin. It keeps a long time unopened, and is both versatile and tasty. Remove the seeds before cooking. Boil or bake till soft and serve with butter, or boil and mash with seasoning and a little orange juice. If you want to make a meal out of a pumpkin, slice it longways down the middle and bake it. While it is cooking fry together onion, christophene, tomato and any left-overs

you might have, melt in quarter of a pound of cream cheese. and stuff the cooked pumpkin with this mixture. Pumpkin makes a delicious soup. Try it in a restaurant or make it yourself.

WEST INDIAN PUMPKIN SOUP. 1 small pumpkin, 1 chopped onion, 1 tablespoon of butter, 1 chicken stock cube, 1/2 pint of fresh cream (or two cans of cream) 1/4 of a glass of white wine. Salt, pepper, grated nutmeg. Skin and seed the pumpkin and chop into small cubes. Lightly saute the onions in butter till cooked. Add pumpkin, stock cube and a minimum of water, boil using a lid. When soft, blend or sieve. Add the cream and wine, flavor with salt, pepper and nutmeg to taste. If too thick, thin with milk or water.

AVOCADO. Local avocados are absolutely delicious, and reason enough to come down in the summer (available June to November, but peak season around August and September). Never store them with citrus. They can be eaten as they are flavored with a little salt and lime juice, or stuffed with mayonnaise and shrimp etc. If they get a little over-ripe, mash them with lime, finely chopped onion and seasoning. This makes an ideal "dip" to enjoy with your sunset drink.

OKRA - a spear shaped green pod with slimy green seeds. Avoid the large ones which tend to be fibrous. They tend to be somewhat slimy if boiled, much less so if sliced and fried. Good in soups.

SWEET POTATO - a local potato which is sweet and tasty - takes a little longer to cook (about 30 minutes). Nice with pork. Try mashing it with a little orange juice.

EDDO, TANNIA, YAM. These are an assortment of brown hairy roots. They can be a bit dry, though mashing with oodles of butter and milk helps. Ask the ladies in the market for suggestions.

CHRISTOPHENE is ridged, pear shaped, comes either green or white and grows on a vine. Somewhat bland in flavor, it makes an excellent vegetable dish, or may be added to curries or stews. One should peel it and remove the seed. This is best done under water, or with very wet hands, otherwise it leaves a mess on your hands that gives the impression your skin is peeling off. It is good just boiled with salt, pepper and butter, it is even better put in a white cheese sauce. It may also be used raw as a salad ingredient.

TROPICAL FRUITS.
(these may be eaten raw or combined in a fruit salad).

PAW PAW (Papaya) - a lush tropical fruit that contains a digestive enzyme, making it an ideal desert. It starts green and is ready to eat when it turns yellow and becomes slightly soft. It is available year round but delicate and hard to store, it must be eaten the same day it becomes ready. Slice like a melon and remove the seeds, add a squeeze of lime to flavor.

CITRUS (oranges, grapefruit, tangerines, etc.) occur mainly in the winter. The quality varies from absolutely superb to dry and unusable. When you are shopping, buy one from the market lady to "try" - she will open it with a knife for you to taste. This is the only way to tell how good they are. Oranges are usually green in colour. This is how the local ones come, despite the outside colour the inside is orange and ready to eat. Limes are generally available year round - they are essential for making rum punch, flavoring fish etc.

GUAVA - Available July to December. A green-yellow fruit a little bigger than a golf ball. They may be eaten raw, are excellent stewed with sugar. They are used locally to make a delicious sweet called "Guava cheese".

CASHEW FRUIT (French Cashew, Plumrose) - available June to August. Pink fruit with a white flesh. Do not peel, but remove the stone. Delicious when chilled, good in fruit salad.

PINEAPPLE. These are available for most of the year, and very inexpensive in Martinique - harder to come by and more costly elsewhere. Local pineapples can be absolutely delicious. Test for ripeness by pulling on a central leaf - if it pulls out

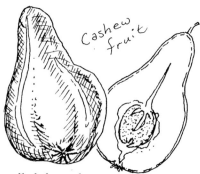

Cashew fruit

easily it is ready.

PASSION FRUIT. Available May to November. A small yellow fruit with a slightly crinkly skin and very strong flavor. Makes an excellent drink and locally made passion fruit juice is usually available in the supermarkets.

BANANAS (available year round) - It is worth mentioning that local bananas, which are naturally ripened, are delicious. As well as the "normal" banana, there are many other similar looking fruit some of which are good eaten raw, and some of which need cooking. Consult your market lady! "Eating" bananas make excellent desserts, try the following:

SKIPPER'S BANANA FLAMBE (for 4) 4 bananas, 1/2 cup of dark rum, 1/2 cup fresh orange juice, 2 tablespoons brown sugar, a slosh of white rum or vodka. seasoning of nutmeg, cinnamon and allspice. Split the bananas in two and put in a frying pan, add the brown rum and orange juice, sprinkle on the sugar and spices, simmer for about 5 minutes. Pour on the white rum and ignite (if vodka, you will have to warm gently in a pan first).

BANANAS CELESTE from Leyritz Plan-

all the Visa group including Master Card, Euro Card, Barclaycard and Carte Bleu. A = American express. nf=not fixed (in this case 10% tipping is normal). Unless otherwise specified assume a government tax of 5%. inc=included. ac=air-conditioning For full postal address add:Bequia, St Vincent and the Grenadines, West Indies. Tax, service or extras must be added to the rate.

BEQUIA BEACH CLUB, tel:83248. Telex:no. Mgr:Heather Culzac. No of rooms:10. cc: A. Agent:Bruno Fink, Mozartstrasse 20, D7261 Deckenpfronn. Tel:(germany 07056 2655). Year round.D:hb$68. Service:10%.

CRESCENT BEACH LODGE, Box 33, tel:83400. Mgr:Cardinal Simon. No of rooms:3. cc:no agent:Georgetown travel. Year round.S:bed$30 year round.D:bed$40. For fb add $25 pp per day. Service:10%.

FRANGIPANI HOTEL, Box 1,tel:83244/ 83255. Mgr:Marie Kingston. No of rooms:12. cc: V, A. HSSbb$35-55 HSD.bb$40-80 LSS.bb$20-40 LSD.bb$30-55. Service:10%. facilities:.Tennis, scuba, sailboards etc.

FRIENDSHIP BAY RESORT, Box 9, tel:83222. Telex:7483 FRIENBAY VQ. Owner:Joanne and Eduardo Guadagnino. No of rooms:27. cc: V, A. Agent:Ralph Locke, HSShb$85-135 HSD.hb$150-200 LSS.hb$75-100 LSD.hb$85-150. Off season 8 day packages available from $500 per person per week. Service:10%. facilities:.Tennis, scuba, windurfers etc.

JULIES GUEST HOUSE, Box 12, tel: 83304. Mgr:Isola McIntosh. No of rooms:25. cc:no Year round.S :hb$17-21 year round.D:hb$38-38. Service:nf tax:inc.

KEEGANS GUEST HOUSE, Lower Bay, tel:83254/ 83530 Mgr:Grace John. No of rooms:7. cc:no. Agent:no. Year round.S:hb$17-20. Year round double:hb$24-36. Service:10%.

LOWER BAY GUEST HOUSE, tel:83675. Mgr:Seton Simmons. No of rooms:9. cc:no. Year round.S:bb$16 year round double:bb$25. Service:10%.

MITCHELL'S GUEST HOUSE, Box 17, tel:83370. Mgr:Papa Mitchie. No of rooms:7. cc:no. Agent:no. Year round.S:bed$7-8 year round.D.bed$14-16. 4 person apartment also available. Service:nf tax:inc.

OLD FIG TREE, Box 14, tel:83201. Mgr:Adlene and Geoff Wallace. No of rooms:6. cc:no. Agent:no. HSSbed15$ HSD.bed$25 LSS.bed$12 LSD.bed$25. Service:10%.

SPRING ON BEQUIA, tel:83414. Telex:7557 SPRING. Mgr:Candy and Rosie Leslie. No of rooms:10. cc: V, A. Agent:Spring on Bequia, Box 19251, Minneapolis, Minnesota 55419. Tel:612 823 1202/ 9225 HSS.bed$85 HSD.bed$125 LSS.bed$60 LSD.bed$90. For hb add $25 pp per day. Service:10%.

SUNNY CARIBBEE PLANTATION HOUSE, tel:83425 (fax#809 4583612). Telex:7500 cw agency VQ SUNNY CARIBBEE. Mgr:Jaques Ducau. No of rooms:12. cc: V, A. Agent:Unique Hotels Worldwide, HSS. bb$40-50 hb$60-90 HSD.bb$50-110 hb$90-150 LSS. bb$30-50 hb$50-70 LSD.bb$40-70 hb$80-110. Special VIP and honeymoon packages available from $870 per couple per week. Service:12%. facilities:tennis, scuba.

SELF-CONTAINED ACCOMODATIONS

ST VINCENT AND GRENADINES REALTY, tel:83679. Will book house rentals, charter boats, hotels and guest houses. Agent:Georgetown Travel, Lichfield Landing, Pawley's Island, S.C.29585 U.S.A. Tel:803 237 8487

FRIENDSHIP COTTAGES, Mrs Joan Stowe, Box 5,Tel:83223. cc:no, 3 cottages, 2, two bedroom, 1 three bedrom, fully furnished with porch. Maid and rental car available. Rates oa.

LAVINIA GUNN, Box 126, St Vincent, tel:71513/ 84224. Quality 3 bedroom holiday home in Friendship Bay.

RESTAURANTS

All rates in EC. Dollars. Unless otherwise stated they include a three course meal and half the bottle price of the cheapest wine, or if more appropriate, two beers. cc=credit card information - V includes all the Visa group - Master Card, Barclaycard, Europcard, Carte Blue etc. Service nf. Means not fixed - normally one would tip around 10%. Inc means it is included in the price. P.E. means Port Elizabeth.

BEQUIA BEACH CLUB. Friendship Bay, Mgr:Heather Culzac. Tel:83248. Price:$36-56. Service:nf. Tax:inc cc::A. Food:local, German, international.

CLUBHOUSE. P.E Mgr:Marie Kingston. Tel:83577. Vhf.Ch 68. reasonably priced plates and snacks. Service:10%. Tax:inc cc:V, A.

CRESCENT BEACH LODGE Industry Mgr:Cardinal Simon. Tel:83400.inexpensive snacks and plates. Service:10%. Tax:5%. cc:no.

DAPHNE'S. P.E., Mgr:Daphne Grant. Tel:83271. Price:$35, more for lobster. Service:nf. Tax:inc. cc:no. Food:creole.

DE REEF. Lower Bay, Mgr:Sylvester Simmons. Tel:83203. inexpensive local snacks/plates, seafood. Service:nf. Tax:inc cc:no.

FRANGIPANI. P.E.. Mgr:Marie Kingston. Tel:83244/55. Vhf.Ch 68 . Price:$36-54. Thursday night barbecue $45 without drinks. Service:10%. Tax:inc. cc:V, A.

FRIENDSHIP BAY HOTEL. Friendship Bay, Mgr:Joanne and Eduardo Guadagnino. Tel:83222. Vhf.Ch 68. Price:$53-66 light lunches available. Service:10%. Tax:5%. cc:V.

GREEN BOLEY. Belmont. Owner:Lyston Williams. Tel:83247. rotis/plates. Service:nf. Tax:inc. cc:no

HARPOON SALOON. P.E., Mgr:Novita Cambridge. Tel:83272. Vhf.Ch 16, 68. Price:$22-44, inexpensive snacks available. Service:nf. Tax:inc. cc:V, A. Food:local, pizzas.

JULIES GUEST HOUSE P.E., Mgr:Isola McIntosh. Tel:83304. Vhf.Ch 68. Price:$30-34. Lunch plates $6-12 service:nf. Tax:inc. cc:no. Food:local.

KEEGANS GUEST HOUSE. Lower Bay, Mgr:Grace John. Tel:83254/ 83530. Price:about$23 with beers snacks available. Service:nf. Tax:inc. cc:no food:local.

LOWER BAY GUEST HOUSE. Lower Bay, Mgr:Seton Simmons. Tel:83675. Price:$25-35. Service:nf. Tax:inc. cc:no food:local.

MACS PIZZERIA . P.E., Mgr:Judy Simmons. Tel:83475. Vhf.Ch 68 . Price:two people sharing pizza, and eating salad and desert with 2 beers each:$15-30.Tuesday night barbecue $35 without drinks. Service:nf. Tax:inc. cc:no. Food:pizza, salads, specials, baked goodies .

OLD FIG TREE. P.E., Mgr:Adlene Wallace. Tel:83201. Vhf.Ch 68. Price:$36-50 inexpensive snacks and plates available. Service:nf tax:inc. cc:no. food:local, pizzas.

PORTHOLE. P.E., Mgr:Noeline Taylor. Tel:83458. Price:$31 inexpensive snacks/plates available. Service:nf. Tax:inc cc:no. Food:local.

S AND W SNACK BAR. P.E., Mgr:Sylvester and Joan Simmons. Tel:83447. inexpensive fish and chicken, rotis, chips. Service:nf. Tax:inc. cc:no.

SPRING ON BEQUIA. Spring, Mgr:Candy and Rosie Leslie. Tel:83414. Vhf.Ch 68 -may have to ask a taxi to relay. Price:$45. Sunday curry lunch special $27 includes taxes but without drinks. Service:10%. Tax:5%. cc:V, A. Food:local seafood and fresh produce cooked with an eclectic approach. Closed July to October.

SUNNY CARIBEE PLANTATION HOUSE. P.E. Mgr:Jaques Ducau and Chester Peters. Tel:83425. Vhf.Ch 68 . Price:$55-60. Service:12%. Tax:5%. cc:V, A. Food:French with local flavor.

COCO'S BEACH BAR. Sunny Caribbee Tel:83425. Vhf.Ch 68. snacks and plates. Service:12%. Tax:5%. cc:V, A. Food:hamburgers, barbecued fish or meat with rice etc .

WHALEBONER BAR AND RESTAURANT. P.E., Mgr:Albert and Angela Hinckson. Tel:83233 83232. Price:$36-46, inexpensive snacks and plates available. Service:nf. Tax:inc. cc:no. food:local

SHOPS

BEQUIA BOOKSTORE. Tel:83258. Mgr:Ian Gale. cc:no. Goods:books, charts, maps, souvenirs.

BOB DEMMANS AIR BRUSH T SHIRTS. at the Crab Hole. Tel:458 3290 mgr:Bob Demmans. cc:V, A. Goods:air brush t shirts, pareos, wall hangings, etc.

CINDERELLA'S HIDEAWAY. Tel:83331. Mgr:Inez Hazell. cc:no. Goods:applique, clothes, dolls.

CLUBHOUSE. Tel:83577. Mgr:Marie Kingston. cc:V, A. Sports equipment and wine and cheese.

DAPHNE'S BOUTIQUE. Nr shell station. Tel:83271. Mgr:Daphne Grant. cc:no. Goods:locally made clothes, silkscreen.

DORIS FRESH FOODS. Tel:83625 vhf ch 68. Mgr:Doris Sachs. cc:no. Goods:fresh produce, meat, ice.

FRIENDSHIP BAY BOUTIQUE. Friendship Bay Hotel. Tel:83222. Vhf.Ch 68. Mgr:Joanne and Eduardo cc:V, A. Goods:handicrafts, clothes .

FRIENDSHIP BAY DELICATESSEN. Friendship Bay Hotel. Tel:83222. Vhf.Ch 68. cc:V, A. Goods:delicatessen, bread, ice.

GREEN BOLEY BOUTIQUE. Tel:83347. Mgr:Rita Williams. cc:A. Goods:locally made handicrafts & clothes.

HELMSMAN. Tel:83577. Mgr:Janke Richardson. cc:V, goods:elegant sports and beachwear.

KNIGHTS SUPERMARKET. Tel:83339. Mgr:Kelvin Knights. cc:no. Goods:supermarket.

LOCAL COLOR. Tel:83202. Mgr:Elaine Scott-Morgan, Joan Chappell. cc:V, A. Goods:handicrafts, fashion, decor, cosmetics.

MELINDA. Tel:83409. Mgr:Melinda Parke. cc:V, goods:Minda's handpainted t shirts.

NOAH'S ARKADE. Tel:83424. Mgr:Moreen Simmons. cc:V, A. Goods:handicrafts, casual wear, batiks, books.

S AND W SUPPLIES. near Bequia marina. Tel:83447. Mgr:Sylvester Simmons. cc:no. Goods:supermarket, some hardware.

SHORELINE MINI-MARKET. Tel:83458. Mgr:Noeline Taylor. cc:no. Goods:supermarket, yogurt, ice .

SOLANA'S BOUTIQUE. Tel:83554. Mgr:Carmette Gooding. cc:V, A. Goods:handicrafts, clothing, gifts.

WHALEBONER BOUTIQUE. Tel:83233 83232. Mgr:Albert and Angela Hinckson. cc:no. Goods:locally made handicrafts & clothes.

ST VINCENT.

If calling from abroad use area code: (1) 809 45. For full postal address add: St Vincent, West Indies.

HOTELS

notes:(all rates in $U.S.). Mgr means manager, or owner manager. oa = on application. bed = bed only bb = bed and breakfast hb = half board fb = full board. HSS means high season single, HSD means high season double, LSS means low season single, LSD means low season double. cc = credit card information - V means Visa and normally includes all the Visa group including Master Card, Euro Card, Barclaycard and Carte Bleu. A = American express. nf = not fixed (in this case 10% tipping is normal). Unless otherwise specified assume a goverment tax of 5%. inc = included. ac = air-conditioning Tax, service or extras must be added to the rate.

BELLA VISTA INN (guest house), Kingstown Park, Tel:72757. Mgr:Pearl Osborne. No of rooms:7. cc:no. HSSbed$12-13. HSD:bed$15-19. LSS.$10. LSD.$15. Service:5%.

COBBLESTONE INN, Box 862, Tel:61937/71177. Mgr:Ann Joshua. No of rooms:19. cc:V, A. Year round.S:bb$36. Year round.D:bb$49. Service:10%.

C.S.Y. Box 133, Tel:84308. Fax:(809) 456 9255. Mgr:Ken Guynes. No of rooms:19. cc:V, agent:C.S.Y. Box 491, Tenefly N.J.07670 (USA) tel:800 631 1593/ 201 568 0390. HSSbed$50. HSD:bed$65. LSS.bed$40. LSD.bed$50. Service:10%. Tax:5% facilities:special full board weekly rates available through Anchor Travel at C.S.Y. New Jersey address.

EMERALD VALLEY COUNTRY CLUB AND CASINO, Box 1081, Tel:87421/31. Mgr:Diane Collen. No of rooms:12. cc:no. HSD:bed$180 HSS.bed:$160. hb supplement:$40 p.p. LSD.bed:$100 LSS.bed$80. Service:nf Facilities:tennis, golf club nearby.

GRAND VIEW BEACH HOTEL, Box 173, Tel:84811. Telex:7557 GRAND VIEW. Mgr:Tony and Heather Sardine. No of rooms:12. cc:V, A. Agent:Robert Reid, Hotels of Distinction, Tropical Enterprises, Inns of the Caribbean. HSSbed$79. HS.Double:bed$103. LSS.bed$52. LSD.bed$72, for hb add $28 per head per day. (rates to increase slightly for 88-89 season onwards). Service:10%. facilities:swimming pool, fishing, squash court, tennis.

HADDON HOTEL, Box 226, Tel:80945/61897. Telex:7568 STAR. Mgr:Sonja Israel. No of rooms:18. cc:V, A. Year round.S:bed$19-$25, hb$34-$40. Year round.D:bed$27-$34, hb$56-$64. Service:nf.

HERON HOTEL, Box 226, Tel:71631. Telex:7557 HERON. Mgr:Mrs McKenzie. No of rooms:15. cc:V, A. Year round.S:hb$35. Year round.D:hb$57-62. Service:10%.

INDIAN BAY HOTEL, Box 538, Tel:84001. Telex:7557 INDIAN BAY. Mgr:Marcia Nevisson. No of rooms:11. cc:V, A. Agent:Nina Chouvan. HSSbed$40, hb54. HS.Double:bed$45, hb$72. LSS.bed$35, hb$50. LSD.bed$40, hb$68. Service:10%. facilities:all rooms self contained.

KINGSTOWN PARK GUEST HOUSE, Box 41, Tel:61532. Telex:7557 KING PARK G.H.. mgr:Nesta Paynter. No of rooms:20. cc:no. Year round:bed$11-14, hb$20 p.p. Apartments also available. Service:nf.

LAST RESORT HOTEL, Box 355, Tel:84231. No of rooms:11. cc:V, A. HSSbed$35. HSD:bed$45. LSS.bed$30. LSD.bed$35. Service:10%.

MARINERS INN, Box 839, Tel:84287. Mgr:Rhonda Walker. No of rooms:25. cc: V, A. HSShb$60 HSD.hb$90 LSS.hb$50 LSD.hb$40. Service:10%.

MERMAID INN, Box 639, Tel:74628. Mgr:Bob Scott. No of rooms:7. cc:no. Year round.D:bb$40. Service:nf. Tax:inc. Facilities:30 foot twin outboard boat available. Also self-contained rooms for $111 per week, or $300 per month.

MOON (THE), Box 120, Tel:84656. Telex:7500 CW AGENCY K ADAMS. Mgr:Kenneth Adams. No of rooms:10. cc:no. Year round.S:bed$15. Year round.D:bed$19. Service:nf.

OLIVES GUEST HOUSE, Box 692, Tel:61821. Mgr:Mr Richards. No of rooms:10. cc:no. Year round.S:bed$11. Year round.D:bed$20. Service:nf.

SEA BREEZE GUEST HOUSE, Arnos Vale, Tel:84969. Mgr:Louisa Daize. No of rooms:7. cc:no. Year round.S:bed$12. Year round.D:bed$17. Service:nf. facilities:some cooking facilities.

SUNSET SHORES, Box 849, Tel:84411. Telex:7557 SUNSET SHORES. Mgr:Compton and Angela King. No of rooms:19. cc:V, A. Agent:Robert Reid. HSSbed$75-90, hb$103-118. HSD:bed$94-107, hb$150-163. LSS.bed$52-65, hb$80-93. LSD.bed$66-76, hb$122-132. Service:10%. facilities:pool.

UMBRELLA BEACH HOTEL, Box 530, Tel:84651. Mgr:Simone Depoint. No of rooms:10. cc:V, A. Year round.S:bed$28. Year round.D:bed$38. Service:nf Facilities:all rooms self-contained.

VILLA LODGE, Box 1191, Tel:84641. Telex:7500 VILLALODGE Mgr:Rosemary Kent. No of rooms:10. cc:V, A. HSSbed$85, hb$120. HSD:bed$95, hb$165. LSS.bed$65, hb$100. LSD.bed$75, hb$110. Service:10%. facilities:pool.

YOUNG ISLAND RESORT, Box 211, Tel:84826. Telex:3217547. Mgr:Vidal Browne. No of rooms:29. cc:V, A. Agent:Young Island, Box 800, Waccabuc, New York 10957. Tel:800 223 1108 telex:423282 fax:914 763 5362/5562. Also Unique Hotels. HSShb$225-350. HSD:hb$275-400. LSS.hb$150-325. LSD.hb$200-375. Service:10%. facilities:day charter boats, tennis, scuba, sunfish, snorkeling, sailboarding. Summer specials fb from $1450 per person per week

APARTMENTS

Notes:(all rates in $US.) oa=on application. One double means one double bedroom (2 persons). Two doubles means two double bedrooms (4 persons). For season/occupancy and credit card abreviations see hotel listing. Unless otherwise stated add 5% for govt tax. Inc=included. Tax, service or extras must be added to the rate. .

BELLEVILLE APARTMENTS, Villa, Box 764, Tel:84776. Mgr:Jackie Minors. No of units:6 (1,2 & 3 bedroom). Rates $170-$300 per week. Service:inc. Tax:inc. cc:no.

BREEZEVILLE APARTMENTS, Villa Box 222, Tel:84008. Telex:7557 BREEZEVILLE. Mgr:Bobby Brisbane. No of units:8. Daily rate from:$65 for single to $100 for 4. Service:10%. Tax5%. cc:V, A. Facilities:pool.

MACEDONIA ROCK HOTEL APARTMENTS, Cane Hall, Box 1070, Tel:84076. Mgr:James Mcintosh. No of units:10. Year round.S:bed$17. Year round.D:bed$20. Service:inc. Tax:inc. cc:no.

RATHO MILL APARTMENTS, Box 803, Tel:84076. Mgr:Reggie Adams. No of units:15. Year round one double:$28. Year round two doubles:$38. Year round three doubles:$48. Service:nf. cc:no.

RICK'S APARTMENTS, near airport, Box 63, Tel:61242/71181/61361. Telex:7561 HILLOCKS VQ. Mgr:AC Hillock. No of units:6 (2 bedroom). Year round rate:$23. Service:nf. Taxinc. cc:no.

RIDGE VIEW TERRACE APARTMENTS, Ratho Mill, Box 803, Tel:61615. Telex:7252. Mgr:Clifford Frank. No of units:5. One and two bedroom units: $175-290 per week service:nf. Tax:inc. cc:no.

STAR GARAGE, Box 144, Tel:61743. Telex:7568. Mgr:Silky de Silva. No of units:2. Price oa.

TREASURE ISLAND BEACH RESORT APARTMENTS, Indian Bay, Box 111, Tel:84934. Mgr:Douglas Brisbane. No of units:11. HSD:$25-50. HS. doubles:$60. LSD.$25-40. LS. doubles:$50. Service:10%. cc:V.

YVONNETTE APARTMENTS, Indian Bay, Box 71, Tel:84021. Mgr:Roxanne Arthur. No of units:7. Year round one double:$32. Year round two doubles:$50. Year rond three doubles:$65. Service:10%. cc:no.

RESTAURANTS

All rates in EC. Dollars. Unless otherwise stated they include a three course meal and half the bottle price of the cheapest wine, or if more appropriate, two beers. cc=credit card information - V includes all the Visa group - Master Card, Barclaycard, Europcard, Carte Bleu etc. Service nf. Means not fixed - normally one would tip around 10%. Inc means it is included in the price.

A LA MER. Indian Bay Hotel. Mgr:Marcia Nevisson. Tel:84001. Price:$39-$58. Service:10%. tax 5%. cc:V, A. Food:local.

BASIL'S BAR at Cobblestone. Mgr:Basil Charles. Tel:72713. Price:$47-$82. Service:inc . Tax:5%. cc:V, A. Food:seafood and international, lunch buffet $25 without drinks, Friday night seafood buffet, lobster, fish and shrimp $50 without drinks .

BIMINI RESTAURANT. Blue Lagoon. Mgr:Mary Barnard. Tel:69324. Price:$28-$75. Service:10%. Tax:5%. cc:V, A. Food:Caribbean, creole.

BOUNTY. Halifax St. Mgr:Tracy Connell. Tel:61776. inexpensive snacks. Service:inc Tax:inc cc:no.

CHICKEN ROOST. Opposite airport. Mgr:David Dunn. Tel:64932. Service:no. Tax:no. cc:no. Food:fast foods - all kinds of chicken and more exotic foods such as goat roti also ice cream parlor open till midnight.

C.S.Y. Blue Lagoon. Mgr:Ken Guynes. Tel:84308. Price:$48-$77. Service:10%. Tax:5%. cc:V, Food:seafoods, steaks. Happy hour in the bar nightly 5-7 pm

C.S.Y. BEACH BAR. Blue Lagoon. Mgr:Ken Guynes. Tel:84308 . Price inexpensive snacks. Service:nf. Tax:inc. cc:no food:local and international snacks. Friday night ethnic night - mexican, chinese or italian barbecue etc $20-$30 excluding drinks happy hour 5-7 nightly and all day Sunday.

DANO'S. Middle St. Mgr:Rosal Daniel. Tel:72020. Price:inexpensive breakfast, lunch plates. Servce:inc. Tax:inc. cc:no.

DOLPHIN. Young Island Cut. Mgr:Bjorn Banke. Tel:84238, vhf ch68 . Price:$52-$84 also snacks Service:10%. Tax:inc. cc:no. pub food.

EMERALD VALLEY COUNTRY CLUB. Penniston Valley. Mgr:Diane Collen. Tel:8742/31. Price:$31-73. Service:nf tax:5% cc:no.

FRENCH RESTAURANT. Young Island Cut. Mgr:Simone and Miguel Depoint. Tel:84972, vhf ch68. Price:$75-$98. service:nf. Tax:inc. cc:V, A. Food:good french cuisine.

GRAND VIEW BEACH RESTAURANT. Grand View Beach Hotel. Mgr:Heather and Tony Sardine. Tel:84811. Price:$63. Service:10%. Tax:5%. cc:V A. Food:Caribbean. Meal time 7- 7.30 p.m.

HERON HOTEL. Bay St. Mgr:Mrs Mckenzie. Tel:71631. Price:$38. Service:nf. Tax:5%. cc:no. Food:local.

JULIETTE'S. Middle Street. Mgr:Juliette Campbell. Tel:71645 . Price:lunch plates only, $8-12. Service:nf. Tax:inc. cc:no food:local.

KENTUCKY FRIED CHICKEN. Grenville Street. cc:no. Food:Kentucky fried chicken.

KINGSTOWN PARK GUEST HOUSE. At Kingstown Park. Mgr:Nesta Paynter tel:61532. Price:$35-40. Service nf. Tax:inc cc:no. Food:local food to order.

MARINERS INN. Young Island Cut. Mgr:Rhonda Walker. Tel:84287. Price:$37-$47. Service:10%. Tax:inc. cc:V, A. Food:Caribbean. Friday night jump up and barbecue $20-$25 without drinks.

MOLLIES. Bay St. Mgr:Marlene Arthur. Tel:72556. Service:no. Tax:no. cc:no food:fastfoods.

MERMAID INN. Young Island Cut. Mgr:Bob Scott. Tel:74628. Price:$37-$60. Service:nf. Tax:inc. cc:no. food:local - curried goat, seafood etc. chinese snacks.

PAPA SPOONS RASTA RANCH. Calliaqua playing field. Mgr:Papa Spoon. Tel:no. Price:each calabash bowl full:$1-2 (without drinks). Service:nf. Tax:inc. cc:no food:Ital - peas, beans, calalou, and corn, all natural.

PIZZA PARTY. St James Place. Mgr:David Dunn. Tel:71032. Service:no. Tax:no. cc:no food:pizza and fast foods.

STEPHENS HIDEOUT. At Wallilabou. Mgr:Girlyn and Elford Stephens. Tel:82325, vhf ch 16 or 68. Price:$34. Service:nf. Tax:no. Food:local speciality fresh water crayfish and calalou soup.

SUNSET SHORES. Young Island Cut. Mgr:Compton and Angela King. Tel:84411. Price:$45-$70. Service:inc. Tax:nf. cc:V, A. Food:caribbean seafood and meats.

VILLA LODGE. Villa Lodge Hotel. Mgr:Rosemary Kent. Tel:84641. Price:$48. Service:10%. Tax:inc. cc:V, A. Food:caribbean.

YOUNG ISLAND RESORT. Young Island. Mgr:Vidal Browne. Tel:84826. Price:five course set dinner:$95-$108. Service:10%. Tax:5%. cc:V, A. Food:seafood and international. Sat night barbecue with steel band $80 without drinks. Friday night cocktail party on Fort Duvenette (includes snacks and drinks $27).

SHOPS

BIMINI BOUTIQUE. Blue Lagoon. Tel:69334. Mgr:Mary Barnard. cc: V, A. Goods:charts, books, skin care products, t shirts, clothes, souvenirs.

BATIK CARIBE. Bay Street. Tel:61666. Mgr:Marnie Palmer. cc:V, A. Goods:batik clothing, toys, gifts etc..

GREAVES SUPERMARKET tel:71074. Mgr:Nigel Greaves. cc:no.

C.S.Y. BOUTIQUE. Blue Lagoon. Tel:84308. Mgr:Ken Guynes. cc:V, Goods:charts, clothing, books, handicrafts etc.

DOCK SHOP. Young Island Dock. Tel:84826. Mgr:Carlita Gill. cc:V, A. Goods:scrimshaw, pottery, handicrafts, clothes.

EDWIN D LAYNE AND SON. spans Bay and Middle St. Tel:61411. Mgr:Grace Morris. cc:A. Goods:department store.

ELLE. Upper Middle Street. Tel:72296. Mgr:Sonja Sprott. cc:no. Goods:fashion, fabrics, costume jewelry.

FIRST BASE DESIGN PRINTHOUSE. North Union. Tel:86161. Mgr: Monica & Gordon Keddie. cc:no. Goods:silkscreen t shirts, fabrics etc - also commercial design and art work.

GIGGLES. Cobblestone Arkade. Tel:71174. Mgr:Terry Wiliams. cc:A. Goods:clothing, costume jewelry.

HARBOUR VIEW BOUTIQUE. Young Island Cut. Mgr:Odette. cc:A. Goods:t shirts, fashion, cosmetics skin care products.

HIBISCUS ARTS AND CRAFTS. Frenchies Tel:61470. Mgr:Mrs Eileen Cummings. cc:no goods:straw goods, handicrafts, exotic souvenirs, carvings.

MADE IN DE SHADE. Upper Middle Street. Tel:72364. Mgr:Leslie Barnard. cc:V, Goods:swim sear, casual wear, dresses.

MARINERS BOUTIQUE. Scuba Shop, Young Island Cut. Tel:84228 also vhf ch 68. Mgr:Sue Halbich. cc:V, A. Goods:clothes, t shirts, sunblock, maps, local books.

NOAH'S ARKADE. Bay Street. Tel:71513. Mgr:Lavinia Gunn. cc:V, A. Goods:handicrafts, local books, maps, skin care products, clothes.

NORLAN. Pitt Stop, also avilable other boutiques Tel:72454. Mgr:Norlan Pitt. cc:no. Goods:handpainted t shirts.

ROGERS PHOTO STUDIO. bay Street. Tel:71572. Mgr:Fitzroy Rogers. cc:no. Goods:cameras, film, same day processing.

SPROTTIES. Bay Street. Tel:61647. Mgr:Joy Sprott. cc:V, A. Goods:silk screen clothing, table ware and fabrics, all made locally in Sprotties factory.

STECHERS. Cobblestone Arkade. Tel:71442. Mgr:Mrs Williams. cc:V, A. Goods:porcelain, china, crystal, jewelry, perfumes.

ST VINCENT HANDICRAFT CENTER. just out of town. Tel:71288. Mgr:Mrs Patterson. cc:no. Goods:straw craft and handicrafts.

SUNRISE BAKERY. near airport. Tel:71074. Mgr:Nigel Greaves. cc:no. Goods:supermarket.

TOUCH OF CLASS. Upper Middle Street. Tel:72706. Mgr:Cora Ross-Cambridge. cc:no. Goods:shoes, handbags, costume jewelry, skin care products.

VOYAGER. Halifax Street. Tel:61838. Mgr:L.S.Jiandani. cc:no. Goods:handicrafts, souvenirs.
Y DE LIMA. Bay Street. Tel:71681. Mgr:Mrs Lorna Williams. cc:V, A. Goods:jewelry, sunglasses, china etc.

TOURS OPERATORS

BAREFOOT HOLIDAYS, Box 39, tel:69334. Telex:7506. Mgr:Martin Barnard. Type:sells package holidays, also island tours, day tours to the Grenadines, etc. Agents:JRC travel, BMIT cc:V A.
GRENADINES TOURS Box 1098, Tel:84818. Mgr:Marnie Palmer. Type:"shared charter concept". Buy a ticket like scheduled airlines, but flight timing is flixible. Day trips to the Grenadines, also sea tours to the Falls of Baleine etc. Agent:Anchor Travel.cc: V, A.
SAILORS TOURS, Box 684, tel:71712 Mgr:Trevor Bailey type:all kinds of island and air tours. Agents:Hunter Associates, suite 1830, 370 7th Ave NY.10001. Tel:212 244 1161. Sailors also has keep fit clinic.cc:no.

CAR RENTALS

All rates in US. Dollars. HS = high season, LS = low season. YR = year round. DD = damages deposit
HILLOCKS AGENCIES, Sharp Street, tel:61242. Mgr:AC Hillock. No cars auto:3. No manual:3. Types:sedans, pick up truck. YR rate from:$28. (weekly from $170). Extras:no. DD:$190. cc:no.
JOHNSON'S U DRIVE, Box 339, tel:84864. Mgr:Mr Johnson. No cars auto:2. No manual:4. Types:sedans. YR rates:$22-32.. extras:mileage charge under 3 days. DD:$300. cc:V, A.
KIM'S AUTO RENTALS, Box 600, Tel:72797. Mgr:Jack Joachim. No cars auto:6. No manual:18. Types:sedans. 4 wheel drive. YR rates:$32-56. (weekly from $190-280). Extras:no. DD:$300. cc:V. A. But not for single day hire
LUCKY RENTALS, tel:61215, 71913, 61733. Mgr:Sam Goodluck. No cars 10 some auto, some air conditioned. YR rates:$187-225 per week. Extras:no DD:$280 cc:V
STAR GARAGE, Box 144, . tel:61743. Telex:7568. Mgr:Silky de Silva. No cars auto:6. No manual:16. Types:sedans, 4 wheel drive. YR rates:$31-46. (weekly one day free). Extras:$1.2 a mile after 60 a day. DD:$1000. cc:V, A.

AIRLINES AND CHARTER

AIR MARTINIQUE Box 870, Tel:84528. Mgr:Leroy Wilson. Type:2 flights daily to Union and two flights daily to St Lucia and Martinique. One flight daily to and from Mustique. Agent:Air France.
GRENADINES TOURS Box 1098, Tel:84818. Mgr:Marnie Palmer. Type:"shared charter concept". Buy a ticket like scheduled airlines, but flight timing is flixible. Daily flights between Barbados & St Vincent, Barbados & Union, Barbados & Mustique, St Vincent & Mustique agent:Anchor Travel.
LIAT, Box 616, Tel:71821/(airport 84964). Type:3 or 4 flights daily to Barbados, 1 direct to St Lucia, 2 to Grenada. One daily between Barbados and Mustique. Agent:all major carriers.
MUSTIQUE AIRWAYS, Box 1232, Tel:84380. Telex:7452 CHARTER VQ. Fax:809 456 4586. Mgr:Jonathan Palmer. Type:5 to 9 seater planes for charter. Agent:Anchor Travel.
ST VINCENT AIRWAYS, Box 1445, Tel:64176. Telex:7500 STV AIRWAYS. Mgr:William Kent. Type:luxurious Piper Seneca, full air conditioning, color radar etc,. For charter.

OTHER

BARCLAYS BANK. Granby Street. Tel:61706. Mgr:Monty St John. Agents for Visa and Master Card.
CARIBBEAN INTERNATIONAL TRAVEL. Granby Street. Tel:71841. Mgr:Ken Murray. cc:local agent for american express, cards and travelers checks. Also travel agent.

ST LUCIA.

If calling from abroad area code is (1) 809 45. For full postal address add: St Lucia, West Indies.

HOTELS

Notes:(all rates in $U.S.). Mgr means manager, or owner manager. oa = on application. bed = bed only bb = bed and breakfast hb = half board fb = full board. HSS means high season single, HSD means high season double, LSS means low season single, LSD means low season double. YR means year round. cc = credit card information - V means Visa and normally includes all the Visa group including Master Card, Euro Card, Barclaycard and Carte Bleu. A = American express. nf = not fixed (in this case 10% tipping is normal). Unless otherwise specified assume a goverment tax of 8%. inc = included. ac = air-conditioning Tax, service or extras must be added to the rate.

ANSE CHASTANET HOTEL, P.O Box 216, Soufriere, Tel:47354/5. Telex:0398/6370. Mgr:Nick Troobitscoff. No of rooms:30. cc:V, A., diners. Agent:Scott Calder International. HSSbed:$96-$160. HSD:bed:$108-$180. LSS.bed:$60-$100. LSD.bed:$80-$118. Service:10%. Tax:8%. Facilities:scuba full water sports.

CLUB ST LUCIA, Box 915, Tel:20551/20543. Telex:6228 fax:20281. Mgr:Richard Michelin. No of rooms:150. cc:V. A. Agent:ITR, Travel and Resorts, Adventure Tours. Weekly rates HSS.fb$1230-1430. HSD:fb$1760-2060. LSS.fb$930. LSD.fb$1360. Service:inc. Tax:inc. Facilities:pool, full water sports tennis.

BLUE LAGOON GUEST ROOMS, Box637, Castries, Tel:28453. Telex:no. Mgr:Mr and Mrs Jupierre. No of rooms:8. cc:no. Agent:. YR.D:bed$20-25. Service:nf. . Two bedroom cottages also available:$35.

BONNE APPETITE, Box 884, Castries, Tel:22757. Telex:no. Mgr:Ezra Charles. No of rooms:10. cc:no. HSSbed$25. HSD:bed$35. LSS.bed$20. LSD.bed$25. Service:inc. Tax:inc.

CLOUD'S NEST, Vieux Fort, Tel:46226. Telex:no. Mgr:Gildette Williams. No of rooms:6. cc:no. Rates:oa. Service 10%.

COUPLES, Box 190, Tel:24211/5. Telex:6203. Mgr:Alfred O'Driscoll. No of rooms:222. cc:V, A. Diners. Agent:all wholsalers. Rates:oa facilities:tennis, sauna, jacuzzi, bicycles, pool..

CREOLE INN Box 967, Castries, Tel:24158. mgr:Pearl St.Helen.. no of rooms:4. cc:no. YR:bed$12-15. YR:bed$22-25. Service:nf. Tax:inc.

CUNARD LA TOC, la toc, Tel:23081/9. Telex:lc6320. Director: Michael Marko. No of rooms:300. cc:V, A. Diners. Agent:Cunard, 555 fifth ave, new york. Tel: 1 800 222 0939. Cunard,30-35 pall mall, London. Tel:01 930 4321 also Scott Calder. HSD:bed:$200-425. LSD.bed$130-265. Service:10%. . Facilities:golf, tennis, pools, full water sports, health center..

DUBOIS GUEST HOUSE, Box 1380, Castries, Tel:22201. Mgr:Hermina Dubois. No of rooms:4. cc:no. HSSbed$15. HSD:bed$30. LSS.bed$12. LSD.bed$24. Service:10%.

EASTWINDS, Box 338, Tel:25331/6. Telex:6343 LC. Mgr:Peter Kouly. cc:V, A.. rates oa.

EDGEWATER BEACH HOTEL, Box 1114, Tel:24872. Telex:no. Mgr:Jane Tipson. No of rooms:6. cc:V, A. YR.S:bed$30. YR.D:bed$40. (extra $5 during christmas, easter and carnival) service: 10%. . Facilities:some rooms ac., close to main bus route.

GROS PITON MOTEL, Soufriere, Tel:47314/47461. Mgr:Michael Jaques. No of rooms:8. cc:no. Rates:YR.bed$23 pp.

HALCYON BEACH CLUB, po Box 338, Tel:25331/6. Telex:6343 lc. Mgr:Peter Kouly. No of rooms:140. cc:V, A. HSSbed:$110-140. HSD:bed:$140-165. LSS.bed:$60-80. LSD.bed:$80-100. Service:10%. Hb sup.:$32 pp. Facilities:pool, tennis, water sports.

HOME HOTEL, Soufriere, Tel:47318. Telex:no. Mgr:Mary Francis. No of rooms:7. cc:no. HSS$oa. HSD:$oa. LSS.bed$11.60. LSD.bed$19.50. Service:inc. Tax:inc.

HUMMINGBIRD YACHT CLUB, Soufriere, Tel:47232. Mgr:Joan Alexander. No of rooms:10 (some still under construction). cc:V. YR.D:bed:$40. Service:nf. Facilities:pool.

ISLANDER HOTEL, Box 907, Castries, Tel:20255/28757. Telex:6209lc. Mgr:Greg Glace. No of rooms:40 double, 20 self contained studios.. cc:V, A. HSSbed$75-85. HSD:bed$85-95. LSS.bed$45-50. LSD.$55-60. Service:10%. Facilities:pool.

KIMATRI, Vieux Fort, Tel:46328. Mgr:Kenny Williams. No of rooms:30. cc:no. YR.S:bed$25. YR.D:bed$35. Service:10%. . Cottages and apartments also available.

LE SPORT, Box 437, Tel:28551. Telex:LC6330. Mgr Nigel Nicol. No of rooms:128. cc:V, A. Diners. Rates:HSS.fb$205-235 HSD.fb$370-430. LSS.fb$180-210. Low season double:fb$320-380 facilities:thalassotherapy, all kinds of sports including archery and fencing..

MARIGOT BAY RESORT, Box 101, Castries, Tel:34357. Telex:6230/6232. Mgr:Johnny Parle. No of rooms:47. cc:V, A. Agent:Moorings Resorts, 1305 us 19th south. Suite 402, Clearwater, fla 33546. Tel:800 535-7289 813 535-1446. Robert reid. HSSbed:$85-120. HSD:bed:$90-125. LSS.bed:$65-75. LSD.bed:$70-80. (many units self-contained, larger units available) service:10%. Facilities:pool, water sports etc.

MODERN INN, Vigie, Tel:24001. Telex:no. Mgr:Mr Joseph. No of rooms:5. cc:no. YR.S:fb$17. YR.D:fb$26-28. Service:inc. Tax:inc. Facilities:some rooms ac Some rooms self-contained.

PARROTS HIDEAWAY, Box 1592, Castries, Tel:20726. Telex:no. Mgr:Lucian Parrot. No of rooms:7. cc:no. YR rates:bed$18 pp.(reductions on long term) service:nf.

SERENITY LODGE, (mail to 40 Micoud St, Castries). Tel:21987. Mgr:Morgan Cyril. No of rooms:9. cc:no. HSSbed$20-25. HSD:bed$45-50. LSS.bed$16-20. LSD.bed$40-45. Service:10%. . (one self contained apt available).

ST LUCIAN HOTEL, Box 512, Tel:28351/5. Telex:6326. Mgr:Lawrence Saunders. No of rooms:222. cc:V, A. Diners. HSS$oa. HSD:$oa. LSS.bed$70. LSD.bed$90. Service:10%. . Facilities:pool, tennis, full water sports, disco..

SUNDALE GUEST HOUSE, Box 138, Castries, Tel:24120. Telex:no. Mgr:Joan Kingshot. No of rooms:5 doubles. cc:no HSS.bb$25. HSD:bb:$35. LSS.bb:$22. LSD.bb:$32. Service:10%. . (also 2 self contained flats available).

TAPION REEF HOTEL, Box 370, Tel:27471/27552. Telex:6216. Mgr:Renato Venturi. No of rooms:32. cc:V, A.. HSS.$bed40-45. HSD:bed$55-60. LSS.bed$30-35. LSD.bed$40-45. Service:10%. Facilities:pool, units are self-catering.

TROPICAL HAVEN MINI HOTEL, Castries, tel:23505. Mgr:F B Williams. no of rooms:12 with 4 apts.LSS:bed$18. LSD:bed$30-35, HSS:bed$20 HSD:bed$40-45.

TROPICAL INN, 5 Church St.,Soufriere, Tel:47248. Mgr:Mrs Victor. No of rooms:6. cc:no. YR rate:bed:$8 p.p plus $1.15 for use of kitchen. Service:nf. Tax:inc.

VIGIE BEACH HOTEL, Box 388, Vigie Beach, Tel:25211. Telex:6219. Mgr:Winsbert St Marthe. No of rooms:50. cc:V, A. HSS$45-90 business rates:$22-35. HSD:$60-120. Business rates:$30-50 LSS.$27-67. LSD.$40-87. Service:10%. Facilities:pool, water sports.

APARTMENTS

Notes:(all rates in $US.) oa=on application. One double means one double bedroom (2 persons). Two doubles means two double bedrooms (4 persons). For season/occupancy and credit card abreviations see hotel listing. Unless otherwise stated add 8% for govt tax. Inc=included. Tax, service or extras must be added to the rate.

BOIS D'ORANGE VILLAGE, Box 1741, Castries, Tel:28213. Telex:6231SIMCOLC. Mgr:Simeon Sealy. No of rooms:14 (one bedroom). cc:V, A. Agent:Edmondial inc, 1405 bishop St., suite 320, montreal, que. H3g 2e5. Tel:514 844 4445. Telex:055 62171 mtl. HS.:$50. LS.:$35, larger units available. Service:10%. Facilities:pool.

CARIBBEES APARTMENT HOTEL, Box 568, Castries, Tel:24767. Mgr:Malcom Brashaw. No of rooms:17. HSS$42 HSD.$55. LSS.$30 LSD.$40. Service:10% tax:18%. cc:A,V.

CLOUD'S NEST, Vieux Fort, Tel:46226. Mgr:Gildette Williams. No of units:20 one, two and three bedroom. Rates:$45-90. Service:nf. cc:no.

FRIENDSHIP INN, Sunny Acres, P.OBox 1457, Castries. Tel:24201. Mgr:Esther Eudoxie. No of rooms:10. HSS:$30. HSD:$40. LSS.$25. LSD.$35. Service:10% tax 8%. cc:no.

HARMONY APPARTEL, Box 907, Castries, Tel:20336. Telex:6222. Mgr:Bob Etts. No of rooms:21 one and two bedroom apartments. cc:V. One bedroom:$53-76. Two bedroom:$74-120. LS.Monthly rates from $1290 service:10%. . Facilities:pool.

MORNE FORTUNE APARTMENTS, (top of the morne) Box 376, Castries, Tel:22531/23603. Mgr:Pat Headly. No of units:12 (1 and 2 bedroom). Daily rates winter:$76-105. Summer:$63-85. Service:10%. . cc:no.

SEAVIEW APARTEL, Box 527,Castries, Tel:24358/20627. Mgr:Jean Marie. No of units:6 doubles. Daily rates:$50. Service:inc. Tax:inc. cc:no.

THE STILL BEACH AND ESTATE RENTALS, Soufriere, Tel:84776. Mgr:Desmond Duboulay. No of units:one 2 bedroom, one 4 bedroom. Rates:$from $100 per week per couple. Service:no. Tax:inc. cc:V.

VILLA APARTMENTS, Box 129, Castries, Tel:22691. Mgr:Errol and Laura Hunt. No of units:20. (1 and 2 bedrrom) daily rates:$65-95 monthly rates oa. Service:10%. . cc:no.

VILLA BEACH COTTAGES, Box 129, Castries, Tel:22884. Mgr:Errol and Laura Hunt. No of units:5 (one and two bedroom). Rates:$45-55. Service:10%. cc:no.

RESTAURANTS

All rates in EC. Dollars. Unless otherwise stated they include a three course meal and half the bottle price of the cheapest wine, or if more appropriate, two beers. cc=credit card information - V includes all the Visa group - Master Card, Barclaycard, Europcard, Carte Blue etc. Service nf. Means not fixed - normally one would tip around 10%. Inc means it is included in the price.

A FRAME. Rodney Bay. Mgr:Chris and Jenny Calderbank. Tel:28725. Price:$29-$77. Snacks available. Service:nf. Tax:inc. cc:V (but not m.Card and V derivatives), A. Food:local flavor

AFTER DECK. Rodney Bay Marina. Mgr:Ed Morez. Tel:20665. Price:$31-$86, snacks available. Service:nf. Tax:inc. cc:V, A. Food:international with Caribbean flavor.

BONNE APETTITE. Morne Fortune. Mgr:Ezra Charles. Tel:22757. Price:$30-$70. Service:nf. Tax:inc. cc:no food:Caribbean/ international.

(THE) BREAD BASKET. Rodney Bay Marina. Mgr:Nicholas Taylor. Tel:20647. Service:nf. Tax:inc. cc:no. Food:croissants for breakfast, sandwiches for lunch, cakes, buns, bread, ice cream, etc.

CAPONES. Rodney Bay, tel:20284. Price:$54-89. service 10%. cc:V,A. food:Italian in American tradition also pizzas, snacks, great ice cream parlour (Sweet Dreams).

CHANTICLEER. Halcyon Beach Club. Mgr:Peter Kouly. Tel:25331/6. Price:$41-$115. Service:10%. Tax:8%. cc:V, A. Food:prime ribs, international

(THE) CHARTHOUSE. Rodney Bay. Mgr:Nick Ashworth. Tel:28115. Price:$46-$94. Service:10%. Tax:inc. cc:V, A. Food:steaks, seafood and spare ribs.

CHUNGS. Choc. Mgr:Mr Chung. Tel:24795. Price:$20-$40. Service:10%. Tax:inc. cc:no food:chinese.

(THE) COAL POT Vigie Creek. Mgr:Sonia Elliot. Tel:25643. Price:$43-$95. Service:10%. Tax:inc. cc:V. Food:French, creole.

DOLITTLE'S. Marigot. Tel:34357. Price:$54-$84. Service:10%. Tax:8%. (also fixed menu at $50 inc of tax) cc:V, A. Food:international with Caribbean flavor

DUTCH DOOR. Northern Main Highway. Mgr:Allan Fernand. Tel:28358. Price:$25-$46. Service:nf. Tax:inc. cc:no. Food:local seafood and snacks

EAGLES INN. Rodney Bay. Mgr:Dominic Gatineau. Tel:28757. Price:$45-$76. Service:10%. Tax:inc. cc:V, A., food:local, snacks available. Happy hour 1700-1900.

FLAMINGO St Lucian. Mgr:Lawrence Saunders. Tel:28351/5. Service:10%. Tax:8%. cc:V, A. Diners food:snacks and a la carte menu.

GIORGIOS Rodney Bay. Mgr:Giorgio tel:28315. price:$35-76. service 10%. cc:V,A. food:Italian.

HALCYON BEACH CLUB, la choc tel:25331/6. Mgr:Peter Kouly. price:$47 fixed menu. Service:10%. Tax:8%. cc:V, A. Food:international

ISLANDER. Rodney Bay. Mgr:Greg Glace. Tel:28358. Price:$45-$76. Service:10%. Tax:8%. cc:V, food:Caribbean/international

HUMMINGBIRD.Soufriere. Mgr:Joan Alexander. Tel:47232. Price:$31-$76. Service:10%. Tax:inc. cc:V, food:wide range of local and international, snacks available.

HUMMINGBIRD. St Lucian. Mgr:Lawrence Saunders. Tel:28351/5. Price:$59 for set meal without drinks. Service:inc. Tax:inc. cc:V, A. Diners. Food:international with local flavor.

HURRICANE HOLE HOTEL.marigot. Tel:34357. Price:$54-$84. Service:10%. Tax:8%. (also fixed menu at $50 inc of tax) cc:V, A. Food:international with Caribbean flavor

IL PIRATA. Vieux Fort. Mgr:Rosalba Nelli. Tel:46601. Price:$48-$71. Service:10%. Tax:inc. cc:no. Food:Italian

JJ'S BAR. Marigot. Mgr:Jigot. Tel:no. Price:dinner plates $20 without drinks. Food:local

JIMMIES. Vigie Cove. Mgr:Jimmy James. Tel:25142. Price:$39-$69.(snacks also available). Service:10%. Tax:no. cc:V. Food:seafood.

(THE) LIME Rodney Bay. Mgr Theodore ("Tee"). tel:20761. price:$35-$69, also excellent inexpensive snacks cc:V,A. food:Caribbean, also good fish and chips etc.

MOTAR AND PESTLE. Harmony Appartel. Mgr:Bob Etts. Tel:20336. Price:$48-75. cc:V. Food:West Indian and eastern specialties.

PISCES. Choc Bay. Price:$oa. cc:A. Food:creole

THE PITONS. La Toc. Tel:23081/9. Price:$85-$150. Service:10%. Tax:8%. cc:V, A. Diners food:first rate French cuisine

RAIN. Columbus Square. Mgr:Al Haman. Tel:23022. Price:$29-$77 with $85 for special recreated 1885 champagne banquet (7courses 4 wines). Snacks and pizza available. Service:10%. Tax:inc. cc:V, A. Food:all kinds.

SAN ANTOINE The Morne. Mgr:Michael and Alison Richings. Tel:24660. Price:$57-$124. (Less expensive lunches) service:10%. Tax:inc. cc:V, A. Food:classic French

SUBWAY. Jeremie St. (White House). inexpensive snacks. cc:no

THE RIB SHAK. Rodney Bay. Service:nf. Tax:inc. cc:no. Food:inexpensive fast foods:spare ribs, fried chicken, barbecued meat on a bun

TAPION REEF. Tapion Reef Hotel. Mgr:Renato Venturi. Tel:27471/27552. Price:$30-$75. Service:10%. Tax:8%. cc:V, A. Food:Caribbean/international.

THE TERRACE. La Toc. Tel:23081/9. Price:$68-$100. Service:10%. Tax:8%. cc:V, A. Diners
food:international with local flavor
TIMOTHY'S. Jerome St. cc:no. Food:inexpensive local snacks, rotis etc.
THE STILL. Soufriere. Mgr:Desmond Duboulay. Tel:47224/47452. Price:$21-$45. Service:10%. Tax:inc.
cc:V. Food:local

SHOPS

BAGSHAWS. La Toc Point. and Pte Seraphine. Tel:22139/26039. Mgr:Alice Bagshaw. cc:V, A.
Goods:silk screened everything, special post cards.
BATIK STUDIOS. Hummingbird Restaurant. Tel:47237. Mgr:Joan Alexander. cc:V. Goods:hand made
batik hangings and clothes.
CARIBELLE BATIK. Old Victoria Road, The Morne. Tel:23785. Mgr:Brendan McShane. cc:V A..
goods:batik everything.
IMAGES, Pte Seraphine. Tel:26885. Goods:perfumes, souvenirs.
J.Q. CHARLES, Castries, Pte Seraphine. Tel:22721. Goods:big store many different departments and
locations.
LES ABRES, Pte Seraphine, tel:27590. Goods:spirits, china, crystal.
ISLAND CONNECTION, Pte Seraphine, tel:26909, cc:V,A. Casualwear, gifts.
MARIGOT BOUTIQUE. Dolittles and Hurricane Hole Hotel. Tel:34357. cc:V, A.. goods:handicrafts,
clothes, batik.
MELI, Pte Seraphine. Tel:27587. cc:v,a. Jewelry, china, gifts.
NOAH'S ARKADE, Pte Seraphine, Castries, most hotels.Tel:27488/22523. cc:v,a. Goods:handicrafts.
RAIN BOUTIQUE. Inside Rain's restaurant. Mgr:Jaqui Devaux. Tel:23022. cc:V, A. Goods:everything
from casual day to elegant evening with costume jewelry to match. Men's and women's sections.
REFLECTIONS, Pte Seraphine. Tel:27575. cc:a,v. Goods:sports/swim wear.
TOP BANANA. Club St Lucia and in the St Lucian. Tel:20551/28351. cc:V, A.. goods:an eclectic
collection of off beat and useful items selected with artistic flair (open sundays and holidays).
TOUCH OF CLASS. Pte Seraphine. Tel:27443. cc:V,A. Goods: general gifts.
WINCRAFT, Pte Seraphine. Tel:27580. cc:V,A. Goods: ceramics, t-shirts, gifts.
WINDJAMMER, Pte Seraphine and in Vigie, tel:27460. cc:V,A. Goods:casual wear.

CAR RENTALS

All rates in US. Dollars. HS = high season, LS = low season. YR = year round. DD = damages deposit
ABC CAR RENTALS, Box 93, Castries Tel:26445. Mgr:. No of cars auto:2. Manual:5. YR rates:$29-33.
Weekly $174-198. DD:$1900. Extras:mileage over 60 a day or 500 a week. cc:A, V. Optional collison
waiver $10 per day.
AVIS, Box 1010, Castries Tel:22202/22700. No of cars auto:30. Manual:40. HS.Rates:$40-65.
LS.Rates:$35-55. DD:$1900. Extras:mileage after 40 a day, optional collsion waiver $10 a day. cc:all
NATIONAL CAR RENTAL, Box 542, Castries, Tel:28721. Telex 6245. Mgr:John Elliot.. no of cars
auto:8. Manual:50. HS.Rates:$36-48. LS.Rates:$35-44 (weekly from 228). DD:$1200. (optional $10 a day
insurance reduces to $300) extras:mileage over 45 a day. cc:am.Ex, diners, V, europ car, nat. Car.
SEAVIEW CAR RENTALS, Box 527,Castries, Tel:24358/20627. Mgr:Jean Marie.. no of cars auto:2.
Manual:4. YR rates:$34 .DD:190. Extras:no. cc:no
SLYS.Tel:25057. Mgr:Geoff Deveaux. No of cars auto:4. Manual:16. YR rates:from:$27 per day. DD:$560.
Extras:optional insurance:$8. cc:V.
U-DRIVE, Box 945, Castries, Tel:24777 22878. No of cars auto:3. Manual:30. HS.Rates:$40-60.
LS.Rates:$30-40 weekly $200-300. DD:570. Extras:mileage after 40 per day. Optional collison insurance
$10 per day. cc:all

TOURS, FISHING, AND DAY SAILS.

ALISON MARINE tel:26811 (Bob Elliot) day sails on Unicorn and Bucaneer.
BARNARDS TRAVEL, Bridge St. Tel:21615. all kinds of island and out of island tours. cc:V, A.
CARIB TRAVEL AGENCY, Jeremie St. Tel:22151/23176/21592. all kinds of sightseeing tours and
tranfers.cc:V, A.
JEM MARINE CO LTD., tel:46182/25057. (Peter McDoom) day sails on 42ft trimaran "Surf Queen".
Also other cruises including cocktail cruises.
JOSEPH'S TOURING SERVICE. Gros Islet. Tel:28619 Mgr:Joseph. German spoken. cc:V
MAKO WATERSPORTS. Rodney Bay, tel:20412 mgr:"Mako" sportsfishing. cc:no
MARIGOT BAY RESORT. Tel:34357. Day sails and half day sails available.

M AND C TOURIST DEPT. Tel:22811. all kinds of tours.
SAIL LTD, A Frame. Tel:28725. Mgr:Chris and Jenny. Day sails, half day sails, sunset cruises, sailing lessons.
ST LUCIA REPRESENTATIVE SERVICES, Micoud St. Tel 23762. All kinds of tours.
SUNLINK, Club St Lucia. Tel:28232. Mgr:Linda Grey. All kinds of tours and activities. agents:ITR. cc:V
SUNFUN TOURS, tel:20896. mgr Mary Bicar. All kinds of island tours, tranfers etc. cc:All

AIRLINES

AIR CANADA. tel:reservations:23051/3. Vieux Fort:46038/46249. weekly flight to Canada.
AIR MARTINIQUE. Tel:22463. Two daily flights to Martinique and St Vincent and the Grenadines.
AMERICAN AIRLINES. tel:reservations 46777/46779. info:46795. Daily flights to San Juan with connections to the U.S.A.
BWIA. tel:23778/23789. Hewanorra:46249/46259. Daily flights to Maimi, bi-weekly to New York.
BRITISH AIRWAYS. Tel:23951/21214. Hewanorra 46172. Weekly flights to London.
LIAT. tel:23051/3 holidays:22348. Many daily flights to all other Caribbean islands.
SCY AIRWAYS. Tel:22686/7. Hewanorra:46660. Charters and day tours on Cessna 411.

OTHER

BARCLAYS BANK, Bridge St, Tel:23306 23685 and Jeremie St Tel 24041. are agents for VISA and MASTER CARD.
CARIB TRAVEL AGENCY, Jeremie St, Tel:22151/23176/21529 are agents for AMERICAN EXPRESS.

MARTINIQUE.
If calling from outside Martinique use area code 596. For postal address: FdeF means Fort de France.
Add Martinique, French West Indies.
HOTELS
Notes:(all rates in French francs). Mgr means manager, or owner manager. oa = on application. bed = bed only bb = bed and breakfast hb = half board fb = full board. HSS means high season single, HSD means high season double, LSS means low season single, LSD means low season double. cc = credit card information - V means Visa and normally includes all the Visa group including Master Card, Euro Card, Barclaycard and Carte Bleu. A = American express. nf = not fixed (in this case 10% tipping is normal). Unless otherwise specified there is no tax to add. inc = included. ac = air-conditioning, sc measns self-cntained rooms available. Tax, service or extras shown must be added to the rate.
ALAMANDA, Trois Ilets, Tel:66 03 19. No of rooms:24. YR.S:bed:ff:410. YR.D:bed:ff:540. Facilities:ac, sc. (joined with Caraibe Auberge)
AUBERGE ATLANTIC, Vauclin, Tel:74 40 36. No of rooms:11. cc:no. YR.S or double:bed:ff:110.
AUBERGE DE ANSE MITAN, Trois Ilets, Tel:66 01 12/05 24. Mgr:mme Athanase Lea. No of rooms:20. cc:am.Ex, V, diners. HSSbb:ff:250, hb:330. HSD:bed:ff:330, hb:440. LSS.bb:ff:200, hb:250. LSD.bb:ff250, hb:400. Service:10%. Facilities:ac, sc.
AUBERGE DU VARE, Case Pilot, Tel:78 80 56. No of rooms:12. HSSbb:ff:190, hb:255. HSD:bb:ff:267, hb:397 LS.Rates:oa. Facilities:ac, pool.
BALISIER, 21 Rue Victor Hugo, Tel:71 46 54. No of rooms:23. YR.S:bed:ff:240. YR.D:bed:ff:274. Facilities:ac.
BAMBOU, Trois Ilets, Tel:66 01 39/ 66 00 20. Telex:912065. No of rooms:118. Agent:Nouvelle Frontieres. YR.S:bb:ff:350, hb420. YR.D:bb:ff:400, hb540. Facilities:ac, pool.
BAKOUA, Trois Ilets, Tel:66 02 02. Telex:912666. Mgr:Christian Vesin. No of rooms:139. cc:all. HSD:bed:ff:about 1900. LSD.bed:ff:1200. Facilities: pool, ac, tennis, sc.
CARAIBE AUBERGE, Trois Ilets, Tel:66 03 19. No of rooms:19. YR.S:bb:ff:240-380. YR.D:bb:ff:290-430. Service:inc. Tax:inc. Facilities:ac (joined with Alamanda).
CARAYOU, Trois Ilets, Tel:66 04 04. Telex:912575. Mgr:M.Dominique. No of rooms:200. cc:all. HSSbb:ff:810-910, hb955-1055. HSD:bb:ff:1050-1150, hb:1340-1440. LSS.bed:ff:oa. LSD.bed:ff:oa. Facilities:ac, pool, tennis, disco.
CHEZ ANNA, 26 Perrinon St, 97200 FdeF, Tel:71 55 62. Mgr:changing No of rooms:14. cc: no. YR.S:bed:ff:130 YR.D:bed:ff:180.
CHEZ AMI FRITZ, Brin d'Amour, Trinite, Tel:58 20 81. Telex:912 121. Mgr:Daniel Rebert. No of rooms:5. cc:V, diners. YR.D:bb:ff:600-700.
CHEZ JULOT, Vauclin, Tel:74 40 93. No of rooms:10. cc:V. YR.S:bb:ff:170, HSD.bb:ff:230. Facilities:ac.
CLUB MED. Ste-Anne, Tel:76 74 52. Mgr:changes every 6 months. No of rooms:300. Agent:Club Med 106-108 Brompton Rd, London SW3 1JJ telex:299221. Club Med, 7975 North Hayden Road, Scottsdale, AZ. USA 85261 telex:669496. Rates oa. Facilities:watersports, tennis, exercises, etc..

DIAMANT LES BAINS, Diamant, Tel:76 40 14. HSSbb:ff:350. HSD:bb:ff:450. LSS.bb:ff:250. LSD.bb:ff:350. Service:inc. Facilities:ac, pool..

DUNETTE, Ste- Anne, Tel:76 73 90/ 76 74 31. Mgr:Mme Norbert. No of rooms:18. cc:V. HSS300-330. HSD:430-480 LSS.bb:ff:220-250. LSD:bb:ff:310-360. Facilities:ac.

EDEN BEACH, Trois Ilets, Tel:66 01 19. Mgr:Mme Sable. No of rooms:15. cc:no. HSD:bb:ff:346. LS:oa. Facilities:ac, sc.

GRAIN D'OR, Carbet, Tel:78 02 27. Mgr:Mme Sonnier. No of rooms:7. cc:V. YR.S:bb:ff:180. YR.D:bb:ff:280. Facilities:ac, pool.

IMPERATRICE, Rue de la Liberte, FdeF, Tel:63 06 82. Telex:29678MR. No of rooms:24. cc:V, A., Diners. YR.S:bb:ff:265-317. YR.D:bb:ff:340-392. Facilities:ac.

LA BATELERIE, Schoelcher, Tel:61 49 49/ 71 72. Telex:912515. No of rooms:200. cc: A., V, diners. Rates around:1000-2000 oa (some changes going on). Facilities:ac, pool, tennis, casino, disco, sc.

LA BONNE AUBERGE, Trois Ilets, Tel:66 01 55. Mgr:M.Marie Clare. No of rooms:16. cc:A., V, Diners. HSSbb:ff:237. HSD:bb:ff:300. LSS.bb:ff:188. LSD.bb:ff:242. Facilities:ac, sc

LAFAYETTE, 5 Rue de la Liberte, FdeF, Tel:73 80 50. No of rooms:24. cc:all. mgr:Simone Brousillon. HSSbed:ff:325. HSD:bed:ff:365. LSS.bed:ff:290-320. LSD. bed:ff:351-355. Tax:5ff per head per day. Facilities:ac.

LA NOUVELLE VAGUE, Ste- Pierre, Tel:77 14 34. Mgr:Jacky Laujin. No of rooms:5. cc:all. YR.D:bb:ff:200.

LA PAGERIE, 97229 Trois Ilets, Tel:66 05 30. Telex:912 581 MR. Mgr:m.Magloire. No of rooms:98. cc: A., V, diners. Agent:. HSSbed:ff:539. HSD:bed:ff:656. LSS.bed:ff:469. LSD.bed:ff:570. Facilities:ac, pool, sc.

LA PETIT AUBERGE, Ste-Luce, Tel:62 57 94. Telex:no. Mgr:Procureur. No of rooms:12. cc: A., V agent:Nouvelle Frontieres, 87 Bd de Grenelle, 75738, Paris. Tel:42 73 05 68. HSD:bb:ff:330. LSD.ff:bb:262. Service:10%. Tax:inc.

L'AUBERGE DE LA MONTAGNE PELEE, Morne Rouge, Tel:52 32 09. Telex:no. Mgr:Mme. Manquant. No of rooms:8. Cc:,V. YR.S:bed:ff:187-220. YR.D:bed:ff:242-275. Service:10%. Facilities:sc.

LE BLENAC, 3, Rue Blenac, FdeF, Tel:70 18 41. No of rooms:8. YR.S:bed:ff:150-180. YR.D:bed:ff:180-220. Facilities:ac.

LE CALALOU, Anse a L'Ane, Trois Ilets, Tel:68 31 67/ 68 31 78. Telex:912790. No of rooms:36. YR.S:hb:ff:580-630. YR.D:hb:ff:860-930. Facilities:ac.

LE CHRISTOPHE COLOMB, Carbet, Tel:78 05 38. No of rooms:10. YR.S:bed:ff:150. YR.D:bed:ff:250. Facilities:ac, sc.

LE DUPARQUET, 68, Av des Caraibes, FdeF, Tel:70 28 36/ 72 61 45. No of rooms:20. YR.S:bb:ff:265. YR.D:bb:ff:350-380. Facilities:ac.

LE GOMMIER, 1-3 Rue Jaques Cazotte, FdeF, Tel:71 88 55. No of rooms:28. Rates:oa. Facilities:ac.

LE GIBSY, Habitation Seguineau, 97214 Le Lorraine, Tel:53 73 46. Telex:no. Mgr:m. Le fevre. No of rooms:7 expanding to 30. cc:A., V YR.S:bed:ff:300. YR.D:bed:ff:400. Facilities:ac.

LE MATADOR, Trois Ilets, Tel:66 04 05/ 66 05 36. Mgr:Francois and Raymonde Crico. No of rooms:8. cc:all. YR.S:bb:ff:310, hb:390. YR.D:bb:ff:420, hb:580. Facilities:ac, sc.

LE REFLET DE LA MER, Trois Ilets, Tel:68 32 14. No of rooms:6. YR.S:hb:ff:220. YR.D:hb:ff:350. Facilities:ac.

LE REVE BLEU, 50 Rue Lazare Carnot, FdeF, Tel:73 02 95. No of rooms:6. YR.S:bed:ff:135. YR.D:bed:ff:160. Facilities:ac.

LES BRISANTS, Francois, 97240 Tel:54 32 57/ 40 29. Mgr:m. Mme Marie Louis. No of rooms:6. cc:V, diners, A. YR.D:bb:ff:260, hb:380. Facilities:ac.

MADIANA, Schoelcher, Tel:61 28 78. Telex:912038. No of rooms:20. YR.S:bed:ff:300. YR.D:bed:ff:350. Facilities:ac, sc.

MADININA, Trois Ilets, Tel:66 00 54. Mgr:M.Choukroun. No of rooms:20. cc:all. YR.S:bed:ff:253. YR.D:bed:ff:385. Service:10%. Facilities:ac.

MALMAISON, 7 Rue de la liberte, FdeF, Tel:63 90 85. Mgr: m. Croulard no of rooms:20. cc: A. HSSbed:ff:330. HSD:bed:ff:360. LSS.bed:ff:230. LSD.bed:ff:260. Facilities:ac.

MANOIR DE BEAUREGARD, Ste-Anne, Tel:76 73 40. Telex:912349. Mgr:Mme Styr. No of rooms:27. cc: A., V, diners. HSSbb:ff:405. HSD:bb:ff:5760. LSS.310 LSD.395. Facilities:ac, pool.

MAROUBA CLUB, 97221 Le Carbet, Tel:78 01 88. Telex:912 138. Mgr:m. Consani. No of rooms:100. cc:no. Agent:Nouvelles Frontieres. YR.S:bed:ff:400. YR.D:bed:ff:540. Facilities:pool ac.

MERIDIEN, Trois Ilets 97229, Tel:66 00 00. Telex:912641. Mgr:E.Cotasson. No of rooms:297. cc: all. Agent:Air France.HSS.bed:ff:1950. HSD:bed:ff:1950. LSS.bed:ff:850. LSD.bed:ff:990. Facilities:ac, pool, tennis, scuba, casino, disco.

MOTEL DU PHARE, Pte des Negres, FdeF, Tel:61 61 67. No of rooms:10. YR.D:bed:ff:250-280. Service:inc. Tax:inc. Facilities:ac, sc..

NOVOTEL, DIAMANT, Tel:76 42 42. Telex:912349. Mgr:jean michel beyrat. No of rooms:173. cc:all. Agent:Accor, 509 Madison Ave, N.Y. 1022. Tel:212 752 7430 telex:661831 HSS.bed:ff:1000. HSD:bed:ff:1200. LSS.bed:ff:600. LSD.bed:ff:700. Facilities:ac, pool, disco, scuba.

Martinique

PLANTATION LEYRITZ, Basse-Pointe, Tel:78 54 32/ 78 53 92.(78 53 08?) telex:912462. Mgr:M. Lucy de Fossarieu. No of rooms:53. cc: A., V diners. HSSbb:ff:800. HSD:bb:ff:900. LSS.bb:ff:500. LSD.bb:ff:620. Facilities:ac, pool, sc, disco tennis.

RESITEL, 48 Rue Schoelcher, FdeF, Tel:71 42 82. No of rooms:14. YR.D:bed:ff:250-335. Service:inc. Tax:inc. Facilities:ac, sc..

RIVAGE HOTEL, BP 45 Trois Ilets, 97229 FdeF, Tel:66 06 56. Telex:912913 MR. Mgr:Jean Claude riveti. No of rooms:16. cc: V, HS. Double:bed:ff:265-365, bb:315-415. LS.:oa service:10%. Facilities:ac, pool, sc.

SAINTE-AUBIN, BP 97220, Trinite, Tel:69 43 77. Telex:917 678 MR. Mgr:M.Mme. Foret. No of rooms:20. cc: A., V. YR.S:bb:ff:290. YR.D:bb:ff:410.service:10%. Facilities:ac, pool.

VICTORIA, 1 km Route de Didier, FdeF, Tel:60 56 18 / 71 59 14. Mgr:Maurice Victoire. No of rooms:24. cc: A., V agent:(U.S.A):(305 756 8009/ 757 5914. HSSbed:ff:280. HSD:bed:ff:340. LSS.bed:ff:250. LSD.bed:300. Facilities:ac, pool, sc.

VICTORIA AIRPORT HOTEL, Ducos, Tel:56 29 82. No of rooms:7. HSSbb:ff:250. HSD:bb:ff:320. LSS.bb:ff: . LSD.bb:ff:. Facilities:ac.

VILLA CLUB ANSE CARITAN, Ste-Anne, Tel:76 74 12. Telex:912551. No of rooms:94. cc: A., V. HSSbb:ff:405. HSD:bb:ff:610. LSS.bb:oa. LSD.bb:oa. Facilities:ac, pool, sc, disco.

SELF-CONTAINED APARTMENTS

(Prices in French francs, all taxes and service included unless otherwise specified) for classification of seasons etc.- see hotel listings. One double means one double bedroom (2 people) two doubles means two double bedrooms (4 people).

BRISE MARINE, Ste-Luce, Tel:62 57 17. Mgr:Jean Viallet. No of rooms:12. cc:V HSD.bed:ff:328. LSD.bed:ff:285. Cottages that sleep 4 to 5 people also available from 328 to 370 ff.

BUNGALOW CARIBOU, Tartane, Trinite, Tel:58 39 40. No of rooms:8. YR.D:bed:ff:200-270. Facilities:ac.

BUNGALOWS DE LA PRARIE, Francois, Tel:53 34 16. Telex:912630 mgr:M.Gouyer. No of chalets:10. cc:no. YR bugalow rate:ff:400.

DIAMANT BLEU, Diamant, Tel:76 42 15. Telex:912378. Mgr:Martine Monplaisir. No of rooms:22. cc:V agent:air tours. HSD:bb:ff:330 (or bed 2240 per week), LS:oa facilities:ac, pool.

DOUCE VAGUES, Ste-Luce, Tel:62 47 47. Mgr:Mme Renaud St Cyr. No of rooms:20. cc:no. HSSbed:ff:220. HSD:bed:ff:285. LSS.bed:ff:190. LSD.bed:ff:246. Facilities:ac.

RESIDENCE GRAND LARGE, Ste-Luce, Tel:62 54 42. No of rooms:18. YR.D:bed:ff:285. Facilities:ac, sc.

STUDIOS LA CARAVELLE, Tartane, Trinite, Tel:58 37 32. Mgr:Christiane Toris. No of studios:10. cc:no. YR rate:bed:ff:200. Facilities:sc.

RESTAURANTS

All rates in French francs. Unless otherwise stated they include a three course meal and half the bottle price of the cheapest wine. In Martinique prices always include services and tax. Cc = credit card information - V includes all the Visa group - Master Card, Barclaycard, Europcard, Carte Bleu etc. A. = American Express.

ANSE CARITAN. St Anne. Mgr:M.Vallet. Tel:76 74 12. Price:ff:120-260. cc:all. food:French.

AUBERGE ATLANTIC. Vauclin. Tel:74 40 36. Price:ff:55-120. cc:no. Food:local.

AUX PATES FRAICHES. FdeF. Mgr:Alberto. Tel:63 21 34. Price:ff:95-207. Service:nf. cc:no. Food:Italian.

AUBERGE DE ANSE MITAN. Anse Mitan. Mgr:Athanase Lea. Tel:66 01 12/ 05 24. Price:ff:100. cc:A., diners. Food:French (best give them advance notice).

AU REGAL DE LA MER. Anse Mitan. Tel:66 04 00. Price:150-400.

BAIE DES FLAMANDES (Abri Cotier). FdeF. Mgr:M. Lison. Tel:63 66 46. Price:ff:85-180. cc:V, food:French and creole, lunch-time snacks available.

BAMBOU. Anse Mitan. Tel:66 01 39. Price:ff:about 150. Food:local, usually entertainment.

CALIFORNIA SALOON. Anses d'Arlet (Petit). Mgr:Hans d'Arlet. Tel:no. Price:ff:80-150. cc:V, food:French, creole.

CHEZ AMI FRITZ. Trinite. Mgr:Daniel Rebert. Tel:58 20 81. Price:ff:150-430. cc:V, diners, A. Food:French.

CHEZ GABY. Grand Anse d'Arlet. Mgr:Gabriel. Tel:68 65 04. Price:ff:80-90. cc:no. Food:French and creole.

CHEZ JULOT. Vauclin. Tel:74 40 36. Price:ff:120-200. cc:V, food:creole.

DELIFRANCE. Anse Mitan. Mgr:Mme Roy de Belle Pliene. Tel:no. cc:no food:patisserie, boulangerie.

ETS AGLAE. Ste-Luce. Tel:62 50 09. Price:ff:60-150. cc:no. Food:local.

LA BELLE EPOCH. Rt Didier. Mgr:Rosso Joseph. Tel:70 36 22/ 71 89 26. Price:ff:190-340. cc:V, food:.

LA BONNE AUBERGE. Anse Mitan. Mgr:M.Marie Clare. Tel:66 01 55. Price:ff:148-385. cc:V, diners. Food:French.

LA DUNETTE. Ste-Anne. Mgr:Mme Norbert. Tel:76 73 90. Price:ff:110-273. cc:V. Food:French.

LA FONTANE. Route de Balata. Mgr:Mme Zamie. Tel:64 28 70. Price:ff:225-440. cc:V, A.. food:French.

LA GUINGUETTE. Ste-Pierre. Mgr:M. Lutbert. Tel:77 15 02. Price:ff:64-277. cc:all. Food:French creole seafood.

LA LANGOUSTE. Anse Mitan. Price:100-250. la marine. Anse Mitan overlooking marina. Food:changing menus.

L'AMPHORE. Anse Mitan. Mgr:Ghislaine Bruere-Dawson. Tel:66 03 09. Price:ff:150-350. cc:V, diners. Food:French and creole, lobster a speciality.

LA NOUVELLE VAGUE. Ste-Pierre. Mgr:Jackie Laujin. Tel:77 14 34. Price:ff:70-250. cc:all. Food:french, creole.

L'ARC EN CIEL. Rond Pt Didier. Mgr:Mme Yenel. Tel:73 61 75/ 60 56 78. Price:ff:150-300. cc:V, A. food:gastranomic French, creole.

L'AUBERGE DE LA MONTAGNE PELEE. Morne Rounge. Mgr:Mme. Manquant. Tel:52 32 09. Price:ff:120-230 cc:V. Food:French.

LA VAGUE DU SUD. Ste-Luce. Mgr:Mme Henry. Tel:62 44 96. Price:ff:65-265. cc:V. Food:French, creole seafood.

LA VILLA CREOLE. Anse Mitan. Mgr:Guy Bruere- Dawson. Tel:66 05 53. Price:ff:150-250. cc:V, diners. Food:French and creole.

LE BOUNTY. Anse Mobouyas (Ste-Luce). Tel:62 57 65. Price:ff:130-350. cc:V, A. Food:French.

LE MATADOR. Anse Mitan. Mgr:Francois and Raymonde Crico. Tel:66 05 36. Price:ff:155-310. cc:all. Food:French and creole.

LES BRISANTS. Francois. Mgr:M, Mme Marie Louise. Tel:54 32 57/40 29. Price:ff:118-211. cc:V, Diners, A.. food:creole.

LES TAMERINIERS. Ste-Anne. Mgr:Jean-Claude Edmond. Tel:76 75 62. Price:ff:118-275. cc:no. Food:French, creole.

LE VIVIER. Anse Mitan. Mgr:Louis Yang Ting. Tel:66 03 19. Price:ff:106-200. cc:V, A.. food:seafood.

MADININA. Anse Mitan overlooking the marina. Mgr:M.Choukroun. Tel:66 00 54. cc:all food: under revision.

PLANTATION LEYRITZ. Basse Pointe. Mgr:m Mme Lucy de Fossarieu. Tel:78 54 32/ 78 53 92. Price:ff:90-200. cc:all. Food:French, creole.

POI ET VIRGINIE. Ste-Anne. Price:ff:120-275. Food:French, creole.

RIVAGE HOTEL. Anse Mitan. Mgr:Jean-Claude and Maryelle Riveti. Tel:66 06 56. Food:reasonably priced snacks and plates.

THE CREW. FdeF. Mgr:Jean. Tel:33 04 14. Price:ff:78-165. Service:nf. cc:V. Food:French.

TIFFANYS. Schoelcher. Mgr:Claude Pradines. Tel:71 33 82. Price:ff:160-270. cc:V, A. Diners. Food:French and creole.

SHOPS

BORA BORA. Pte Du Boute. Tel:66 01 68. Mgr:Mme. Riveti. cc:V, . Goods:supermarket.

CALYPSO. Anse Mitan. Tel:66 07 91. cc:A. Goods:high class artisinale.

CITRON VERT. Anse Mitan. Tel:66 05 56. cc:V, goods:hand painted t shirts, handicrafts, costume jewelry.

GALERIE VERMEIL. Anse Mitan. Tel:66 03 64. Mgr:Mme arnoux. cc:A. Goods:silk screen fabrics and paintings by Serge Arnoux.

LA CASANADE. Anse Mitan. Tel:68 61 57. Mgr:Francette Assencio. cc:no. Goods:wonderful confections, ice creams.

LA GALERIE. Ste-Anne. Tel:76 92 36. Mgr:m, Mme. Beaumont cc:V, goods:souvenirs.

LA MALLE DES ISLES. Ste-Anne. Tel:76 70 51. Mgr:M. Lacour. cc:V, . Goods:books, maps.

L'ISLE AUX TRESORS. Anse Mitan. Tel:66 05 93. Mgr:Martine Hillion. cc:V, goods:handicrafts, clothes.

PALM BEACH. Anse Mitan. Tel:66 05 23. Mgr:M. St rock. cc:V. Goods:handicrafts.

CAR RENTAL

(all rates in French francs) DD means damages deposit. YR means year round

AVIS. 4, Rue Ernest Deproge FdeF tel:70 11 60, also at airport tel:79 26 86. Pte Du Boute tel:66 04 04 telex:912376 MR. Mgr:M. De jaham. No of cars auto:4. No manual:220. Types:sedans. YR rates:262-558. Extras:66f insurance. DD:6000. cc:V, Diners, A.

BUDGET, 12, Rue Felix Eboue. Tel:63 69 00. Telex:912 541. Also at airport: 51 22 88, Anse Mitan 66 00 45. Mgr:M.Malidor. No of cars: lots. Types:sedans from uno to mercedes. YR rates:199-1190 (weekly 1500-5000). Extras:insurance 68f per day.. DD:1500f. cc:V, diners.

EUROCAR tel:73 33 13. Telex:912 470. Types:sedans. Rates:148-330. Extras:1.1-3.5 per km, also insurance. DD:oa.

EXPRESS RENT A CAR tel:60 28 06. Telex:912929. Types:sedans. YR rates:208-247. Extras:insurance 57. DD:2000. cc:A, V, Diners.

FUNNY. Tel:63 33 05. FdeF, St Anne, Anse Mitan. Types:motor bikes and scooters. YR rates:91-215. DD:1500. cc:A. Visa, diners

HERTZ, 24 Rue Ernest Deproge, FdeF. Tel:60 64 64. Telex:912000 MR. Types:sedans. Rates:273-473. Extras:insurance.

LOC CARAIBES, Station Shell, Place Bertin, 97250, Ste-Pierre. Tel:77 15 89/ 77 13 21. Types:sedans rates:oa.

SAFARI CARS, Anse Mitan Trois Ilets. Tel:66 06 26 telex:no. Mgr:M Pinville. No of cars auto:5. No manual:40. Types:sedans. HS rates:188-450 (weekly 1057-3080). Low season rates:160-400 (weekly 900-20500). Extras:insurance 55f per day. DD:2000. cc:all. Motor bikes also available from 90-120 per day).

TOUR OPERATORS

CARIBTOURS, Pointe Du Bout, Trois Ilets, Tel:66 02 56. Mgr:Jacques Vitu. All kinds of tours arranged, within Martinique, and air tours to other islands. cc:V, A.

JET TOURS, Marina Pointe Du Bout, Trois Ilets, Tel:66 05 07/ 03 05. All kinds of land and air tours.

STT VOYAGE. 23, Rue Blenac, FdeF, Call:71 68 12

FLECHION VOYAGES, Rue Schoelcher, FdeF, Call:73 35 35.

AIRLINES

AIR CANADA. Lamentin Airport, tel:51 29 81. Twice weekly to Montreal and Toronto.

AIR FRANCE, Rue de la Liberte, FdeF. Tel:63 75 52/ 63 69 97 (airport 51 51 51). Daily flights to Paris and San Juan, two flights a week to Miami.

AIR MARTINIQUE. Lamentin airport, tel:51 09 90. Twice daily flights to St Lucia, St Vincent and the Grenadines.

AMERICAN AIRLINES, Lamentin Airport, tel:51 12 29. Flights most days to San Juan.

EASTERN AIRLINES, Lamentin Airport, tel:51 11 26. Flights most days to Miami.

LIAT, Lamentin Airport, tel:51 10 00/ 51 21 11. Several flights a day to St Lucia and Barbados (with links to the rest of the Windwards).

OTHER

AMERICAN EXPRESS office upstairs in Roger Albert, Rue Vitor Hugo.
Most banks cater to VISA CARD

HELP US HELP YOU. Your opinion counts! Please let us know.....

Your name /address (optional)...
Which establishments (restaurants, hotels etc) gave you:
Good service and value...

....

Poor service or value...

....

How can we improve this guide?...

Please elaborate as much as you like and use additional paper. Send it to:
Chris Doyle, Box 308, St George's, Grenada. West Indies.